Praise for

Have Your Home and Money Too
by P.J. Wade

"Finally, a comprehensive examination of the reverse mortgage option. An objective opinion has been long overdue. P.J. Wade, a recognized authority in the field of housing opportunities, brings her expertise to us in a clearly written and factual manner."

— Dale Ennis, Publisher, *Canadian MoneySaver*

"An excellent guide for mature homeowners and their advisers interested in evaluating reverse mortgages as an alternative form of home equity conversion. This book should also be required reading for lenders designing and marketing reverse mortgage products."

— Joe O'Brien, retired from Canada Mortgage and Housing Corporation

"In addition to useful information about how to find and prudently negotiate a reverse mortgage, P.J. Wade's book provides a thoughtful review of the many factors that older persons should consider before deciding to 'age in place.'"
— Ethel Meade, Co-Chair,
Older Women's Network, condominium owner

"Makes the dynamics of using the cash value in your home easily understandable. It is written to coach you through the many alternatives to access YOUR equity in YOUR homes. "
— Marina & Ron Ringler,
Co-ordinators, Consumers for Home Equity Conversion (CHEC)

"A carefully crafted, thorough, and thoughtful treatment of reverse mortgages."
— Peter Kingston, President,
Diversified Financial Corporation, mortgage broker

"This practical, common-sense advice will be invaluable for seniors and lawyers advising them."
— Malcolm S. Archibald, Q.C., Weir & Foulds

"A very innovative, thought-provoking concept in money management… easy to read and understand…should be required reading for anyone over 50."
— Margaret Eberle,
Past-President, Federated Women's Institutes of Ontario

ABOUT THE AUTHOR

Have Your Home and Money Too grew out of P.J. Wade's commitment to consumer empowerment and her interest in innovative housing options. An acknowledged consumer advocate, P.J. developed Canada's first independent reverse mortgage seminars. On the encouragement of members of the senior's community, P.J. wrote the widely-acclaimed consumer handbook on reverse mortgages that formed the foundation for *Have Your Home and Money Too.*

A much sought-after speaker and frequent guest on television and radio, P.J. is a nationally recognized authority on the mature market. A leader in Canada's home equity conversion movement, P.J. was invited to speak at the 1991 U.S. National Home Equity Conversion Conference in Washington, D.C. She is also the first Canadian to complete the American Reverse Mortgage Counsellor Training Program spnsored by the U.S. federal government and the American Association for Retired Persons.

P.J. is a regular columnist for Ontario's *Today's Seniors* and a featured writer for other publications including the *Globe and Mail.* She is also an active member of a number of seniors' organizations.

As The Catalyst, P.J. Wade "gets things started" for individuals, businesses, and organizations interested in mastering and/or initiating change. P.J. offers her innovative retirement and life planning programs in employer-sponsored seminars, at the University of Toronto, and through other organizations. In her work with consumers and businesses, P.J. draws on 20 years experience in strategic planning, and marketing for a wide range of service-based industries.

P.J. is currently based in Toronto.

HAVE YOUR HOME AND MONEY TOO

*The Canadian Guide to Reverse Mortgages,
Home Equity Conversion, and Other
Creative Housing Options*

P. J. Wade
"THE CATALYST"

John Wiley & Sons

Toronto • New York • Chichester • Brisbane • Singapore

John Wiley & Sons Canada Limited
22 Worcester Road
Rexdale, Ontario
M9W 1L1

Although great care has been taken in the compilation and preparation of this publication, P.J. Wade/The Catalyst cannot accept responsibility for any errors or omissions or for the results of agreements entered into by readers. The author strongly urges anyone considering a reverse mortgage to seek professional advice from independent legal, housing, and financial advisers.

Canadian Cataloguing in Publication Data
Wade, P. J.
       Have your home and money too: the Canadian guide to reverse mortgages, home equity conversion, and other creative housing options
Includes index.
ISBN 0-471-64091-3
1. Home equity conversion — Canada. 2. Mortgage loans, Reverse — Canada. I. Title.
HG2040.45.W33 1994 332.7'22'0971 C94-930569-3

Production Credits
Jacket design: Selwyn Simon
Text design: JAQ
Printer: Trigraphic

Printed and bound in Canada
10 9 8 7 6 5 4 3 2 1

Contents

Acknowledgements

Many people generously shared their thoughts, experiences, concerns, and expertise to ensure future consumers would be fairly treated. A special thank you to the wonderfully helpful people across the country who talked to me about their lives and their homes. Those who agreed to do case study interviews deserve special acknowledgement for their candour. And finally to my support team, especially Vic and Beverly, a warm thank you and hearty congratulations.

Research for this publication was enhanced by contributions of time and information from a number of homeowners, professionals, financial experts, researchers, lawyers, journalists, and current consumers, both across Canada and in the United States. The professional advisers I interviewed deserve full credit for their candour and genuine interest in seeing improvements in their industries. The lenders—current and potential—also provided invaluable assistance. Special acknowledgement is due the Canada Mortgage and Housing Corporation, Consumers for Home Equity Conversion, the American Association of Retired Persons, the (US) National Home Equity Conversion Centre, and Hinton & Wild (Home Plans) Ltd. in England.

Home Is Where the Money Is

Are you house-rich but cash-poor? Would you like a few extra dollars for travel and personal indulgences? Or, although you live comfortably, are you attracted to the prospect of tax-free income? Are you looking for something to do with your time that will also generate extra money? Or, are you interested in sharing your home to overcome your sense of isolation while earning income at the same time? In other words, would you like to have your home and money too? If you own your own home, alone or with others, whether it is a house, semi-detached home, townhouse, or apartment condominium (or anything in between), you have a number of options. *Have Your Home and Money Too* will get you started.

Over the years as a creative life planner, journalist, and speaker, I have talked to countless homeowners who are struggling to keep the home they love or who deprive themselves of the frills of life in order to keep their home. Usually, these homeowners are unaware of the ways the home itself can play an active part in solving their problems. Or, worse, they are burdened with misinformation and false impressions, and so never explore the very alternatives that could lead to a financial solution and their peace of mind. *Have Your Home and Money Too* fills the information void. Although this is not a "get-rich-quick" book, the ideas in it can be used in a variety of ways, either to generate a few dollars a month or to create a steady income. The only real limitation is the homeowner's imagination, once needs and interests have been identified.

I hope this book will revolutionize your concept of home, your perception of home ownership, and your ideas on the buying of property. The time has come for "home" to undergo a transformation—not in the physical sense, rather in our attitude towards home and all it entails. Home is more than somewhere to keep your stuff. Homeowners can no longer afford to include their homes as only a passive component in their retirement plans, and one that also carries a heavy caretaker responsibility. Home must now be viewed as a dynamic financial resource.

Over the years that I have been writing and speaking about reverse mortgages, home equity conversion, innovative housing options, and change itself, I have talked to many homeowners across the country. Too many of them have suffered hardship because they signed a contract regarding their home that they did not read or, if they did read it, did not understand. Since failure to read or to understand what you have signed is not grounds for cancellation of a contract, these homeowners were bound by the terms and conditions of the contract they signed. This book provides homeowners with the questions to ask *before* signing any one of a variety of agreements regarding their home, including a reverse mortgage contract.

I hope to convince readers that signing an agreement regarding your home is at least as important as buying a pair of walking shoes. How do you buy shoes? Do you go out to buy shoes without a clear idea of why you need them? Do you buy the ones in the store window without trying them on? Do you buy the same pair a friend raves about, without even looking to see whether there is something that would suit you better? Do you try on only one shoe of the pair because you are in a hurry? Do you buy them without checking in the mirror first to see how they fit at the heel? Do you end up buying a pair of dress shoes instead because that salesperson is nicer than the one selling walking shoes? Do you buy a pair of shoes that don't fit just because they are the only ones available? Anyone who answers yes to even one of these questions, will probably know just how uncomfortable or unbearable life can be when your feet hurt. A poorly fitting reverse mortgage or other housing option is even more unbearable. Why do people who would never use these approaches to buy a pair of shoes, fall into these patterns when buying a reverse mortgage or hiring a professional adviser? And people do.

The decisions associated with the housing and financial concepts presented in this book are not to be made lightly or quickly. "Trying on" any option in this book means asking more than "How soon do I get the first cheque?" The best tool for determining the fit of an option is questions. Keep asking until you completely understand. Asking a lot of questions is not a sign of stupidity, but signing a contract without asking a lot of questions may be. Remember, the skill of astute consumers lies in using questions to peel away the jargon and sales pitch in order to learn exactly why a product or service is right or wrong for them.

By translating the jargon of reverse mortgages and the other creative housing options available to the homeowner, *Have Your Home and Money Too* empowers the homeowner to action. This book provides the foundation of understanding necessary so that the homeowner can hear, as well as read, between the lines when dealing with salespeople and other professionals.

Decisions about home equity conversion are already being made and reverse mortgage transactions have already taken place. Until now, the consumer has been alone. My 1991 consumer handbook on reverse mortgages filled the gap temporarily. This expanded version of the guide will now provide consumers with a "portable counsellor" as they investigate their financial and housing options. The many professionals unfamiliar with reverse mortgages and other home equity conversion methods will find this reference guide valuable reading for themselves and their clients.

Although this book is a "portable counsellor", it is not meant to be used alone, either as a decision-making tool or an information source. Take these ideas and custom-design your solution with the help of professional or personal advisers. Research the idea until you find a solution you can live with comfortably. A note of caution though, even if you feel a reverse mortgage is right for you, examine the other ideas in the book before you make a decision. If after reading this book you are relieved to learn you have many choices and feel more at ease with your circumstances, then this book will have served its purpose, whether you actually implement an idea or not.

A word about reverse mortgages: I believe that reverse mortgages and home equity conversion represent a powerful opportunity for older homeowners. These innovations offer tremendous choice for those interested in aging in place. However, I would like to make it very clear that I base my positive viewpoint on the home equity conversion concept and its potential for supporting aging in place, not on the products that are currently available in this fledgling marketplace.

I hope *Have Your Home and Money Too* catalyses the home equity conversion movement and sparks some new activity, particularly government involvement in a special reverse mortgage insurance program to encourage lenders to enter the market. This program, in turn, will give a tremendous boost to home equity conversion, especially the reverse mortgage industry.

A reverse mortgage could be your best friend or your worst enemy. The decision to convert home equity should not be entered into quickly or taken too lightly. Although many positive aspects are presented by lenders, their agents, and their salespeople, their views are decidedly biased. This book is designed to tip the scales in favour of the consumer by providing clear explanations of the advantages and disadvantages of reverse mortgages, as well as many other creative options.

P Wade

The Catalyst

PART ONE

The Home Equity Conversion Revolution

CHAPTER 1

Have Your Home and Money Too

Whether you need a little extra money so that you can take a cruise each year, visit your children more often, pay property tax increases, or simply indulge in a hobby, this book contains suggestions for you. *Have Your Home and Money Too* also presents ideas for those who need money to modernize a heating system, build an accessory apartment, buy a new car, or start a business. Or perhaps you would like to delay selling your home for awhile, to keep your ailing spouse at home, or to raise your standard of living with the tax-free dollars locked in your home? In short, if the question you are asking is, "How can I have my home and money too?" this book is designed for you.

The ideas presented here are based on three premises: people care where they live; people care how they live; and home ownership is something people value. Dorothy in *The Wizard of Oz* said it best, "There's no place like home." Although this statement is as true today as it was in 1939 when the movie was made, as we enter the twenty-first century, the concepts of "home" and "home ownership" are evolving. "Home" continues to mean more to us than the building's physical shell. Independence, security, and flexibility are still deeply rooted in the sense of personal identity associated with home ownership. However, as will be revealed in this book, "home ownership" offers additional financial management opportunities for homeowners. Finally, homeowners can have their home and money too.

Change is all around us. Even one of the last bastions—our conception of home—is gradually being altered. Homeowners are beginning to realize the benefit of treating "home" not as something the homeowner is responsible for preserving, but instead as an investment that can be used to preserve the homeowner's lifestyle as aging progresses. As fewer and fewer homeowners measure their self-worth or the value of their lives by how much they leave their heirs, managing home ownership will become a focus in retirement planning.

The financial twists and bumps of the 1990s' recession have led many people to look on the role of home ownership in retirement in a very different light. Now the home can be counted as an active financial resource in retirement planning, not merely the eventual "lump of cash" that it has been in the past. No longer are selling or mortgaging the home the only cash liberation methods available to the homeowner. Today people are looking for ways to tap into the value accumulated in their homes while they continue to enjoy the rights of ownership. Now through their homes, owners have a means of generating additional returns on the investment originally made in buying the property.

Using clear, simple terms, this guide explores the full range of options available to homeowners who wish to use their home to generate money without having to sell and move. The guide provides the information necessary to access the value apparently locked in the home and use the home itself to create additional income. In exploring ways to improve their standard of living, homeowners can use the ideas and information presented here to balance both the sales rhetoric and the ignorance of others. Written with a "how to do it right" approach, topics are carefully examined so that homeowners can see the potential as well as the pitfalls of each idea. This book is not meant to warn people off a concept but to empower homeowners with information, insight, and a sense of direction, so they will be able to "do it right." This do-it-for-yourself book encourages readers to develop their own variations of the innovative and creative options presented here.

Today, homeowners preparing for retirement want to have their home and money too. They would like the same accessibility to the money tied up in their homes that they have to the savings held in their bank accounts. Many would like a method of "spending their home" while still living in it. Homeowners and financial advisers alike now see home ownership as a vehicle for storing tax-free capital, which can be liquidated as required at a later date. In other words, now we can live *in*, as well as *on*, our retirement income.

WHAT IS THIS BOOK ALL ABOUT?

This book is based on the author's personal experience, on extensive research, on hundreds of interviews, and on a creative attitude towards housing. Some of the ideas presented here are new to Canada, others, such as home-based business, are established concepts but not yet common as retirement activities. The power of asking questions is a central theme, and questions are provided for the consumer investigating many of these options.

Have Your Home and Money Too will help you overcome the greatest barrier to a new view of home ownership—a natural resistance to change. People can be slow to accept new ideas. They are often suspicious of new methods and wary of being taken advantage of if they act on a new concept. This innovative guide fosters open-mindedness and creativity by supporting the consumer's perspective. Ideas are presented in the same way that wise individuals approach every new idea, that is, with a willingness to understand and an eye to the possible opportunities. "Buyer beware," is however, the underlying theme: after all, the home is the owner's resource and the owner is the one who must make the most of it and make the money last.

The advantages and disadvantages of each innovation and alternative are presented so that readers can make up their own minds. Homeowners are invited to try ideas on for size by seeing if they can find a way that an option—or a variation on an idea— would suit their needs, now or in the future. The challenges faced by homeowners are acknowledged and discussed, including the scarcity of unbiased and detailed information, the importance of affordability, high-pressure sales techniques, individual isolation, and the threat of rising costs. Resources, such as independent advisers, effective decision making, and time, are explored as well.

In this book, the terms, "homeowner," "consumer," and "borrower," refer to either gender, as well as to individuals and couples. Here "home" refers to the land and the house plus any other buildings or landscaping, and is considered equivalent to "property." "Home ownership" signifies ownership of a house, semi-detached home, or townhouse, or ownership of any type of condominium, including townhouses—and apartment-style condominiums.

This chapter introduces home equity conversion as an opportunity for unprecedented choice and freedom, while warning that conversion is not a panacea. As mentioned, a reverse mortgage can be your best friend or your worst enemy. Chapters 2 through 6 provide the information and guidance necessary to make reverse mortgages a friend rather than an enemy. In Chapter 2, "The Revolution of Choice," home equity conversion is identified as a revolutionary opportunity for today's homeowners. This discussion and the investigation of reverse mortgages that follows show the reader that this is not just another mortgage, but a fundamentally new financial concept, offering new choice and flexibility to homeowners. To put reverse mortgages in perspective, the home equity conversion marketplace in the United States is profiled to reveal its steady, if slow, steps forward.

Chapter 3, "Variations on a Theme," launches a detailed examination of the most common type of home equity conversion: reverse mortgages. Reverse mortgages are compared with traditional mortgages to put the general issues of mortgages and the specific concerns of home equity conversion in focus for the reader. This comparison gives the reader a clear view of the implications of arranging a reverse mortgage. After a detailed discussion of the various types of reverse mortgages, the development of the Canadian reverse mortgage market is examined to provide the consumer with an inside view of the industry. By examining the risks for lenders who offer reverse mortgages, the concepts behind current reverse mortgage products and the concerns regarding home equity conversion are revealed to the consumer.

"Is a Reverse Mortgage Right for You?" is the question answered in Chapter 4. The profile developed for an ideal candidate is contrasted with that of a homeowner who would not suit this home equity conversion method. The overall perspective gained from this exercise is useful for the reader interested in evaluating the personal worth of this innovative option. The section, "Decisions, Decisions, Decisions," acknowledges the fact that homeowners have never made a decision like this before.

The choice of arranging a reverse mortgage is not one to be made lightly or quickly as the reader will see in Chapters 5 and 6. These chapters examine the details that are important in researching and evaluating a reverse mortgage. Chapter 5, "Where Do I Start?" discusses ways the consumer can determine value, security, and flexibility in reverse mortgage products. Chapter 6 provides the reader with a set of questions to ask lenders when investigating the reverse mortgage option, as well as insight into the reverse mortgage contract itself. These two chapters are intended to clearly and simply present the information vital to consumers.

Chapter 7 details the ideal characteristics to look for in an independent adviser. Chapter 8 presents the reader with other types of home equity conversion, including property tax deferral plans, as well as sale leaseback and life estate programs. Chapter 9 takes a look at the future of home equity conversion and examines issues that must be dealt with to ensure that the consumer is well served both now and as the market develops.

Chapters 10 through 12 present other alternatives to selling and moving, arranging a traditional mortgage, or converting home equity. In exploring these options, the book effectively outlines the advantages and disadvantages for an number of innovative income-generating alternatives including: accessory apartments, home sharing, joint ownership, and home-based businesses.

To assist readers in using this book as a reference guide, an extensive Glossary, an innovative Quick Question Index, and a standard Index have been provided. Throughout the book cross-references to other chapters also appear for the reader's convenience.

HOME EQUITY CONVERSION REVOLUTION

The whole concept of retirement has changed. Gone is the time of quietly waiting for the end and making do. Retirement is now embraced as an extension of life —a third age. Coupled with this change is a growing realization that there are not yet enough housing or financial alternatives available to those who choose to live this independent lifestyle.

Home equity conversion offers a revolutionary new choice to homeowners. This innovation gives homeowners the freedom to choose when—and whether—to move from their homes. They also gain the power to improve their standard of living without the physical and emotional disruptions of moving. No longer is selling the home the only answer for older homeowners, should financial pressures become overwhelming.

Home equity conversion refers to methods the homeowner may employ to release or to utilize the equity, or accumulated value in the home, while retaining ownership and possession. For instance, reverse mortgages convert equity into cash, and property tax deferral plans use the equity as security in a pay-later approach. Both are home equity conversion methods. Using the "have your cake and eat it too" analogy, the homeowner is able to enjoy the pleasure of home ownership while "eating" or spending the equity. Conversion programs are particularly attractive because they take the pressure off the homeowner's present income by postponing repayment of a mortgage or by delaying payment of an expense, such as property taxes, until some future date. However, home equity conversion does not create equity, it gives the homeowner access to equity that currently exists.

Home equity conversion also reinforces a current shift in traditional thinking. In the past, parents worked a lifetime building an estate to pass on to their children. However, people are now living longer, healthier lives. Today, children are often well established and have usually reached retirement age themselves before their parents die. Most no longer need their parents' money to "give them a start in life." Now children are normally more intent on helping their parents live comfortably than on inheriting assets their parents could use. Children want parents to use their money to enjoy life in much the same way as they themselves intend to when they reach their parents' age.

Home equity conversion has the power to bring about far-reaching change. Instead of automatically moving to a retirement facility, an increasing number of older homeowners are *aging in place*, or staying at home as they age. Home equity conversion can allow aging in place to become more feasible, by providing the financial framework to support this choice. As a result, community home support networks and personal service businesses could thrive, while offering a diversity of local employment opportunities. Communities would benefit in both financial and social ways. Ultimately, many facets of community life could be affected, for the better.

The news about home equity conversion has been rippling steadily throughout the country. This quiet revolution in home ownership is building momentum, while home equity conversion gains growing recognition as an instrument of change for individuals and for society.

CHAPTER 2

The Revolution of Choice

Today in Canada, more than 80 percent of homeowners over the age of 65 hold their properties mortgage-free. For many of these older individuals, their home is their largest financial asset—"the nest egg"—representing more than 60 percent of their net worth.

This is the problem. The wealth of many older homeowners is locked up in their properties. Furthermore, the increasing costs of property maintenance, insurance, and taxes continuously devour income and erode savings. Ironically, while the home is a powerful symbol of independence and freedom, this valuable asset can also become a terrible financial burden.

Many comfortably well-off homeowners are aware of the tax advantage of releasing the *equity*, or accumulated value, in their homes. Using home equity conversion to gain access to this money, without selling the home, means the homeowner has tax-free dollars to spend. However, these homeowners are frustrated by the scarcity of options for tapping into their equity.

Conventional approaches to the "cash-poor, house-rich" dilemma and to tax planning have been either to arrange a traditional mortgage or to sell the home.

Homeowners, determined to stay in the home they know and love, may consider arranging a traditional mortgage. (These

Equity is the homeowner's share of the accumulated value in the home. Equity is the monetary value of the home that belongs to the home-owner after mortgages and creditors' claims are deducted. For example, if a house, valued at $250,000, has a $100,000 mortgage against it and no other creditors' claims, the equity, or net value, to the homeowner is $150,000 ($250,000–$100,000). Equity accumulates as the property value increases and/or as an original traditional mortgage is gradually paid off. Before home equity conversion, this equity was eventually released to the homeowner, or the estate, when the property was sold.

mortgages are also known as for-ward, standard, or straight mort-gages.) However, homeowners must have sufficient income to satisfy a mortgage lender that they can afford to repay the mortgage debt. Lenders use calculations based on gross income —that is, on the borrower's ability to repay the debt—to deter-mine the amount of debt a borrower will be allowed to carry (see page 20). The size of the traditional mortgage is based on the homeowner's ability to repay the debt: therefore, if the bor-rower's income is low, the traditional mortgage may be too small to be con-sidered useful by the borrower.

At retirement, an individual's in-come usually drops drastically—often by 40 percent or more. Therefore, most older homeowners cannot satisfy the income requirements for a mortgage of any useful size. For this reason, the traditional mortgage option is closed to most retired householders.

Selling the home may be an acceptable solution for home-owners who feel their houses are too big for them, or who have found an attractive housing alternative. However, surveys have shown that most older people would prefer to stay in their homes as they age. Furthermore, in many rural communities, housing alternatives are often limited, forcing older individuals to move out of the area altogether.

Selling the home may offer a remedy for financial stress, but the full impact of the sale can be far-reaching, even traumatic. The decision to sell the home involves not only financial, but also complex personal and social considerations. Often this valuable asset has been a home for many years. A home defines a person's life through the roles it plays: a place for friends and family; a place of comforts and conveniences; a place of memories; and a place of belonging. The homeowner's life usually revolves around the privacy, independence, and flexibility that ownership offers. The home can also represent a personal statement by the owner: the pleasure that "pride of ownership" can generate is one example. When the home is sold, every aspect of life can change dramatically. In moving to a new home, an individual must adjust to a new location, a new lifestyle, and a new focus.

Home equity conversion (HEC) offers a third choice—the new alternative—for older homeowners who cannot, or will not, arrange a traditional mortgage and who wish to stay where they are. Older homeowners can improve their financial well-being by using home equity conversion to unlock the equity in their home. At the same time, they will retain ownership and possession of the property. The homeowner will be free of repayment responsibilities until a predetermined time in the future.

This book explores several methods of converting home equity, including reverse mortgages, sale leasebacks, property tax deferral plans, and life estate arrangements. Each approach has distinct benefits and pitfalls. Some types of conversion are more easily arranged than others. This chapter discusses the advantages and disadvantages of reverse mortgages. Chapter 8 explores other methods of home equity conversion.

WHAT IS A REVERSE MORTGAGE?

A reverse mortgage is a variation on the traditional mortgage concept. Reverse mortgages and traditional mortgages are legal claims against the property as security for a loan. In a traditional mortgage, the debt is usually repaid in monthly instalments over many years. **A reverse mortgage enables the homeowner to convert equity into cash without selling the home or repaying the debt immediately.** The homeowner retains ownership and possession of the home while using the equity in the property. The homeowner receives the equity as an amount of cash: in a lump sum, in regular payments, or in a combination of these two options. No repayment of the reverse mortgage takes place until a specified time in the future: when the homeowner sells, when the homeowner moves permanently, when a preset period—perhaps 5 or 10 years—ends, or when the homeowner dies.

Reverse mortgages contradict the old saying, "You can't have your cake and eat it too." With home equity conversion, homeowners can have the "cake"—the home—and they can "eat it too"—take out equity as cash. If the reverse mortgage is a good "fit" and satisfies the homeowner's needs, the cake analogy is complete. Although the reverse mortgage is "consuming" the equity, the property is still completely available to the homeowner.

Yes, the equity is being eroded and, as we will see, may even be completely exhausted as the interest accumulates. However, if the homeowner has taken this reality into account when arranging a reverse mortgage, then the homeowner has decided that having the cake and eating it too is worth the reduction in equity. Without home equity conversion, there would be no other acceptable way to have the home and the cash at the same time, as far as the homeowner is concerned.

And that is precisely when home equity conversion is ideal— when there is no other way. If a homeowner puts aging in place at the top of the "wish list," then all available options should be carefully considered. A reverse mortgage should only be selected when it is clearly the best choice, from all perspectives, for helping the homeowner stay in the home.

A Mortgage by Any Other Name

Reverse mortgages are frequently explained by comparing them to traditional mortgages. The flaw with this approach is that it is based on the assumption that everyone understands what a mortgage is. In reality, most people know very little about mortgages, even if they have actually been a borrower or lender themselves. Since building the explanation of a fundamentally new concept on misunderstandings of another is bound to lead to confusion, a general discussion of mortgages must precede our investigation of reverse mortgages. Although the following material on mortgages may induce "information overload," I encourage you to read on. This background is vital to your truly understanding and appreciating the discussion of reverse mortgages in Chapters 3, 4, and 5.

Reverse mortgages and traditional mortgages are both variations on the mortgage concept. In general, *mortgage* **usually refers only to traditional mortgages. In this book,** *mortgage* **will**

refer to both traditional and reverse mortgages simultaneously. The following statements are true for mortgages, and are therefore true for both traditional and reverse mortgages. However, there may be variations from province to province regarding details or procedures. Contact the provincial government department or ministry that regulates mortgages and mortgage brokers in your area for further information.

A mortgage is a *contract*, or legally binding agreement, between a lender, the *mortgagee*, and a borrower, or *mortgagor*. It is the security given to the lender by the borrower. The mortgage is *registered* against the ownership of the property at the appropriate land registration office to establish the lender's legal claim for the money lent to the borrower. In exchange, the borrower is given a pre-arranged amount of money, called the *principal*, by the lender. As the principal is reduced by regular repayments, it becomes known as the *balance* or *outstanding balance*. The lender usually also receives *interest*, a charge paid by the borrower for the use of the money from the lender. The borrower and the lender agree on the borrower's repayment schedule and describe the schedule in the mortgage contract or document. The *term* of the mortgage is the length of time the mortgage loan will be in effect, as specified in the contract. The term can be any period from 6 months to 30 years. (Most lenders do not offer the complete range of term options.) As the balance may not be completely paid off at the end of one term, renewing or refinancing the mortgage for one or more terms will be necessary until the balance is paid off. Borrowers have the right to *discharge* the mortgage, that is, remove the mortgage claim from *title*, their property ownership registration, once the outstanding balance has been repaid in full, including all interest due.

Most mortgages are arranged to purchase a property, to undertake renovations to the home, to satisfy personal needs, or to solve a crisis in the family.

♠ **Mortgages involve a contract** between a borrower, known as the *mortgagor*, and a lender, called the *mortgagee*. To keep these terms straight, remember the borrower or mortgag*or* must pay up "*or* else." At the same time, the lender or mortgag*ee* thinks, "G*ee*, isn't it nice to get all this interest." The mortgagee or lender could be a bank, a trust company, an insurance company, a credit union, a private investor group, or an individual. The lender may also be represented by agents, brokers, or mortgage brokers who sell the lender's mortgages under their own business names for a commission, but are not employed by the lender. Lenders use their own funds, or those of investors. The mortgage contract identifies the mortgagor and the mortgagee, as well as describing the unique contractual relationship between them. The document also includes a set of terms and clauses that describe the mortgage in detail, specifying the rights and responsibilities of each party. For simplicity, the terms "borrower" and "lender," rather than "mortgagor" and "mortgagee," are used in this book.

♠ **Mortgages provide cash to the borrower at a cost.** The cost to the borrower includes the lender's expenses in setting up, administering, and eventually discharging the mortgage. The borrower's cost also includes the interest charged by the lender against the outstanding balance.

♠ **The maximum size of the mortgage is established by an appraiser, who is hired by the lender, at the borrower's expense.** The appraiser estimates the *lending value* of the property, which represents the maximum amount of money that could safely be lent against the property. Lending value refers to an estimate of property value that reflects the value the lender could expect to generate if forced to liquidate the property quickly. A quick sale would become important should legal action for borrower default become necessary. The lending value is equivalent to 100 percent of the value of the home, from a lender's perspective. Lenders will then offer the borrower a mortgage, usually for an amount less than this maximum value, for instance 50 percent or 75 percent of the appraised or lending value. (Note that lending value is less than *market value*, which is the highest price a willing buyer will pay in an open competitive market. One important factor for achieving market value is exposing the property to potential buyers for a reasonable time period, relative to average sale times.)

Appraisers are qualified specialists who offer professional services for establishing property value. The appraiser's report also describes the type and condition of the property, so that lenders can make sure the property meets their mortgage

---

Market value is the worth of a property, or the amount of rent that can be collected, relative to a specific time or real estate market. It is the largest amount of money a knowledgeable, rational, and unpressured buyer or tenant would pay for a particular property in an open, competitive market. In other words, a property is worth what someone is prepared to pay either to buy or rent it. The market value focuses on the buyer's or tenant's actions, not on the owner's costs, needs, or dreams.

Lending value, used by mortgage lenders to establish the amount of money a consumer may borrow, is a very conservative estimate of value and often considerably lower than market value.

---

criteria. For example, if the property is in disrepair, the lending value would fall. To protect the lender's investment in the mortgage, a portion of the mortgage funds may be withheld until repairs are completed.

- **The mortgage is registered against the ownership of the property to protect the lender's investment.** Registering the mortgage, or recording it at the land registration office, ensures that the property cannot be sold before the mortgage is completely repaid. The borrower must pay off the outstanding balance, including any interest due. Once the mortgage is repaid to the lender, it can be legally discharged, or removed from the ownership registration, so that there is no longer a registered claim from that lender against the property. The home is now *free and clear* of the mortgage debt. All the equity now belongs to the homeowner, unless there are other creditors' claims registered against the property, also expressed as *title is free and clear*.

- **Every mortgage is unique.** Mortgages vary with the borrower, the lender, and the property, as well as the terms and the purpose of each mortgage.

- **The borrower makes *covenants* or legally binding promises to the lender.** The mortgage may include any or all of the following covenants or borrower's legal responsibilities:

- to maintain the property in good repair;
- to keep the property insurance in good standing and up-to-date;
- to pay the property taxes;
- to pay the condominium fees, if applicable; and
- to repay the principal and pay any interest due.

🏠 **The mortgage document gives the lender certain legal rights**, including the right to:

- enter and inspect the property, arrange any necessary repairs, and add the cost of these repairs to the mortgage debt;
- pay the property insurance if it is insufficient, or if it lapses, and add this cost to the mortgage debt;
- pay the property taxes if they fall in arrears and add this cost to the mortgage debt; and
- take legal action against the borrower and recover the mortgage debt should any one of the covenants be broken.

While the mortgage gives the lender many rights or powers, the lender does not acquire the rights of ownership by signing the mortgage contract. When you mortgage your property, whether with a traditional mortgage or a reverse mortgage, *you*, the borrower, remain the owner. As long as the mortgage is kept in good standing by upholding the covenants, the borrower has the right of possession of the property.

For either type of mortgage, if the borrower breaks one of the covenants, provincial mortgage laws give the lender the right to take legal action to collect the debt. For instance, the mortgage contract, with certain restrictions, gives the lender the power to sell the property after gaining possession. Here, the lender does not become the owner of the property, but has the legal right to sell it and apply the proceeds of the sale to the outstanding debt. The borrower could still be responsible for any deficiency if the sale does not produce enough money to pay off the debt. However, any excess funds go to the borrower.

The law offers the lender other legal remedies to collect the debt, including suing for foreclosure. *Foreclosure* is a legal action taken by the lender to gain ownership of the property through the courts. As with all legal remedies, until the lender's legal action is complete, the borrower retains the right to pay off the debt and put the mortgage in good standing or to sell the property to pay off the mortgage debt.

Understanding the Differences

While reverse mortgages and traditional mortgages share the many similarities outlined above, the differences between them are of greater significance. These distinctions make reverse mortgages an exciting option for Canadian homeowners. The key differences outlined below highlight the main advantages and disadvantages of reverse mortgages compared with traditional mortgages. These features will be discussed in detail in the next four chapters.

♠ Traditional Mortgages in Reverse

Traditional mortgages: As the homeowner (borrower) *makes* regular repayments of principal and interest to the lender, the balance owing on a traditional mortgage gradually *decreases*. At the same time, the homeowner's share of the equity in the home gradually *increases*. The traditional mortgage terminates, usually 10 to 25 years later, when the original debt, including all accumulated interest and any penalties, has been completely repaid. At this point, the homeowner possesses all the equity in the property.

Reverse mortgages: Here, things happen in reverse. Since the homeowner *receives* payments from the lender, the balance owing on a reverse mortgage *increases*. At the same time, the homeowner's share of the equity in the home *decreases*. The reverse mortgage terminates at a specified time in the future: when the homeowner sells; when the homeowner moves permanently; when a preset term ends; or when the homeowner dies. When the reverse mortgage terminates, the total accumulated debt of the reverse mortgage, including any fees or penalties, must be repaid to the lender.

The equity in the home may be completely depleted even before the reverse mortgage terminates, as interest accumulates against the debt. (See "Interest on the Interest," page 21, for further details.) In this case, the mortgage debt, including accumulated interest, will exceed the value of the property. However, the borrower is usually limited to repaying the portion of the debt equal to the value of the property; the lender must absorb the extra debt. The homeowner is not required to sell the home to repay the reverse mortgage debt. However, sale of the property may prove to be the most common method of paying off a reverse mortgage. Any funds from the sale left after the mortgage debt is settled, belong to the homeowner or the estate.

♠ Basis for Qualification

Traditional mortgages: Qualification for a traditional mortgage is based on the borrower's ability to repay; that is, on the borrower's income. Most lenders dictate that the combined payments for principal, interest, and taxes should not exceed approximately 30 percent of the family's total gross income. The traditional mortgage will be set at a percentage of the appraised value. The appraised value of the property represents 100 percent of the lending value. A homeowner may be eligible to borrow up to 90 percent of the appraised value of the property from most lenders. However, mortgaging up to or more than 100 percent of the value may also be possible.

Reverse mortgages: In contrast, the borrower's income is not a factor in qualifying for a reverse mortgage. In fact, a homeowner with no income at all can arrange a reverse mortgage. Qualification for a reverse mortgage is based on:
- the appraised value of the property
- the age and sex of the homeowner(s)

Lender policy establishes the maximum lending limit for the reverse mortgages the lender offers. This limit is set as a percentage of the appraised value of the property. Most lenders keep their upper borrowing limit under 50 percent of the appraised value, for instance, a maximum of 30 percent to 40 percent of the appraised value of the property. This is to ensure that, as interest accumulates, the mortgage does not exceed 75 percent of the appraised value. Using the lender's borrowing criteria, a limit is established for each borrower that is at or under the lender's maximum lending percentage.

♠ Age is an Asset

Traditional mortgages: As the lender's security is tied to the homeowner's ability to repay the mortgage, older homeowners may be at a disadvantage when applying for a traditional mortgage. Lenders are very aware of the decrease in income that is associated with retirement, and of the limited employment opportunities that may be available to older homeowners.

Reverse mortgages: Here, age is a positive factor. In fact, reverse mortgages are designed *for* the older homeowner. Often, the minimum qualifying age is set at 60. Furthermore, the lender's payments to the homeowner are based on projections of the homeowner's life expectancy. Therefore, the older the homeowner, the greater the reverse mortgage payments possible from the lender.

♠ On the Receiving End

Traditional mortgages: The responsibility of making regular, usually monthly, repayment can reduce the advantage gained by arranging a traditional mortgage for some homeowners. A few may even have to resort to using the mortgage money they borrowed to make the required regular repayments.

Reverse mortgages: One of the most attractive differences between these two types of mortgages is that with reverse mortgages, homeowners receive payments instead of making them. The equity in the home is converted into cash by the reverse mortgage. The homeowner receives this cash in a lump sum, in regular payments, or in a combination of these two options. The payment period for the homeowner may last a few years or a lifetime, depending on the terms of the reverse mortgage contract.

♠ Interest on the Interest

Traditional mortgages: Most residential mortgages are repaid in blended monthly payments of principal and interest. With blended payments, the Federal Interest Act restricts the frequency of compounding interest to either semiannual or annual calculations. For most traditional mortgages, interest is compounded semiannually and charged against a decreasing balance.

THE "RULE OF 72"

Compounding interest involves charging interest on the interest. When saving money, compounding is a positive accelerator of the saving process, as it builds the balance more quickly. When borrowing money, compounding becomes a debt accelerator, as it is the factor that makes the debt grow more quickly.

The amount of interest charged in a period, for instance over one year, is added to the balance to create a new amount on which to calculate interest. For example, at the end of the first year, the interest charged on $50,000 would be $4,500, if the rate was 9 percent, compounded annually. In the second, the interest would be charged on the new balance of $54,500. Eventually, the original amount of money will double in size to $100,000 as the interest accumulates. **To determine the doubling point, divide 72 by the percentage of interest.** Continuing with the example above, the $50,000 would double to $100,000 in (72 ÷ 9) 8 years, if the interest rate remained at 9 percent. At 6 percent, the $50,000 would double in 12 years; at 12 percent it would double in 6 (72÷12) years.

Other types of traditional mortgage repayment plans are not restricted in the frequency of interest compounding.

Reverse mortgages: While semiannual compounding is common in reverse mortgages, the frequency of compounding in these mortgages has no legal limit. In contrast to the interest charged in traditional mortgages, the interest in reverse mortgages is compounded against a steadily increasing balance. For instance, if the borrower receives the payment in a lump sum, interest compounds against the total principal as well as against the accumulating interest, from the date the mortgage is signed.

♠ Borrower Default and Lender Risk

Traditional mortgages: The most common cause of borrower *default,* or breach of the mortgage contract, is the borrower's failure to make the required principal and interest payments. To protect lenders against loss, the National Housing Act stipulates that all mortgages over 75 percent of the appraised value of the property, called *high-ratio mortgages*, must be insured against borrower default. As lender risks are reduced, lenders are more receptive to offering *high-ratio mortgages*. Canada Mortgage and Housing Corporation (CMHC), the federal housing agency, provides mortgage insurance for lenders and pays off the debt if the borrower defaults on the mortgage. The premiums are paid by the borrower.

Reverse mortgages: The reverse mortgage industry is still in its infancy. Patterns of mortgage default have not emerged as yet. Since reverse mortgages are not repaid until some future date, default could occur at the termination date if the homeowner refused or was unable to move at the end of the term, so that the home could be sold to repay the debt. However, as discussed in the previous section, the lender could take power of sale action against the borrower to force the sale of the property, or the lender could sue for foreclosure to take over ownership.

Default could also occur if the borrower failed to maintain the home in good repair, keep the property insured, or pay the property taxes. While the same remedies would be available to resolve these default situations as with the failure to repay the mortgage debt, the lender may decide on less drastic default remedies. For each of these default situations, the lender could step in and solve the problem for the borrower, and then add any costs incurred in the process to the mortgage balance.

There is, however, a lender risk peculiar to reverse mortgages. Because the mortgage balance is growing constantly as the interest compounds, if property values stay the same or decrease, the mortgage debt could exceed the value of the property. The reverse mortgage could also consume all the equity in the property if the homeowner outlives the lender's estimates of life expectancy. Obviously, if these two situations occur at once, the mortgage debt will probably exceed the value of the home. Provided the mortgage contract carries a clause to limit the homeowner's liability, the borrower has to repay only the portion of the mortgage equivalent to the value of the home. The lender must absorb debt that exceeds the value of the property. Lender insurance for reverse mortgages would cover the lender against this potential loss.

TRADITIONAL MORTGAGES AND REVERSE MORTGAGES: A COMPARISON

	Traditional Mortgages	Reverse Mortgages
Basis for Qualification	Homeowner(s)'s income; appraised value of property	Appraised value of property; age of homeowner(s)
Size of Mortgage	Depends on income of homeowner(s) and appraised value of property	Depends on appraised value of property, and age of homeowner(s)
During the Mortgage	Homeowner(s) *make* regular repayments of principal and interest *to* the lender, as per mortgage contract	Homeowner(s) *receive* lump sum payment(s), regular payments, or a combination of these payment plans, *from* the lender, as per mortgage contract
Debt/Equity Pattern	Decreasing debt, increasing equity	Increasing debt, decreasing equity
When Mortgage Ends	Debt completely repaid; homeowner holds all the equity	Debt at maximum; equity at minimum or completely depleted
Source of Repayment	Income of homeowner(s) or other assets	Equity in property or other assets

HOME EQUITY CONVERSION IN PERSPECTIVE

Although home equity conversion programs are fairly new in Canada, they have existed since Napoleonic times. In fact, reverse mortgages are familiar financial tools in many countries. Those who have lived abroad, or who travel extensively, are often surprised to learn that home equity conversion is only beginning to emerge in Canada as an alternative for older homeowners.

Home equity conversion and reverse mortgages are well known to older homeowners in many western European countries, including Britain. Home equity conversion programs have also emerged in the Pacific Rim countries of Japan, Australia, and

New Zealand. In North America, reverse mortgages were introduced in the United States more than thirty years ago.

The legal frameworks and the program details differ from
country to country, but the concept remains the same: equity in
the home is converted to generate cash or to postpone payment of
an expense such as property taxes. The homeowner does not have
to move and usually retains ownership of the property. Therefore,
home equity conversion allows older homeowners to improve
their standard of living while maintaining continuity with home,
family, and community. The "aging in place" pattern that results
also reduces the need for government-subsidized seniors' housing
or institutional care.

A detailed global review of all the home equity conversion programs available is beyond the scope of this publication. However,
research for this book included an examination of a number of conversion programs in other countries. In some countries, banking
and mortgaging systems are very different from those in Canada, so
that comparisons become quite complicated. Although one aspect
of the British market is outlined in Chapter 9, page 212, to illustrate
a concern regarding consumer protection, the American reverse
mortgage market was selected for a full profile, which is given
below. The U.S. market seemed the natural choice for four main
reasons: (1) Canada is now more closely connected with the United
States than ever before; (2) the growing "snowbird" population,
those with property south of the border, is keen to understand
housing and financial developments that might affect their second
homes; (3) most Canadians have had some contact with the way
things are done in the United States; and (4) the American market
has progressed beyond the pioneer stage.

Reverse Mortgages in the United States

Since the first reverse mortgage was arranged in Maine in 1961, a
growing number of lenders, including banks, private companies,
and local governments, have offered reverse mortgage programs
in the United States. The American reverse mortgage market
entered a new era in 1988 when the U.S. federal government introduced a national reverse mortgage insurance program, both to
reduce lender risk and to encourage lender participation in this

evolving market. At first, the federal Home Equity Conversion Mortgage Insurance Demonstration, known as the HECM Demonstration, made insurance available for 2500 reverse mortgages across the country. Fifty Federal Housing Administration (FHA)–approved lenders participated in the initial pilot program. In November 1990, the national program was expanded, offering insurance for 25,000 reverse mortgages. The 10,000 FHA–approved lenders across the country then became eligible to take part in the reverse mortgage program.

The HECM Demonstration protects lenders against financial loss. The program does not offer borrowers government-subsidized reverse mortgages at below-market prices. In fact, the expense of the mortgage insurance premium that the borrower is required to pay, added to the set-up and administration fees, can make the cost prohibitive for some of the cash-poor, house-rich older homeowners the program was originally designed to assist. Conservative loan limits make the program impractical for owners of higher-priced homes.

The HECM Demonstration, which has five reverse mortgage payment options, allows borrowers to switch payment plans at any time during the life of their reverse mortgage. The flexible withdrawal option, called a line of credit, has proven popular, either alone or in combination with another payment plan. In response to consumer demand, an equity preservation feature was added to the program to guarantee homeowners that all their equity would not be depleted.

The Demonstration program appeals to older borrowers, largely those over 70, who have substantial equity in their homes but little income and few, if any, children. Homeowners who take part tend to have above-average-valued homes but below-average incomes and are heavily dependent on Social Security payments (government pensions).

The U.S. program got off to a slow start for a number of reasons. The complexity of offering five payment options for the reverse mortgage discouraged many lenders. In addition, existing federal and state laws and regulations presented problems in implementing the HECM Demonstration. Because they were written for traditional mortgages and other types of loans, these laws and regulations often contain provisions that are unfavourable to reverse mortgages. Also, the requirement that prospective borrowers receive mandatory counselling from approved housing counsellors caused a bottleneck. The HECM counsellor training program, sponsored by the American Association of Retired Persons (AARP—a nonprofit, nonpartisan organization with more than 32 million members aged 50 and over), has been very effective in training over 1000 counsellors from across the United States. However, the availability of qualified counsellors and the monitoring of counselling quality remain concerns in quite a few of the 47 states involved in the Demonstration. Counsellors must be employed by, or volunteer for, one of the 500 Federal Department of Housing and Urban Development (HUD)-approved agencies. Approved counsellors use computers to demonstrate the various HECM options available, but do not provide financial guidance nor discuss private plans.

In spite of these problems, by reducing risks, the Demonstration did encourage lenders to enter the reverse mortgage market. Many lenders were also attracted to HECM when the Federal National Mortgage Association, a private corporation known as "Fannie Mae," agreed to purchase the reverse mortgages, called HECM loans. The establishment of this secondary mortgage market, a normal feature in traditional mortgage markets, was essential to the development of the HECM Demonstration. Lenders are now able to sell the reverse mortgages to secondary market investors and use the proceeds of these sales to make additional HECM loans available. Also, the administration services offered by Wendover Funding, a private company, allow lenders to subcontract the ongoing responsiblities of reverse mortgage loan servicing.

The HECM Demonstration has raised the profile of reverse mortgages and has created a recognized framework for reverse mortgage lending. The private sector has benefited as well. Private lenders were reported to have arranged more than 9000 reverse mortgages from 1990 through 1992, bringing the estimated total from the 1980s to the early 1990s to approximately 15,000 reverse mortgages from all sources.

Reverse mortgages are not the only known type of home equity conversion in the United States. Deferred payment loans and property tax deferral programs are also available in a number of areas. For instance, property tax deferral programs, which allow homeowners to postpone payment of property taxes, are available state-wide or regionally in 16 states, including Florida and Washington.

While the economic downturn of the early 1990s limited the funding available to some private lenders, on the whole, the reverse mortgage market has shown steady growth in the United States. For example, the HECM program is now operating in 47 of the 50 states, plus Puerto Rico and the U.S. Virgin Islands. In mid-1993, reverse mortgages coupled with income-generating products called annuities were introduced to the U.S. market by two new lenders, one of which is the high-profile Transamerica Corporation. These reverse mortgages will continue to provide the consumer with income through the annuity even after the home is sold. (For an explanation of annuities, see Chapter 3, page 45.) Fannie Mae is, at the time of this writing, introducing a privately insured reverse mortgage line of credit program that has the potential to be available on a large scale. Other lenders are also preparing to enter the market. The United States will undergo many changes as reverse mortgages and home equity conversion gain further acceptance with lenders and homeowners alike: the 1990s may well represent the decade of the reverse mortgage for Americans.

And in Canada ...

The Canadian home equity conversion market is in its infancy. Since the mid-1970s, a great deal has been written and said about home equity conversion options, especially reverse mortgages. For the past few years, in fact, reverse mortgages have been a "hot" media topic. Gradually, the home equity conversion movement has been gaining momentum. The Canadian reverse mortgage marketplace has begun to define itself with a few exploratory products. Property tax deferral programs, another conversion option, exist on a limited scale. When consumer demand intensifies and more lenders enter the market, consumers will enjoy the full advantage of shopping in a competitive home equity conversion market, especially in rural areas. Although this consumer-driven movement has begun, only time will reveal how well consumers' voices have been heard.

Canadian lenders, including the chartered banks, are legally entitled to sell reverse mortgages and many other conversion products. However, they are unlikely to do so to any great extent until there is measurable, consistent consumer demand. Currently, reverse mortgages and other home equity conversion options are not widely available across the country. However, banks, insurance companies, and other financial institutions have expressed interest in home equity conversion. Most financial institutions and related businesses have been monitoring the rising consumer awareness of home equity conversion and reverse mortgages for a number of years.

A few pioneering products have been introduced in Canada by private companies, but without direct or indirect government involvement. To date, government counselling services and consumer protection programs have not developed to a level that would parallel the growth in the emerging Canadian reverse mortgage market.

While the federal housing agency, Canada Mortgage and Housing Corporation (CMHC), has researched the development of the reverse mortgage market in the United States, this agency has not participated directly in the Canadian market. Nor has CMHC created any comprehensive consumer education and protection programs, although it has produced a few pieces of background literature. In 1992, CMHC began a consultation process designed to examine the feasibility of amending the National Housing Act to extend CMHC's mortgage lender insurance program to cover reverse mortgage lenders against loss. CMHC's proposed insurance program may be the catalyst that will galvanize potential reverse mortgage lenders into action.

The explanation of types of reverse mortgages in Chapter 3 will assist readers to analyze the reverse mortgage products currently available in Canada. This chapter also contains background on Canadian reverse mortgage lenders and furthers the discussion of reverse mortgage insurance for lenders. The investigation of reverse mortgages continues through Chapters 4, 5, and 6. Although the reader is encouraged to read this book in sequence for maximum clarity, the Glossary, on page 291, will support those who would like to read ahead.

Chapter 8 explores other types of home equity conversion, including property tax deferral and sale leasebacks. Once again, if you wish to read ahead, the Glossary can assist you.

WHO IS "THE LENDER"?

A reverse mortgage lender, known as the mortgagee, could be a bank, a trust company, an insurance company, a credit union, a private investor group, or an individual. (Note that Banks are not currently lending reverse mortgages however.) Lenders may sell their own reverse mortgage product(s) themselves. They may also be represented by agents, who enter into an agreement to act on the lender's behalf for a sales commission, but who are not employed by the lender. Usually, these acknowledged agents are insurance brokers, mortgage brokers, or financial planners. Agents advertise and sell one or more lenders' reverse mortgage product(s) under their own business name. In this book, *lender* refers to the originator or the supplier of a reverse mortgage product. However, the points and the concerns raised concerning lenders hold true even if the borrower is working through an acknowledged agent. Borrowers would, nevertheless, be wise to clarify whether they are dealing directly with the lender or through an agent.

Lenders may originate the entire reverse mortgage product themselves or only a portion. For instance, the lender may arrange the mortgage component of a reverse mortgage and then purchase the annuity from an insurance company, in order to offer a reverse annuity mortgage product to the consumer as a complete package. (See page 45 for a discussion of annuities and reverse annuity mortgages.)

CHAPTER 3

Variations on a Theme

O f all the questions concerning home equity conversion that I have been asked over the years, the one question I hear most often is: "Which is the best reverse mortgage?" This apparently simple question is anything but simple to answer. No single reverse mortgage product is a "one-size-fits-all" option. However, one *type* of reverse mortgage might suit you better than another. **The "best" reverse mortgage is the one that is best for you today and that is best suited to your plans for the future.**

Building on the mortgage concepts explained in Chapter 2, this chapter introduces the basic types of reverse mortgages. The first section, "Types of Reverse Mortgages," explores the ideas behind the various reverse mortgage designs. The second section, "The Emerging Canadian Market," discusses which of these options are available to consumers across Canada.

While you may be tempted to skip to the second section, give "Types of Reverse Mortgages" a chance. To properly evaluate your options, you should understand and be able to compare the various types of reverse mortgages. Canada's reverse mortgage market does not resemble a supermarket. You cannot simply choose from shelves full of products, all regulated by the government to be safe for consumer use. Home equity conversion in Canada is in its pioneer stage. It is possible that the only home equity conversion option available to you today may be to create your own reverse mortgage. Knowing the "what" and the "why" of reverse mortgages is important in this "Buyer Beware" marketplace. Consumers should be prepared to take responsibility for equipping themselves to make informed decisions.

REVERSE MORTGAGES CLARIFIED

Some of the confusion that consumers experience regarding reverse mortgages arises from the fact that the term "reverse mortgage" is often used to refer to all types and all variations of reverse mortgages. For example, the terms "reverse mortgage" and "reverse annuity mortgage" are often used interchangeably. Rarely are "fixed term" and "tenure plans" identified accurately. And the reverse mortgage line of credit is often overlooked.

In this book, I use the term "reverse mortgage" to refer collectively to reverse mortgages and to related reverse mortgage products. Use of this term means that the statement applies equally to all types of reverse mortgages. For further clarification, see the Glossary on page 291.

How Much Will a Reverse Mortgage Pay?

The maximum loan amount, or total equity advance of a reverse mortgage depends on the factors which are discussed below:

- ♠ the present and future value of the property
- ♠ the age of the homeowner(s)
- ♠ lender profit and costs
- ♠ the amount of equity preserved from conversion
- ♠ the design of the reverse mortgage

♠ The Present and Future Value of the Property

The greater the value of the property and the more stable the local real estate market, the more the reverse mortgage will pay. The lender arranges a professional appraisal to establish the lending value of the property. The general condition of the property can have an impact on the lending value. This is the value that the lender believes represents a realistic selling price for the property even if a quick sale were required. (See Chapter 2, page 16, for more on appraisals.) The lender selects annual property appreciation projections, based on available real estate sales statistics, to determine the future value of the property. For instance, in 1990 value-increase estimates of 5 percent to 7 percent in annual appreciation were typical. Throughout the early 1990s, figures of 0 percent to 4 percent have represented the real estate market appreciation factors currently in use by lenders.

The length of time the homeowner has owned the home is not a factor. The property could be bought today and the equity converted tomorrow if a reverse mortgage could be arranged that quickly.

♠ The Age of the Homeowner(s)

The older the homeowner, the greater the payments. Older is definitely better with reverse mortgages. Very simply, each property represents a finite amount of equity. If this equity is released over a shorter period, it will generate larger individual payments, as there are fewer to make. Reverse mortgage lenders base their calculations on life expectancy projections. These statistics project how long individuals can be expected to live beyond a certain age. That is, the older the individual, the shorter the life expectancy. Gender plays a role in life expectancy, as statistics show that women live longer than men. For example, a 66-year-old woman will live another 18 (to the age of 84) years, a 66-year-old man 14 years (to the age of 80); a 93-year-old woman will live 3½ years, a man 3 years.

Older homeowners also benefit in that there is less time for the interest on the balance to accumulate.

♠ Lender Profit and Costs

Lender profit and various borrowing costs, including interest charges, will reduce the size of the payments. Reverse mortgages are not free. A reverse mortgage has the costs of developing and administering the home equity conversion program built into it, just as costs are built into all financial products. Legal fees, sales commissions, and advertising represent a large portion of the lender's costs. However, lenders who borrow funds to offer as reverse mortgages incur an additional expense: they have to pay interest to the investor who provides the funds for the reverse mortgage. Lender profits derive from the interest differences, or "spreads." An *interest spread* is the difference between what the lender pays to borrow the money for the equity advances, and what the homeowner pays the lender to use the equity advances. For example, the lender might borrow at 10 percent and lend at 11 percent; the interest spread of 1 percent means a 1 percent profit for the lender. Lender profit also derives from the interest spread between the reverse mortgage interest rate and the interest rate on the annuity. For instance, if the annuity provided through or by the lender is 9 percent while the reverse mortgage rate paid by the borrower is 11 percent, the 2 percent spread is lender profit.

The homeowner's direct borrowing costs include application cost, appraisal fees, closing costs (legal costs for finalizing the contract), servicing or administration fees, and interest charges. The direct costs for the lender mentioned above, including legal fees, sales commissions, advertising, and interest charges to investors, are built into the reverse mortgage as indirect costs for the borrower.

⌂ The Amount of Equity Preserved from Conversion

The more equity that is preserved and not converted, the less equity is available for the reverse mortgage payments. The equity left at the end of the reverse mortgage is called *residual equity*. This amount of equity belongs to the homeowner or to the heirs of the homeowner's estate.

⌂ The Design of the Reverse Mortgage

The specific type of reverse mortgage also affects the size of the payments. For example, the longer the *term*, or the length of time the reverse mortgage runs, the lower the payments. Also, in a combination payment plan, a lump sum payment at the beginning of a reverse mortgage will reduce the size of the regular instalments, by reducing the equity advance available.

TYPES OF REVERSE MORTGAGES

Reverse mortgages enable homeowners to convert their equity into cash without selling their home or having to repay the mortgage debt until some time in the future. They allow homeowners to spend the equity in their home while retaining ownership and possession of the property.

As explained in Chapter 2, a reverse mortgage is a contract between a lender, the mortgagee, and a borrower, the mortgagor, who is a homeowner. The reverse mortgage contract describes, in detail, the type of reverse mortgage, including the pattern of payments and the length of time the mortgage will run. Usually, the lender sets the terms and the conditions. However, following discussions and negotiations between the lender and the borrower, the reverse mortgage contract may be modified. If the borrower decides to accept the terms and the conditions of the reverse mortgage, both parties sign the reverse mortgage contract. On the other hand, before signing, the homeowner is free to turn down this lender's reverse mortgage offer. However, the homeowner may forfeit an application fee of several hundred dollars as a result.

The basic reverse mortgage variations are outlined below.

Outline: Variations on the Reverse Mortgage Theme

The discussion that follows examines reverse mortgage *design variables*, or factors, then explores the various types of reverse mortgages. As mentioned earlier, lenders may describe their products with different terminology or use this terminology differently. Also, shared appreciation can be coupled with the other types of mortgages. All of the types listed on page 35 can exist as fixed-term or tenure-plan mortgages. Your goal when investigating a specific reverse mortgage product should be to relate it to one of these basic types. Once you have asked enough questions to be sure which type of reverse mortgage is involved you will be better able to determine the suitability of the product for your needs. Remember, your goal and that of a reputable salesperson should be the same: to be sure you understand. Don't be intimidated by anyone's jargon.

REVERSE MORTGAGE DESIGN VARIABLES

Two of the main design variables, or factors, in a reverse mortgage are:

1) the type of *equity advance* or payment plan, and

2) the *timeframe* of the reverse mortgage: the length of time the reverse mortgage will run.

(1) Equity Advance or Payment Plans

By arranging a reverse mortgage, homeowners borrow on their own money—their equity in the home. Equity, the net value in the home, accumulates as property values increase and/or as an original traditional mortgage is gradually paid off. This equity is eventually released to the homeowner, or to the estate, when the property is sold. However, as explained earlier, a reverse mortgage releases the accumulated value *now*, by lending the homeowner the equity in advance of selling the property. *Equity advances* can be as small as a few hundred dollars a month or as large as lump sums of tens of thousands of dollars.

The reverse mortgage lender gives the homeowner advance payments of equity in return for a fully secured loan against the house. The lender also receives interest on the total equity advance. Note that, just as money borrowed against the home in a traditional mortgage is not taxable income, reverse mortgage equity advances are not considered income. This distinction is an important one, both for the homeowner who receives the money, as well as for the public, in terms of growing acceptance of home equity conversion products. *Reverse mortgages are a source of tax-free dollars because equity advances are not considered taxable income.* (Note that the situation is more complex with reverse annuity mortgages, but the outcome is the same—the money is not taxable income. See Chapter 10 for details.)

The lender may or may not impose restrictions on the use of equity advances.

Lump Sum Plans

A lump sum equity advance may equal the entire reverse mortgage loan (principal), or a sizeable percentage of this amount. A lump sum payment does not equal the total amount of equity in the home. Typically, whether in a single payment or in a series of them, the total equity advance represents less than 50 percent of the equity in the property.

If the reverse mortgage contract does not specify any restrictions, the homeowner may put the money to any use. However, the lender could restrict the use of the lump sum equity advance, or most of this payment, to the purchase of an income-generating annuity. The lender may further restrict the homeowner to purchasing the annuity from

EXAMPLE OF A LUMP SUM PAYMENT

If a house is worth $200,000, the homeowner has $200,000 equity, provided there are no traditional mortgages or other debts against the property. If a 35 percent reverse mortgage were arranged, this mortgage would release $70,000 of the equity. The $70,000 lump sum would go directly to the homeowner, or it would be used, by the borrower or by the lender, to buy an income-generating investment product or *annuity* (see page 45). As a result, a reverse mortgage debt of $70,000 plus interest would accumulate against the house.

one or two insurance companies, selected by the lender. In practice, the reverse mortgage lender usually purchases an annuity in the homeowner's name, thus converting the lump sum equity advance into a stream of income for the homeowner. (See "Reverse Annuity Mortgages" on page 45.)

If a homeowner needs cash to buy a second home, to pay off a debt, to renovate the home, or to start a business, the lump sum equity advance is an attractive option. With this method of payment, the borrower can raise a lump sum of tax-free money and remain in the family home. There is no obligation to repay the reverse mortgage until a date in the future.

Exercise caution before selecting the lump sum payment plan. Since the full amount of the reverse mortgage is advanced from the time the mortgage is signed, interest is compounded on the entire balance over the life of the mortgage. Therefore, total interest costs are highest with this type of payment plan.

Caution is also advised because, once the money is gone, the homeowner will be left with an increasing debt against the property. The borrower may have to sell the property to pay off the reverse mortgage debt eventually. The problem worsens if the reverse mortgage is due, for example, in five years. After even five years, the homeowner may need to sell the home to pay off the debt. Further, if the real estate market is in a slump, the homeowner could be left with insufficient funds to maintain a certain desired standard of living.

Regular Instalment Plans

In this type of payment plan, the homeowner receives the equity advance in regular instalments—monthly, annually, or as frequently as agreed to in the contract—over the lifetime of the reverse mortgage. If the interest rate has been fixed for the duration of the reverse mortgage, the size of the payments will remain constant. If the interest rate changes at agreed-upon intervals during the reverse mortgage, the equity advances may change as the interest rate is reset. In this version of a regular instalment plan, the reverse mortgage debt increases with each payment to the homeowner. Interest is charged against the outstanding balance, which represents the total of the payments received by the homeowner to date, *not* the total amount of the reverse mortgage set in the contract.

Line of credit reverse mortgages can be set up either to allow the homeowner to self-manage the regularity of withdrawals, or to have automatic period deposits made to the homeowner's account by the lender. (See page 49 for details.)

Another variation on the regular instalment plan is found in *reverse annuity mortgages*, which are reverse mortgages coupled with income-generating products called annuities. With this type of reverse mortgage, the interest is compounded against the total amount of the reverse mortgage from the date the mortgage begins. (See "Reverse Annuity Mortgages" on page 45.)

Combination Plans

A reverse mortgage may combine the payment plans described above to custom-fit a homeowner's situation. One common combination is a moderate lump sum payment, usually representing 25 percent to 40 percent of the reverse mortgage, coupled with a reverse annuity mortgage. For example, a retired couple may need a lump sum of $25,000 to buy a car and to replace an aging furnace. They may also want a monthly income to supplement their pensions.

In the case of the lump sum example on page 37, the $70,000 reverse mortgage discussed there would provide the homeowner with up to $24,500 as a lump sum, if the lender's maximum for lump sum payments is 35 percent of the reverse mortgage. The balance of the reverse mortgage could then be used by the homeowner, or by the lender on behalf of the homeowner, to purchase an annuity. An annuity purchased with the remaining $32,500 would generate less income than an annuity bought with the original $50,000 balance of the reverse mortgage. In combination plans, the lump sum amount must be limited in size to ensure that sufficient equity advance funds remain to generate the size and frequency of the regular payments required by the homeowner. These calculations are carried out by the lender using the borrower's criteria. Computers enable lenders to "crunch the numbers" quickly and simply. The lender can show the homeowner the impact of increasing or decreasing the lump sum on the size of the regular instalments.

(2) Timeframes

The length of time the reverse mortgage runs, an important design variable, gives rise to two categories of reverse mortgage:

- fixed-term reverse mortgages
- tenure-plan or lifetime reverse mortgages

Fixed-Term Reverse Mortgages

A fixed-term reverse mortgage must be repaid completely after a specified period, usually 5 or 10 years. Such mortgages can be ideal if the additional income is needed only for a short period. For example, the mortgage may provide income until a homeowner's retirement benefits begin; until an investment matures; until space is available in a desired housing complex; or until a terminal illness has run its course.

Once the homeowner and the lender agree to the term—the number of years the mortgage will run—they are both bound by that term. **The homeowner cannot have second thoughts.** When the mortgage falls due, the debt must be settled, even if the property must be sold to raise the funds for repayment. The lender is not required to renew the reverse mortgage unless a clause in the contract guarantees that the borrower has the option to renew. Refinancing is possible, but not probable, for retired homeowners, so it is best not to count on this faint possibility.

Fixed-term reverse mortgages incorporate lump sum plans, regular instalment plans, or combination plans for payment of the equity advances to the homeowner. Reverse annuity mortgages are a common type of fixed-term reverse mortgage, and they use the regular instalment payment approach. Here, the fixed-term reverse mortgage releases the equity, which is then used to purchase a fixed-term annuity. The mortgage and the annuity usually terminate at the same time.

Reverse mortgage lines of credit are another type of fixed-term reverse mortgage. For a definition and detailed discussion, see "Reverse Mortgage Line of Credit" on page 49.

Case Study:
Fixed-Term Reverse Mortgage Line of Credit

Mr. and Mrs. T both retired early, determined to "enjoy life since we are in good health." Mr. T owned and operated his own business for 42 years while Mrs. T had part-time employment. Their pension income will be limited to the government pension programs. Mr. and Mrs. T have lived in their Toronto home for 33 years and paid off the mortgage years ago.

After their daughter read an article on home equity conversion, she encouraged her parents to put off selling their home and enjoy life now by arranging a reverse mortgage. They agreed a reverse mortgage would give them the money they needed to travel and pay the bills. The children told their parents not to worry about them as they were well established already.

Mr. and Mrs. T called around, located a lender they felt comfortable with, and signed up for a *3-year reverse mortgage line of credit* in May of 1993. They were offered a 4-year term but decided a 3-year term would suit their needs. Interest will be adjusted annually.

The whole process, from first contact with the lender to the date of signing, was approximately 6 weeks, and included extensive counselling with the lender and the Ts' lawyer.

House value (appraised 1993)	$150,000
Reverse Mortgage Line of Credit	$52,000
Line of credit maximum withdrawal limits:	
for year 1	$25,000
for year 2	$14,000
for year 3	$13,000

When the reverse mortgage comes due, they feel they will sell the house and move into a senior's apartment building to reduce their overhead. The money left after paying off the reverse mortgage will enable them to continue to take the trips they so enjoy.

They could have had the entire amount of the reverse mortgage all at once but decided on the line of credit so that they could withdraw what they needed as they needed it. Mr. and Mrs. T are very pleased to be able to have their home and their money too. They do not consider arranging a reverse mortgage equivalent to going into debt as "it is our money—we are just spending our own money in advance." The interest due at the end of each year will be paid out of the line of credit account. They feel a reverse mortgage is ideal for people who "want to enjoy life before they get too old to do so."

Tenure-Plan Reverse Mortgages

A *tenure-plan* (also known as a *lifetime* plan) reverse mortgage runs until the homeowner moves permanently, until the property is sold, or until the homeowner dies. In other words, until the homeowner's tenure of the property ends. As owner occupancy is usually a condition of the mortgage contract, the reverse mortgage may also terminate if the homeowner vacates the property for an extended period. Tenure plans allow homeowners to live in the home for as long as they would like or for as long as they are physically able. The equity advances provide the funds to make this possible. These mortgages use lump sum plans, regular instalment payment plans, or combinations of these two payment options.

Reverse annuity mortgages are a popular tenure-plan variation. In this type of plan, the proceeds of the reverse mortgage are used to purchase a lifetime annuity that pays the homeowner monthly income for life. The reverse annuity mortgage ends when the homeowner dies, sells the property, or moves permanently. However, the annuity income continues for the balance of the homeowner's life, even after the reverse mortgage has ended and the home has been sold.

Laws regulate each type of lender differently and, therefore, dictate the features of a lender's reverse mortgage products. In Canada, only insurance companies can sell financial products that are based on life risk or life expectancies such as annuities. Therefore, only insurance companies can originate tenure-plan (lifetime) reverse mortgages at present. Other lenders can offer reverse annuity mortgages by purchasing annuities from an insurance company.

Case Study:
Tenure-Plan Reverse Annuity Mortgage

Mr. and Mrs. Y still live in the two-storey Toronto home they bought new in 1956. They paid off their mortgage in 1981. Both are retired from the same large office supply company after long careers. By 1991, Mr. and Mrs. Y found that their unindexed pensions were not keeping pace with rising costs. They did "not want to leave [their home] until they have to" as they "are not the type to go into an apartment." However, they were under "pressure to give up the house as maintenance costs were rising."

They attended a seminar by a financial planner and became interested in the reverse mortgage concept. With his assistance, they researched this option. At that time the Canadian Automobile Association magazine carried an article on reverse mortgages that encouraged them further. Their son and daughter, both in their 40s, fully supported their decision to arrange a reverse mortgage. Mr. and Mrs. Y signed up for a *tenure-plan reverse annuity mortgage* in March, 1991. They decide on a 10-year guaranteed annuity with survivor benefits to ensure the payments run until the death of the surviving spouse.

House value (appraised August 1991)	$260,000
Reverse Annuity Mortgage	$66,390
Annuity purchased for	$41,855
Lump sum received in 1991	$22,000
Monthly payments from annuity	$386.00
(* Costs not included here)	

Some of the $22,000 lump sum payment was used on the home and the rest was invested. The revenue from the reverse mortgage enabled them to complete a self-contained apartment for their daughter, replace the roof, rebuild the chimney, and "employ people to do the lawns and shovel snow." As they are "not Florida-types" and live in their home year round, the house is very important to them. They will "stay until they can't."

TYPES OF REVERSE MORTGAGES

The differences between the types of reverse mortgages lie with the legal framework of the reverse mortgage and the manner in which the borrower receives the equity advances. Four basic types are:

- ♠ Simple reverse mortgages
- ♠ Reverse annuity mortgages
- ♠ Reverse mortgage lines of credit
- ♠ Shared appreciation reverse mortgages

Simple Reverse Mortgages

In a simple or straight reverse mortgage, the lender and the borrower agree on the principal, or amount of the reverse mortgage, for instance, $40,000. If the principal goes to the borrower in one lump sum equity advance, interest is charged on the entire $40,000 from the date the borrower receives the cheque. The borrower may decide to use the lump sum to purchase an annuity, but is not required to do so by the reverse mortgage contract. If the borrower wants instalment payments, the lender and the borrower agree to a schedule of regular payments, probably monthly. The lender essentially sets up a $40,000 line of credit for the borrower's reverse mortgage. The lender then makes withdrawals to cover the regular payments to the borrower, charging interest on the sum of these withdrawals. That is, the borrower pays interest on the total equity advance actually received, not on the total value of the reverse mortgage of $40,000.

In either of these payment-plan scenarios, the reverse mortgage could be set up as a fixed-term reverse mortgage, with a pre-arranged termination date set five or more years in the future, or, alternatively, as a tenure-plan reverse mortgage. In a variation on the fixed-term mortgage, the lender could pay the equity advances to the homeowner during the term of the reverse mortgage, but not require repayment of the loan until a later date, or until the homeowner moves away permanently or dies.

Tenure or lifetime payment plans would make the simple reverse mortgage an open-ended loan, potentially running for the lifetime of the homeowner. Currently in Canada, only insurance companies are legally authorized to originate financial products based on life risk, such as lifetime simple reverse mortgages.

Example:
Fixed-Term Simple Reverse Mortgage

A retired Calgary couple, interested in moving to Arizona for the winters, fell in love with a $95,000 home in a scenic suburb of Phoenix. However, they needed to keep their current home for three more years. By then their two children, still living in the home, would have finished university and could move out on their own. The couple knew that they could qualify for a mortgage through the Arizona developer. The monthly payments on a $55,000 traditional mortgage would be well within their budget. Although they had reasonable pension and investment incomes, they had no way to raise the $35,000 cash down payment without selling their home or some of their investments. Then they heard about reverse mortgages.

A *3-year simple reverse mortgage* for $40,000 would give them enough for the down payment and moving expenses. In a slow real estate market their Calgary home would still be worth $270,000. Later, they would have more than enough money from the sale of this house to give each of the children a small financial start, even after paying off both the 3-year reverse mortagage and the Arizona mortgage.

Reverse Annuity Mortgages

Many home equity conversion products available in Canada today are actually reverse annuity mortgages or RAMs, although they are often referred to simply as "reverse mortgages." As explained earlier, a reverse mortgage is registered against a property to release the funds necessary to purchase an income-generating annuity for the homeowner. The homeowner may elect to take some of the equity advance as cash. In turn, the lender may hold back some funds as an administration fee. The lender uses the balance of the reverse mortgage funds to purchase an annuity on behalf of the borrower.

What is an Annuity?

An *annuity* is a contract in which a purchaser gives an insurance company a lump sum of money in return for receiving regular payments for an agreed period of time extending into the future. These income-generating investment products, that often involve tax benefits, provide a guaranteed stream of income in monthly, quarterly, or annual payments. In other words, an annuity is a pension. For instance, before December 31 of your seventy-first year, you may use the proceeds of your registered retirement savings plan (RRSP) to purchase an annuity, with no tax penalties, that can provide you with a pension, that is, an income for the rest of your life.

Buying an annuity is equivalent to making a risk-free investment that guarantees you a specific return for a fixed period or for life. The purchaser of an annuity, called the *annuitant*, gives an insurance company a lump sum of money and the company then pays the annuitant a periodic payment or instalment. This amount is a blended payment, consisting of the original principal and the interest. Insurance companies base their calculations of the size of these payments on life expectancy tables and on the interest rate at the time the annuity is established. The interest rate is usually set at the beginning for the entire annuity period.

Although there are many varieties of annuities available, the basic categories are:

- ♠ *Fixed-term annuities* that pay out periodic instalments for a pre-arranged number of years.

- ♠ *Life annuities* that pay out periodic instalments for one's lifetime, or for the joint lives of a married couple, until the death of the surviving spouse.

- ♠ *Life annuities with a guaranteed period* that pay out periodic instalments, as described above for *life annuities*, but that guarantee payments for a set period, even if the person entitled to the annuity dies within that period. For example, if the guaranteed period runs for the first 15 years of the annuity and the person entitled to the annuity dies in the fifth year, a lump sum payment representing the value of the total unpaid instalments for the balance of the 15-year period will be paid to the deceased's estate.

There are many variations on these basic types, including variations in the features available with each type. For instance, an *indexed annuity* provides annual cost-of-living adjustments for the periodic instalment payments. Features such as this increase flexibility and security for the purchaser of an annuity, but can reduce the total amount paid by the annuity. Special provisions should be made for couples purchasing an annuity. (See Chapter 5, page 115, and Chapter 6, page 143.) For more information on annuities, contact your provincial insurance bureau, or the

Case Study:
Tenure-Plan Reverse Annuity Mortgage

Mr. and Mrs. A have lived in their comfortable two-storey home in Surrey, just outside Vancouver, for over 25 years. Retired from real estate, Mr. A. did not have a company pension, nor did Mrs. A, and their savings were limited. Although the couple had only their Old Age Security and the Canada Pension Plan as incomes to live on, their home was valued at almost $100,000. In 1988, Mr. A was 72 and Mrs. A was 69. Both are still in excellent health.

Mr. A had heard a bit about the conversion programs in England but did not know exactly how they worked. However, after attending a seminar put on by a local reverse mortgage lender, Mr. and Mrs. A became very interested. The reverse mortgage product seemed to fit their needs. Since their children expressed more concern for their parents' wellbeing than receiving an inheritance, Mr. and Mrs. A decided to look into things more closely. The salesperson was extremely helpful and attentive "nothing seemed too minute to explain." At the time, this was the only commercial product available to them. On November 1, 1988, they signed the *tenure-plan reverse annuity mortgage* contract. The annuity had a 5-year guarantee period and has survivorship benefits so that payments will continue until the death of the surviving spouse.

House value (appraised 1988)	$94,000
Reverse Annuity Mortgage	$32,273
Lump sum received in 1988	$3,500
Monthly payments from annuity	$148.00
Current estimated value of home	$210,000
Residual home equity	$177,000
(*Costs not included here)	

They used the lump sum to put a down payment on a new car, which they still have and enjoy. The difference now? "A little more money and we do not pay income tax [on it] and it gave us a new car." Mr. A feels that tax-free status of the reverse annuity mortgage income is an important feature for them.

As real estate values in Surrey have been steadily increasing over the years, Mr. and Mrs. A still have considerable equity remaining in their home. To date they have received more than $10,000 in equity advances through the lifetime annuity. They are very pleased with their decision and will stay in the home as long as they can. "The next move will be to an apartment or something self-contained with no gardening."

government department or ministry responsible for insurance in your province.

Both fixed-term and tenure-plan reverse mortgages can be coupled with an annuity, to create an income-generating reverse mortgage called a *reverse annuity mortgage*. The homeowner retains ownership of the property and receives payments for a

---

Case Study:
Tenure-Plan Reverse Annuity Mortgage

Mr. B, a widower for 10 years, lives alone in the Vancouver ranch-style home he designed years ago. A successful businessman for over 28 years, Mr. B did not retire at 65 but continued to run his business until 1992. At that time a slight medical set-back caused his doctor to suggest full-time retirement to preserve Mr. B's health. As is the case for many small business owners, Mr. B had no company pension and only limited savings.

His son heard about reverse mortgages and the two went to a lender's seminar together. While his wife was still living, the couple had decided to leave everything in their estate to their grandchildren (14 so far). Mr. B feels that "after the kids leave home, parents deserve to live." He believes there will be equity left for his estate, but "if not, well I worked for [the house]."

House value (appraised 1992)	$275,000
Amount of home equity converted approximately	35%
Lump sum received in 1992	$20,000
Monthly payments from annuity	$1,027
Current estimated value of the home	$350,000

Mr. B intended to use the lump sum to buy a new car, but got a terrific deal on a secondhand car for about $11,000 and so put the balance in the bank for emergencies. At 78, Mr. B cheerfully proclaims that with the reverse annuity mortgage "you are at ease." He enjoys the fact that "I never pay as long as I live" nor does he "owe anyone anything." Mr. B's taxable income is approximately $11,000. The reverse annuity mortgage gives him an additional $12,324 a year tax-free. An active individual, Mr. B is free to "enjoy life" now that he has no financial worries. "You do not have to have a million dollars to live in a pleasant way and feel like a millionaire."

fixed period or for life. The reverse annuity mortgage becomes due and payable when the homeowner moves, sells, or dies, or when the fixed period expires.

With a *fixed-term reverse annuity mortgage*, the homeowner receives the annuity payments for a set time. With a *tenure, or lifetime, plan reverse annuity mortgage*, the homeowner receives payments for life from the annuity. In the latter type, the homeowner's payments from the annuity continue for life, even if the homeowner sells the property and pays off the reverse mortgage.

Lenders usually have standing agreements with one or more insurance companies, so the borrower may not have much, if any, choice of source or category with respect to the annuity. Lenders may even limit the annuity features available through their reverse annuity mortgage programs.

Reverse Mortgage Line of Credit

When a reverse mortgage line of credit is arranged, the lender approves the full amount of the reverse mortgage. The homeowner then has ready access to this preset amount of equity. Borrowers can withdraw cash at their own discretion. For instance, if a number of expenses arise one month, the homeowner might need $700, after which two months might elapse without a withdrawal. Then, in the fourth month, the homeowner might withdraw $100. In another case, a lender may allow a lump sum withdrawal of $6,000 at the beginning of the line of credit, and then impose a monthly limit after that. Some homeowners may not withdraw any money from their reverse mortgage line of credit for years. However, they derive great comfort from knowing that the money is there if they need it. Others may choose to withdraw the entire balance at once.

For a homeowner who wants an emergency fund, or extra cash "just in case," the reverse mortgage line of credit can offer peace of mind. However, a line of credit can be risky. With poor money management, a homeowner can exhaust the loan too quickly and have no funds available for needs that might arise in the future. To reduce this risk, the lender may set monthly or annual cash withdrawal limits. As flexibility is a key feature of a reverse mortgage line of credit, the borrower is usually given an

Case Study:
Fixed-Term Reverse Mortgage Line of Credit

Mrs. N., who was was widowed before she was 65, has lived in her home for 30 years, and openly admits she "would rather go from my own home to the cemetery. She struggled financially for many years. Even after her pension benefits began, Mrs. N was still under financial stress, and her son and daughter were not financially able to help her.

A few years earlier she had heard that reverse mortgages were available in Vancouver. In 1991, she saw an article in a local paper indicating that a type of reverse mortgage was now available in her city. The reverse mortgage line of credit program was so new that the procedures were not in place when she first applied. After Mrs. N, with the help of her daughter-in-law, examined the available information, she signed up for a reverse mortgage line of credit.

House value (appraised 1991)		$125,000
Lump sum received in 1991		$3,000
Current debt against the house	approx.	$10,000
Current estimated value of home		$100,000

Mrs. N took a lump sum of just over $3,000 to pay for "certain things badly needed and with the money left, I bought my own funeral, so that is all paid." When her car died, she withdrew another $3,000 to buy a used car. In 1993, she was short of money and the costs of maintaining the house were escalating. To avoid debt, Mrs. N took $600 from her reverse mortgage line of credit. Recently, she needed some money to buy wool to knit her first great-grandchild's baby blanket and so she made another withdrawal. Her 2 children want her to use some of the equity advances to take the trip she has always dreamed of. Mrs N is quite happy spending the money as need arises or to provide things for her family.

Even in Ontario's weak real estate market, Mrs. N feels "very safe as I can get $100,000 for my house at the worst.... I feel much better that I can touch a few hundred dollars when needed but my house is safe.... To have a safe roof overhead is a very good feeling." Without the reverse mortgage, Mrs. N would have had to sell her house, and leave the home and neighbourhood she loves. She happily admits the reverse mortgage line of credit "changed my life."

opportunity to revise the withdrawal program should a current financial responsibility end, or should new needs arise.

Interest is charged only on the amount of cash withdrawn. Therefore, the homeowner can control the rate at which the debt increases, by carefully managing the size and the frequency of withdrawals. The lender may even allow repayment of the reverse mortgage debt by permitting the homeowner to make deposits into the reverse mortgage line of credit account.

The laws that regulate a lender dictate the features of the lender's reverse mortgage products. For example, only insurance companies can sell financial products based on life risk; therefore, a line of credit provided by a credit union cannot be a lifetime program. Only insurance companies can offer lifetime reverse mortgage lines of credit. Credit unions and other lenders are restricted to fixed-term plan lines of credit, which are usually renewable to enhance their practical appeal to borrowers. However, at some point, perhaps when the reverse mortgage reaches 75 percent of the appraised value of the property, the line of credit will be terminated and the full amount of the debt must be repaid to the lender. For example, see the case study on page 41 and the one on page 50.

Shared Appreciation Reverse Mortgages

As the U.S. reverse mortgage marketplace evolved, a variety of features were introduced. For example, *shared appreciation* is a provision in a reverse mortgage contract that reduces the risk for the lender and, therefore, increases equity advances and eventual costs for the homeowner. This provision stipulates that the lender receives a share, or percentage, of any increase in property value, the *appreciation*, which may occur during the reverse mortgage. In exchange for a share of the appreciation, the lender may offer larger equity advances or a reduced interest rate.

In Canada, the Federal Interest Act contains requirements for complete disclosure of the *effective interest rate*, the actual or true rate of interest charged or the total cost of the mortgage. This requirement may limit the use of shared appreciation features in reverse mortgages, as the exact dollar amount of the appreciation would remain an unknown factor until the year the reverse mortgage terminates. However, enterprising lenders find ways to legally circumvent this lending restriction. For instance, if the lender makes assumptions concerning the rate of appreciation of the property, the lender can establish a dollar figure for the expected appreciation. Therefore, the actual maximum cost of the mortgage can be calculated for the consumer. (For more information, see Chapter 5, page 112.)

Other Variations

As the home equity conversion revolution gathers momentum, lenders, borrowers, investors, and governments will, no doubt, find creative ways to modify, and even to "reinvent," the basic types of reverse mortgages. **Consumer demand will fuel product development.**

WHEN DOES A REVERSE MORTGAGE END?

A reverse mortgage ends, terminates, or falls due for repayment, under any one of several circumstances:

- ♠ when the homeowner or homeowners move permanently from the home;

- ♠ when the homeowner or homeowners decide to sell the home;

- ♠ when the fixed-term expires and a preset termination date is reached; or

- ♠ on the death of the homeowner or, for a couple, the surviving homeowner.

If the reverse mortgage is in default, the lender has the option of calling the loan due and taking legal action against the homeowner to recover the debt. If the homeowner fails to honour any one of the reverse mortgage covenants, that is, allows the property taxes or condominium fees to fall in arrears; lets the insurance lapse; or fails to keep the property in good repair. (Alternatively, the lender may decide to try to resolve the problem by paying the taxes, fees, or insurance or by repairing the home. The lender will then add all costs of the remedy to the reverse mortgage debt.) (See also Chapter 6, page 123.)

♠ If the lender exercises an "on demand" provision or a preset maximum debt provision that gives the lender the right to request repayment in full before the end of a fixed-term reverse mortgage or to decline further renewal. (See also Chapter 6, page 142.)

When a reverse mortgage ends, the lender does not automatically assume ownership of the house, just as the lender did not take over ownership when the reverse mortgage began. The homeowner retains ownership of the property, even if the equity in the home has been completely depleted, and even if the debt is greater than the value of the home.

Once the reverse mortgage ends, the homeowner must pay off the entire debt as soon as is reasonably possible or as required by the contract. The homeowner may choose to sell the house to pay off the debt, or to sell off other assets and keep the house. The homeowner may not qualify for refinancing or may have died. Under these circumstances, perhaps a relative who wishes to keep the house in the family could arrange a traditional mortgage, to pay off the reverse mortgage debt. (See also Chapter 6, page 126.)

Beware of Imitators

Don't confuse reverse mortgage lines of credit with "home equity lines of credit," also known as "home equity personal lines of credit" or "home equity loans." Home equity lines of credit are traditional mortgages. As a result, regular repayment of the debt is mandatory. If the borrower does not meet the mortgage repayment responsibilities, the lender has the contractual right to take legal action to collect the debt, including forcing the sale of the home.

Unsophisticated consumers might sign up for a home equity loan thinking they are getting a home equity conversion line of credit. Instead of being able to postpone repayment, they will be faced with obligatory repayments and may find themselves in the midst of an expensive problem. In the United States, consumer protection laws have been tightened to restrict unscrupulous lending practices regarding home equity loans and to end the equity scams that have emerged.

The names of traditional mortgage and savings programs may also be confusing. Words such as "home equity," "home account," and "reserve" are used to target the products to customers who have equity in their homes. These practices and advertisements may be legal and quite clear, if read carefully. However, they may mislead an unsophisticated, reckless, or stressed-out consumer into buying a financial product that does not really fit the consumer's needs. Consumers should not rely on names, illustrations, advertising slogans, or endorsements. There is no substitute for getting the facts and reading everything before you sign.

Consumers often think that the endorsement of a particular product, service, or company by an association or nonprofit group automatically guarantees the consumer's protection. Many assume the endorsement means that the product, service, or company is the best available, that the consumer has legal recourse through the organization if problems arise, and that the organization is presenting a complete picture of all the home equity options available to the borrower. To be absolutely sure these assumptions are accurate, ask questions.

Confusion can also arise in the naming of home equity conversion products. Furthermore, commercial product names and company names may lead consumers to believe they are dealing with government agencies. To date, the only government home equity conversion programs are property tax deferral plans (Chapter 8).

Adopt a "Buyer Beware" attitude to help you in converting assumptions into facts.

THE EMERGING CANADIAN MARKET

This section of Chapter 3 explains the development of reverse mortgages in Canada. Some readers may be surprised or disappointed to hear that despite all the media stories on home equity conversion, and despite all the advertisements for reverse mortgages, consumers still have little choice. But consumers do have the power to change this. To help you understand what "consumer-driven market" means, this section explores the impact of the lenders' perspective on the development of home equity conversion. Once you understand the lenders' viewpoint, you will be better prepared to look at home equity conversion, which is discussed in Part Two of this book, "From the Consumers' Perspective." "Is a Reverse Mortgage Right For You?" in Chapter 4, page 69, and "Where Do I Start?" in Chapter 5, page 97, will walk you through the details and the decisions involved in arranging home equity conversion by means of a reverse mortgage. Chapter 6 examines the selection of a reverse mortgage by exploring the question, "What Am I Signing?"

READER BEWARE!

Please understand that any mention of specific lenders or their products in this book must not be considered an endorsement of either one. At the same time, the omission of the name of a lender or a product is not meant to cast either the lender or the product in a negative light. *Each* reverse mortgage product has pros and cons for *each* borrower. Be cautious when examining and comparing reverse mortgage lenders and their products. Do not base your decision—either to buy or not to buy a reverse mortgage—solely on another person's opinions or analysis. Remember, no matter how helpful they may appear to be, lenders—including their staff, their salespeople, and their agents—are *not* there to provide you with a well-rounded education in home equity conversion. That's *your* job. And this book is designed to help you do that job well.

Reverse Mortgage Pioneers

While home equity conversion options, particularly reverse mortgages, have been researched and written about extensively since the mid-1970s, these options are only now becoming a reality to any appreciable extent. The Canadian reverse mortgage market has just begun to define itself with a few exploratory products. Consumers will not enjoy the advantage of shopping in a competitive market for a while yet, especially in rural areas.

Of all the possible home equity conversion programs, only property tax deferral plans and reverse mortgages are available on any scale in Canada at this stage. While a few cities allow a percentage of the property taxes to be deferred, only British Columbia and Prince Edward Island have province-wide property tax deferral plans, that is, programs that postpone payment of taxes well into the future. Reverse mortgages are the most common type of home equity conversion in Canada, and in North America.

Although reverse mortgages made a brief appearance in Ontario in the early 1970s, home equity conversion in Canada had its widely acknowledged beginning in British Columbia in 1987. Then, a tenure-plan reverse annuity mortgage called Canadian Home Income Plan (CHIP) was introduced for older homeowners by the Canadian Home Income Plan Corporation (also known as CHIP), a private mortgage investment company. However, by 1989, heavy consumer demand had exhausted the funding originally provided by Vancouver-based Seaboard Life Insurance Company, so there was no money for new reverse annuity mortgages. The existing CHIP reverse annuity mortgages were not directly affected by this situation. William Turner, CHIP founder and president, stopped offering the CHIP product and began his search for funding so that CHIP could finance additional reverse annuity mortgages.

In 1986, Royal Trust Corporation of Canada introduced a 5-year fixed-term reverse annuity mortgage. Royal Trust's product is not considered a true reverse mortgage, for two reasons. First, partial repayment of the mortgage balance, using a portion of the annuity income, is required during the reverse annuity mortgage term. Second, because of the dynamics of this product, the borrower's portion of the annuity income is taxable. Royal Trust has not promoted this product actively, however, and, as a result, sales of its reverse annuity mortgage have been low. The Royal Bank of Canada's acquisition of Royal Trust may result in changes to this product offer.

In March of 1990, Security Life Insurance Co. Ltd., under the leadership of president Bruce Hammond, launched Home Equity Plan, a tenure-plan reverse annuity mortgage for older homeowners. Security Life is owned by the Co-operators Group Limited, a Canadian diversified insurance group. Security Life reported over 5000 inquiries within the first seven months of introducing their plan in Ontario, principally in Metropolitan Toronto. However, only a small number of reverse mortgages resulted. In response to consumer interest, Security Life created Term Home Equity Plan, a fixed-term reverse annuity mortgage. This variation of Security's lifetime product was developed for homeowners who needed the income supplement only for a fixed period, usually 5 to 10 years; for example, those waiting until full pension benefits begin or until a weak real estate market recovers. Security Life introduced its reverse mortgage products into British Columbia and then Alberta, using a network of brokers to sell these products. With some exceptions, availability of both Home Equity Plans was restricted to the urban areas of these provinces.

With financing from a pension fund in place in 1990, Vancouver-based CHIP re-emerged in Vancouver and Victoria, and then expanded into the Metropolitan Toronto area. Corporate policy focuses its home equity conversion activity entirely on tenure-plan reverse annuity mortgages. In the same year, an innovative home equity conversion program was introduced in Niagara Falls, Ontario. Cataract Savings and Credit Union created Canada's first reverse mortgage line of credit in direct response to the needs of the credit union's members. (Credit unions have members, not customers.)

Jonathan Barnes, the man behind Cataract's innovative program, then worked with Credit Union Central of Ontario, the provincial association of credit unions, to develop a reverse mortgage line of credit that could be offered through credit unions across Ontario. While older homeowners were the primary target market, the product was expected to appeal as well to younger homeowners interested in returning to school, starting a business, or taking extended leave without pay. Credit unions are directed in their product development activities by members looking for value and services, not shareholders looking for profit. In creating a reverse mortgage line of credit, the credit unions responded to members' needs that seemed best met by home equity conversion. The Credit Union Central plan, called the HomeFund Line of Credit Reverse Mortgage, became available through a number of Ontario credit unions throughout 1992 and 1993. HomeFund will eventually be available across Canada, as the credit union program expands into other provinces (probably British Columbia, Alberta, and Manitoba).

Since credit unions were not legally entitled to offer lifetime reverse mortgages, but members favoured tenure-plans, the developers designed the HomeFund to simulate a lifetime plan by using a life-approximation term, which was calculated using life expectancy statistics. Credit unions, each of which is autonomous businesses, modify the HomeFund program slightly to suit the needs of their member base. For instance, set-up fees, interest rate criteria, and payout plans vary with the credit union which is offering HomeFund. Most credit unions are full-service financial institutions; many are open to the general public.

In 1991, Ivan Wahl, chairman of First Line Trust (now owned by Manulife Financial), announced the Home Equity Pension Plan (HEP). This plan included a simple reverse mortgage, a lifetime reverse annuity mortgage, and a fixed-term reverse annuity mortgage. The Canadian Association of Retired Persons (CARP) marketed the HEP Plan for First Line, beginning with promotion to CARP members across the country. The program was suspended in 1992 because the expense of responding to the tremendous interest in the plan was offset by only a small number of reverse mortgages. As First Line operates its mortgage business on a volume basis, the program was considered unsuitable for them at this stage in the market's development.

In Toronto, the Retirement Counsel of Canada, a private financial planning company, began offering Security Life's products in 1989, and then developed its Home Income Plan in 1990, using its client base to generate the investment funds to finance its reverse mortgages. By 1992, Counsel was lending in outlying areas of Ontario, including in cottage country north of Toronto. President Paul Tyers has expanded the company to approximately a dozen branches across Ontario. The Home Income Plan includes fixed-term and tenure-plan reverse annuity mortgages, as well as simple reverse mortgages.

In 1992, Home Earnings Reverse Mortgage Corporation of Canada was formed to take over marketing the Home Equity Plan from Security Life, a major shareholder in this new venture. Bruce Hammond, now president of Home Earnings, oversees the agency network originally established by Security Life. In response to consumer interest, Home Earnings introduced an open reverse annuity mortgage, that is, a mortgage that can be repaid at any time without penalties, as well as a shared appreciation program to provide a reverse annuity mortgage described as being indexed for inflation. Home Equity Plan is still a reverse annuity program that principally offers tenure-plan reverse annuity mortgages. Expansion into Quebec is in progress.

Reverse mortgages have been called a "boutique" product by the larger financial institutions. Until a national insurance program is introduced, smaller lenders may lead the home equity conversion revolution. For example, the Caisse populaire St.-René Goupil, north of Montreal, introduced Quebec's first home equity conversion program—a reverse mortgage line of credit—to its members in 1993.

A NOTE ABOUT NUMBERS

How many reverse mortgages have been written in Canada so far? I have my estimates; others have theirs. Since reverse mortgage transactions are private and are not specifically regulated by the government, accurate statistics do not exist. Also, one person's reverse mortgage is another person's creative financing. In other words, there is no strict legal definition of "reverse mortgage" that can be used as a benchmark for classifying products. For example, many analysts do not consider the Royal Trust product a reverse mortgage, although it has a niche in the marketplace. At Canada Mortgage and Housing Corporation, the federal housing agency known as CMHC, fixed-term reverse mortgages are not considered reverse mortgages when estimating numbers; only tenure-plans meet CMHC's definition of reverse mortgages. Canadian numbers are definitely lower than those of the United States, but then the U.S. has a head start on us: a number of years, a government insurance plan, and a few more homeowners!

Perhaps, at this stage, the only really significant number is 22, "Catch-22," that is.* Until lenders see consumers buying reverse mortgages, they will not provide products; but, until there are products to choose from, homeowners will not buy reverse mortgages. Many homeowners I have talked to over the years have made the decision to get a reverse mortgage "when the time comes." How do we count these pre-committed individuals? With so few products available, even in the most favoured areas of the country, how can we measure demand by looking at sales? I have talked with many older homeowners in rural areas across the country who would welcome a reverse mortgage, but who cannot find a lender. Yes, the number is definitely 22.

---

* *Catch 22*, the title of Joseph Heller's 1961 novel, is a term that has come to mean an insoluble dilemma.

CANADIAN REVERSE MORTGAGE LENDER CHART*

Reverse Mortgage Variation	Timeframe	REVERSE MORTGAGE LENDERS				
		CHIP[1]	Home Earnings[2]	RCOC[3]	Credit Unions[4]	Royal Trust[5]
Simple Reverse Mortgage	Fixed Term	N	N	Y	N**	N
	Tenure Plan	N	N	Y	N	N
Reverse Annuity Mortgage	Fixed Term	N	Y	Y	N	Y
	Tenure Plan	Y	Y	Y	N	N
Line of Credit Reverse Mortgage	Fixed Term	N	N	N	Y	N
	Tenure Plan	N	N	N	N	N

KEY: **Y** = currently available

N = not currently available

[1] **CHIP** Canadian Home Income Plan (British Columbia, Ontario)

[2] **Home Earnings** Home Earnings Reverse Mortgage Corporation of Canada (was Security Life Insurance Company) (Ontario, Alberta, British Columbia, expansion into Quebec)

[3] **RCOC** Retirement Counsel of Canada (principally Ontario)

[4] **Credit Unions** Credit Union Central of Ontario program plus independent program in Quebec — details vary with credit union

[5] **Royal Trust** Royal Trust Corporation of Canada (Royal Bank of Canada) (national)

(Addresses and phone numbers for the lenders mentioned here are in the Appendix, page 287.)

* All of the information in this table is subject to change. To find out exactly what reverse mortgage options are available to you, call *all* the lenders and explain your situation: reverse mortgage lending is "custom-tailored" financing. You will never be certain whether a particular lender can help with a reverse mortgage or other option until you ask.

** The credit union program does offer a line of credit reverse mortgage payment option that is equivalent to a lump sum simple reverse mortgage in many respects.

Public awareness of home equity conversion and reverse mortgages is growing. Now a common topic in the media, reverse mortgages are described as both "the answer to a prayer" and "a financial curse." The business world's interest in home equity conversion is fueled by the tremendous wealth locked-up in Canadian homes, and the realization that Canada is truly an aging society. Financial institutions, including insurance companies and credit unions, as well as labour unions, pension funds, and entrepreneurs from across the country are continuing to research possible conversion programs. The home equity conversion revolution is poised to switch into high gear.

A Consumer-Driven Movement

For many homeowners across Canada, the search for a reverse mortage, or any home equity conversion product, ends before it begins. The reverse mortgage lenders discussed in the table on page 60 restrict product sales almost exclusively to urban areas in Ontario, British Columbia, and Alberta, since these locations have stable real estate markets. Lenders also target areas with high concentrations of older homeowners, so that marketing and servicing their products can become cost-effective. In Ontario, some lending has taken place in suburban communities and in select recreational areas outside Metropolitan Toronto that feature both of the above characteristics; that is, stable real estate values and high concentrations of older homeowners.

While Canadian lenders are legally free to introduce reverse mortgages, they are unlikely to do so to any extent until there is measurable, steady consumer demand. Home equity conversion through reverse mortgages is definitely a consumer-driven movement.

Is Demand Really There?

In Canada, the population of older homeowners has accumulated hundreds of billions of dollars of equity in their homes. This locked-up wealth is very attractive to financial institutions and consumer service businesses. Home equity conversion is seen as one key to unlocking these billions of dollars.

While there appears to be a use for home equity conversion, is the demand really there? This is the multimillion dollar question. Banks, insurance companies, trust companies, and other potential lenders are monitoring and researching the home equity conversion market to answer this question. Before staking their time, money, resources, and reputations on a conversion venture, potential lenders want to know the proportion of eligible older homeowners who will actually purchase a home equity conversion product.

While the uncertainty of demand is one issue, financial institutions, including banks and trust companies, are reluctant to enter the reverse mortgage market for a variety of other reasons as well, including:

- ♠ The considerable investment in time, personnel, and money required to set up and administer these products before any revenue can be generated;

- ♠ The high cost of the extensive marketing and consumer education programs necessary to overcome the natural aversion of older homeowners to incurring debt and jeopardizing their security base;

- ♠ The lenders' risk in paying out more in equity advances than could be recovered from the sale of the property (a likely occurrence if the borrower outlives the lender's estimate of life expectancy, and/or if the property does not increase in value as the lender had expected);

- ♠ The uncertainty of predicting property appreciation accurately for specific areas over time spans measured in decades;

- ♠ The risk that a particular property will not appreciate in value, even if values in the area generally appreciate, because it has not been kept in good repair by the homeowner or has not been modernized over the years;

- ♠ The difficulty of predicting interest rates decades into the future;

- ♠ The uncertainty of the length of residency of homeowners over the life of the reverse mortgage; and

- ♠ The potentially damaging publicity that could arise from forcing aged, perhaps ailing, homeowners out of their homes when the fixed-term mortgage is due, or if the homeowner fails to meet contractual responsibilities and, therefore, breaches the reverse mortgage contract (see Chapter 6, page 123).

Lenders' reluctance to enter the reverse mortgage market is reinforced by the belief that if they sit tight and wait, the Canada Mortgage and Housing Corporation will eventually introduce lender insurance. This program would reduce lender risks and establish certain reverse mortgage product designs that would outline qualifications for reverse mortgage lender insurance coverage. This "wait and see" attitude is keeping some lenders out of the marketplace—for now.

How Does Lender Risk Reduction Affect Consumers?

Lenders that do offer reverse mortgages have faced the risks of loss detailed above, and have reduced them as much as possible. For example, lenders launch extensive public relations campaigns that are not usually as costly as advertising programs, but that increase credibility in the eyes of the consumer. Public relations programs focus on getting as much media coverage, that is, third-party endorsement, as possible for the client or product. Current lenders further reduce the risk of loss by setting conservative equity withdrawal limits, usually below 50 percent of the appraised value of the property, to ensure that the final balance of the mortgage will not exceed 75 percent of the value of the home. Also, some lenders manage risk by adjusting the interest rate over the life of the reverse mortgage, for instance, they review the rate annually or at five-year intervals, instead of using a fixed rate.

Reverse annuity mortgages, the most common type of conversion product available in Canada today, offer the lender another risk reduction strategy. The borrower receives lifetime annuity payments from an insurance company. Therefore, if the borrower outlives life expectancy projections, the insurance company, not the reverse annuity mortgage lender, is faced with the extra payments. The lender's risk is limited to the possibility that the final balance, plus the accrued interest, will exceed the value of the home—a risk that can be reduced by conservative lending policies. In designing a reverse mortgage to limit the lender's risk of loss, the borrower's costs can be increased. This point can be best illustrated by comparing a reverse annuity mortgage with a simple reverse mortgage of the same size. For instance, with a reverse annuity mortgage of $40,000, the homeowner pays interest on the entire reverse annuity mortgage principal from the start of the mortgage term, since the total equity advance is withdrawn to purchase an annuity. However, for a $40,000 simple reverse mortgage with regular payments, interest is charged only on the actual amount received by the borrower in regular payments, not the $40,000 principal of the simple reverse mortgage. The simple reverse mortgage is, therefore, less expensive for the consumer.

Risk reduction policies also have an impact on the availability of reverse mortgages. For example, until reverse mortgage lender insurance exists, lenders will probably avoid rural areas and locations with low or unstable rates of real estate appreciation. Also, banks are not currently involved in the reverse mortgage market, because they lend on the homeowners' ability to repay the debt, not on the asset itself—the property. Their policies also dictate that they should be able to offer the same product across most, if not all, of their national network, at limited risk. Without a government-backed reverse mortgage insurance program, banks will probably not enter the home equity conversion market, for all of the reasons mentioned above.

Reverse Mortgage Lender Mortgage Insurance

In order to make reverse mortgage products more financially attractive to consumers by creating an open, competitive marketplace, more lenders must be encouraged to enter the market. Competition would also encourage increased flexibility in the types of product features that lenders offer to consumers. A government-backed reverse mortgage insurance plan would widen the availability and the diversity of reverse mortgages, and broaden the base of lenders involved in the market by reducing lender risk, one of the greatest barriers to the full-fledged development of home equity conversion in Canada.

This insurance should not be confused with mortgage insurance for the borrower, which is a type of life insurance, called mortgage life insurance. With mortgage life insurance, the insurance company pays off the traditional mortgage balance if the homeowner dies.

Canada Mortgage and Housing Corporation has researched the U.S. insurance program and over the past few years has studied the possibility of expanding the current mortgage loan insurance program to include reverse mortgages. Currently, although insurance is available for any traditional mortgage lending situation, CMHC is mainly asked to insure *high-ratio mortgages*, that is, traditional mortgages that exceed 75 percent of the appraised value of the home. Borrowers pay the premium, a percentage of the principal, at the beginning of the loan, adding the premium to the principal of the mortgage if they cannot afford to pay this expense separately.

During the summer of 1992, CMHC held a national public consultation on "Innovative Uses of Public Mortgage Loan Insurance" to elicit responses to the creation of a government-backed mortgage lender insurance program for reverse mortgages. Responses confirmed the demand for reverse mortgage insurance. The next major step for CMHC in introducing this insurance program will be to apply to Cabinet for approval to amend the National Housing Act, in order to include reverse mortgages under the current mortgage insurance program. The 1993 federal election interrupted these government policy-making procedures. Consumers may have an opportunity to persuade politicians to introduce the insurance program while the Liberal government's seniors' housing policies are developed and implemented. At this stage of the home equity conversion revolution, it is probably more a question of *when* CMHC's lender mortgage insurance program will be available, rather than *if* it will be available.

CMHC's proposed reverse mortgage lender insurance program may prove to be the catalyst that will galvanize potential reverse mortgage lenders into action.

(Read more about Reverse Mortgage Lender Insurance in Chapter 6, page 152.)

PART TWO

From the Consumer's Perspective

In the world of reverse mortgages, one person's future may be another person's folly. Investigating reverse mortgages is a highly personal task. Your perspective and your needs must be the foundation of your criteria for evaluating the financial and housing options available to you. Therefore, until you understand what you want and what you value in life, deciding whether a reverse mortgage is right for you can be difficult.

Chapter 4 encourages readers to clarify their personal criteria as they survey financial and housing alternatives. For many people, this will mean shifting from an unconsciously held belief system to a clear awareness of what is really important. Facing fears is an important part of this process. After clarifying your values, needs, and dreams, you will be in a better position to select the specific reverse mortgage that is right for you.

The questions and issues raised in Chapter 4 will help you decide whether to arrange a reverse mortgage or to defer your decision until some point in the future. You can analyze the various options presented here and then choose the best path to follow.

Chapters 5 and 6 explain how to evaluate a reverse mortgage. At present, the reverse mortgage market offers only a small number of pioneering products. As more reverse mortgages become available, this book can serve as a useful reference. If you decide to create your own "custom-fit" reverse mortgage, you will have the information necessary to negotiate, with legal assistance, an agreement that suits your needs, as well as those of the private investor who will be your lender.

Once you have developed a frame of reference by examining some key questions, you may still need a sounding board before you make a decision. Chapter 7 will help you decide whether you need a professional adviser and if so, guide you in shopping for professional advice.

CHAPTER 4

Is a Reverse Mortgage Right for You?

You may be wondering, "Is a reverse mortgage right for me?" No one can answer this question but **you**. No one should make this decision **for** you. However, that does not mean you have to make the decision alone. On the contrary, I have always believed that isolation inhibits inspiration. Gaining clear, knowledgeable input from others will make the decision making, if not fun, at least less intimidating.

A bad decision involving reverse mortgages is always serious. A bad decision can mean saying no to a reverse mortgage when yes would have been better or it can result from not knowing that a reverse mortgage exists as an option. Leaving a home you love, when you do not really need to, involves as great a loss as converting home equity unnecessarily. These situations are as detrimental as saying yes when a reverse mortgage is not a wise alternative for you at a certain point in time.

Deciding whether or not to sign up for a reverse mortgage is a unique personal choice. As you read this chapter, the significance of this statement should—excuse the pun—come home to you.

WHO IS THE IDEAL REVERSE MORTGAGE CANDIDATE?

For older homeowners who don't want to move now—or perhaps ever—a reverse mortgage provides a way to liberate home equity

USING A REVERSE MORTGAGE TO CONVERT HOME EQUITY INTO INCOME IS NOT FOR EVERYONE!

while retaining possession and ownership of one's property. However, a reverse mortgage is not a panacea or a "one size fits all" solution.

Since the equity-eroding impact is virtually irreversible for older homeowners, a reverse mortgage should only be considered after all other financial and housing options have been fully explored. This chapter examines the issues behind deciding whether a reverse mortgage is the right choice for you, right now. If this financial option is not right today, it may be the best solution at some time in the future. If you understand reverse mortgages, you may also be able to help a friend or relative who is contemplating this decision.

For those readers who turned directly to this chapter: as this book is a reference guide, flipping from chapter to chapter is quite acceptable. The Glossary, page 291, and the Quick Question Index on page 297 are designed to give you the greatest possible flexibility in using the book. **However, I caution you to base your decisions on *all* the information in the book, not just on one section, especially if your immediate reaction is, "A reverse mortgage is for me."** Once you understand the concepts presented here, you will be better prepared to make the most of home equity conversion, if not now, then perhaps at some time in the future.

Are You an Ideal Candidate for a Reverse Mortgage?

If you are, *all* of the following criteria will apply to you. (Note that while "homeowner" is used here, the plural for couples or joint owners may be substituted, to suit your situation.)

⌂ **The homeowner has a very strong desire and the capacity to live in the home for a fixed or extended period.** This desire to stay should be reinforced by the suitability of the home and the community for "aging in place." Simply wanting to stay where you are is not enough if it is impractical for you to manage the house or if it is unsafe for you to remain in a deteriorating neighbourhood. (Pages 88–94 of this chapter discuss how to determine whether a home is suitable for aging in place.)

♠ **Both or all of the owners of the home are receptive to the possibility of arranging a reverse mortgage.** This does not imply that the owners will definitely agree to a reverse mortgage. It simply means they *might* agree.

♠ **The homeowner, and any family members directly involved, are comfortable with the decision to deplete the estate, perhaps completely, by converting the home equity into income.** One belief associated with reverse mortgages is that the homeowner's children and heirs tend to resist home equity conversion because it robs them of their inheritances. This may be true in some families, but it seems far from always the case. In fact, the opposite is often true. The homeowner's "children" are generally mature, independent adults, often in their 40s, 50s, or even 60s. Most children want their parents to be able to live comfortably. Many would rather have their parents tap into home equity than see them struggling to make ends meet.

♠ **The homeowner can adjust to the increasing debt against the home.** The ability to live comfortably with debt is another important issue here. Some people argue that reverse mortgages do not impose the same pressures associated with repayment and the consequences of nonpayment, compared with traditional mortgages. They point out that there are no monthly payments to miss and that the sale of the house will cover the debt. Those opposed to this viewpoint believe that the prospect of using up all the equity in one's home can be a source of great anxiety. Some homeowners find it difficult to reconcile themselves to leaving only the shell of their estate to their family. Ultimately, homeowners must satisfy themselves that they have planned as well as possible, even if, in spite of precautions, all the equity should be depleted.

♠ **The homeowner meets the lender's age requirements.** Usually, the minimum age for qualification is between 60 and 65. For a change, older is better! In the United States, the average age of homeowners arranging a reverse mortgage falls in the mid-70s. (See Chapter 3, page 33, and Chapter 5, page 105, for more information on age requirements.)

♠ **The homeowner has complete or near-complete equity in the home.** The lender wants the maximum possible security for the reverse mortgage loan. If mortgages or debts are already registered against the property, the lender will be faced with a lower level of security. The degree of mortgage security is based on a first come, first served basis for all debts, with the exception of unpaid property taxes and condominium fees, which take automatic priority over all other registered claims. A lender wants maximum security and the strongest possible claim against the house. This is especially important for reverse mortgage lenders, because the security for the mortgage debt is based entirely on the value of the property. For this reason, the reverse mortgage must be the first legal claim, that is, the *first mortgage*. (Lenders may allow a property tax deferral plan to take priority. See Chapter 8, page 179.)

If you plan to use a reverse mortgage to discharge an existing mortgage, check with the traditional mortgage lender first to find out: (1) whether that mortgage can be paid off in advance; (2) the *maturity date*, the date the mortgage is scheduled to terminate; and (3) what penalties, if any, you will be charged for the privilege of paying off the mortgage in advance. Three months' interest is a common penalty, but you could be liable to pay even larger amounts. (To learn more about prepayment penalties, see Chapter 6, page 139.)

♠ **The type of ownership meets the lender's criteria.** *Fee simple estate*, that is, complete home ownership, is ideal. Condominiums and duplexes may qualify; co-operatives and leaseholds probably will not. (See the Glossary, page 291, for an explanation of types of homeownership. In Chapter 5 this aspect of the lender's criteria is discussed on page 105.)

Obviously, being a suitable candidate is relevant only if reverse mortgages are available in your area. Currently, the reverse mortgage market offers only a limited number of pioneering products. A homeowner interested in arranging a reverse mortgage may have little or no choice among commercially available home equity conversion plans. The greatest diversity of reverse mortgage products is found in the urban areas of Alberta, British Columbia, and Ontario. In Ontario and Quebec, some lending has occurred in small communities and in recreational areas. At the time of this writing, reverse mortgages are expected to be developed in Manitoba and Saskatchewan and to become more widely available in the provinces where lenders are already active.

If the current reverse mortgage lenders do not sell their products in your area, you may still wish to research all these products in anticipation of the expansion of home equity conversion into your area. In this way, you may be able to gauge whether you feel it is worthwhile to wait until reverse mortgages become available. You may also find the research useful, should you decide to create a private, or a "custom-fit" reverse mortgage.

Although from a legal standpoint reverse mortgages can be arranged privately anywhere in Canada, finding a willing private investor to act as lender can be like finding a needle in a haystack. Intra-family arrangements are the most feasible type of private reverse mortgage.

Summary: Characteristics of the Ideal Reverse Mortgage Candidate
- Has a strong desire and the capacity to stay in the home;
- Has achieved agreement with all the other owners;
- Is comfortable with the decision to use, and possibly deplete, the home equity;
- Meets the lender's age requirements;
- Has complete or near-complete equity in the home; and
- Qualifies in terms of the type of home ownership.

REVERSE MORTGAGES DO NOT SUIT EVERYONE, NOR EVERY SITUATION.

Who Is *Not* An Ideal Candidate for a Reverse Mortgage?

- **The lender's eligibility criteria have the greatest impact in determining who is not a suitable candidate for a reverse mortgage.** For example, if you are too young, according to a lender's criteria, you are disqualified as a candidate. Or, if your property is in a rural area or in a region where appreciation of real estate values is weak or unstable, you may not be considered eligible for a reverse mortgage.

In addition, properties with lower lending values and with lower projected appreciation rates may not generate a reverse mortgage large enough to be useful to a homeowner.

♠ **A homeowner is not a suitable candidate if the amount of cash needed is greater than the equity advance approved by the reverse mortgage lender.** For example, if a property were valued at $100,000 and the lender decided on a maximum lending limit of 25 percent of the equity, the reverse annuity mortgage would liberate $25,000 to buy an annuity. The monthly annuity income would be $230. But if a 73-year-old male homeowner needed $350 a month to pay taxes and home maintenance costs, a reverse mortgage would be impractical. (Note that these figures are for illustration only.)

♠ **Homeowners who are comfortable with the idea of moving from their home and/or who have arranged acceptable financial or housing alternatives will not select a reverse mortgage.** Also, some homeowners will qualify for government-sponsored programs that may solve their financial problems. For example, in British Columbia, the property tax deferral plan allows older homeowners to postpone payment of taxes.

♠ **Homeowners whose home and/or community are not practical for aging in place.**

♠ **Homeowners who are committed to bequeathing as large an estate as possible may not be suitable candidates.** Homeowners who wish to leave the family home to their heirs may find home equity conversion a disagreeable concept. While it may be possible to preserve a percentage or a fixed amount of equity when arranging a reverse mortgage, this may not be sufficient to satisfy the homeowner.

♠ **People who find the idea of living with accumulating debt stressful will probably seek another alternative.**

♠ **Reverse mortgages are available only to homeowners, not to tenants who rent a property.**

♠ **Unfortunately, some homeowners who receive biased information, or who remain unaware that reverse mortgages exist, will not become candidates.** Home equity conversion is poorly understood by many people, including some individuals that homeowners might consider knowledgeable. As the automatic reaction to something new or poorly understood is usually "no," information or advice passed on by these individuals may be clouded by their biases.

Why Would a Homeowner Want to Arrange a Reverse Mortgage?

Listed below are some ways in which homeowners have used reverse mortgages. If you can match your projected use for the reverse mortgage equity advances with any of the items on this list, this does *not* mean that a reverse mortgage is definitely right for you. Nor does it mean that a reverse mortgage is the best way to achieve the goals that are listed. The list merely reinforces the basic premise underlying the concept of reverse mortgages and home equity conversion: **because reverse mortgages are not a "one size fits all" solution, each application for a reverse mortgage must be regarded as unique.** The uses that one person would consider practical or essential, another person might see as foolish or frivolous. If the lender does not restrict the uses for equity advances, the homeowner is solely responsible for deciding how to use the money generated by a reverse mortgage. The homeowner's imagination is the only real limitation to possible uses at this stage.

Reverse Mortgage Equity Advances Have Been Spent On ...

♠ Annuities (life or fixed term)

♠ Asset management and tax planning

♠ Buying a new recreational vehicle or a mobile home

♠ Buying a second property

♠ Delaying sale of the home until the real estate market rebounds

- Financing a grandchild's education
- Going back to school
- Helping children buy their first house
- Hiring a home-care support service
- Lifetime dreams, for example, "the trip of a lifetime"
- Major home renovations
- Modernizing heating systems
- Nursing home expenses for an ailing spouse or relative
- Paying off an existing mortgage or debt
- Personal indulgences
- Prepaid funeral expenses and plot
- Pre-pension financial bridging
- Preserving the family cottage
- Property tax and condominium fee payments
- Quitting a corporate position to work full-time as an artist
- Replacing the family car
- Saving a home from legal sale by the lender when the traditional mortgage was in default
- Settling a divorce
- Sharing the estate with the family while the homeowner could enjoy everyone's pleasure
- Terminal illness
- Transition period following a bereavement
- Travel, including an annual cruise
- Waiting for an opening in a retirement facility

Once again, this list represents uses that homeowners have actually chosen for the funds received from their reverse mortgages. I am not suggesting a reverse mortgage is necessarily the best way, or the only way, to accomplish any of these ends.

Who Are Today's Reverse Mortgage Users?

The individuals who arrange reverse mortgages are as varied as the uses for these innovative financial products. However, certain distinct patterns have emerged. Although reverse mortgages are often used to improve the standard of living for cash-poor, house-rich homeowners, many users merely wish to alter or enhance their lifestyle. These homeowners may also consider a reverse mortgage a beneficial asset-management and tax-planning tool. They want to take advantage of the tax-free dollars generated by home equity conversion. Others are motivated primarily by tax considerations.

One important aspect of the developing reverse mortgage market in Canada is that arranging a reverse mortgage does not stigmatize the borrower as a low-income individual. Homeowners in million-dollar properties and those with more than adequate incomes have decided to arrange a reverse mortgage. Reverse mortgages and home equity conversion products are regarded as useful to homeowners of all economic backgrounds. There is no stigma attached to using home equity conversion, because there is no one use or circumstance that predominates in the marketplace.

WHAT DO YOU THINK?

When you give your opinion or offer advice (solicited or unsolicited), are you really being helpful? When a friend, family member, or acquaintance asks for your opinion on reverse mortgages or home equity conversion, will you be able to separate your biases from the true issues for that individual? Is your advice based on what you think the other person wants to accomplish or on what *you* think the individual should do? If you are going to perpetuate your prejudices, at least explain to the other party that your opinion is very biased and for what reasons.

One of the best responses to, "What do you think?", is actually to ask the individual for their opinion and ideas before you give yours. Usually people ask this question to get support or encouragement for a decision. Listen to the individual's analysis of the problem and the potential solutions. Jumping in with "well, if it were me" ideas before you have a clear picture of the issues involved may just complicate the situation.

The Reverse Mortgage Quiz

In view of everything you have read so far, should you consider a reverse mortgage a possible answer to your financial and housing needs? Check off your answers to see where you stand.

	YES	NO
1. Can you relax and enjoy the money from the reverse mortgage, knowing that debt is compounding against the value of your home?	☐	☐
2. Are you committed to spending the equity in your home now?	☐	☐
3. Do the benefits of home ownership clearly outweigh the burdens, now and in the foreseeable future?	☐	☐
4. Can you accept full responsibility for home maintenance, taxes, and insurance, given that failure to meet these obligations could authorize the lender to request full repayment of the mortgage debt?	☐	☐
5. Have you set short- and long-term budgets to ensure that the money released by the reverse mortgage will be adequate to cover rising maintenance costs, escalating insurance costs, increasing tax pressures, and inflation, as well as possible personal or medical expenses?	☐	☐
6. Can you manage financially if the home equity is substantially or completely used up, and/or if the need to move into alternative housing arises?	☐	☐
7. Have you had candid discussions with your spouse and with other family members to determine their true feelings about depleting, or perhaps exhausting, the equity in the home? *(This question will not apply to everyone.)*	☐	☐
8. Are you making a decision about a reverse mortgage without feeling pressured and after having taken sufficient time to "live with" the implications before plunging in?	☐	☐
9. Are both or all of the homeowners making this decision together, or is someone giving in to the other(s)?	☐	☐
10. Regarding the neighbourhood and the property, is the house a practical setting for aging in place? (See page 88 for more details.)	☐	☐
11. Do you know precisely what your alternatives are if you do not arrange a reverse mortgage?	☐	☐

If you answered no to any of the questions in the quiz, a decision in favour of a reverse mortgage may be premature, impractical, or ill-advised for you at this stage. If you have not resolved all outstanding issues with family members, you may benefit from rethinking the whole situation. Getting professional financial, housing, or legal advice would also probably be helpful, especially as further research and evaluation may be wise at this point. A negative answer on the quiz indicates there still may be more for you to learn or explore.

On the other hand, if you answered yes to *all* of the questions in the quiz, *you might be a suitable candidate for a reverse mortgage.* I say *might be* because making a decision to arrange a reverse mortgage should be based on careful thought and research, not on the results of a quiz. It is possible to answer yes to some of these questions on a superficial level, when in fact the issues behind a question have not been thoroughly addressed.

DECISIONS, DECISIONS, DECISIONS

Gathering accurate, unbiased information about the reverse mortgage products available to them is the first challenge for consumers. The next challenge is to relate this information to personal needs, so that the consumer can select a suitable product. As yet, Canada has no specific legislation that governs reverse mortgages or that regulates standard terms and documents. Therefore, consumers are faced with having to make complex product comparisons. Chapters 5 and 6 provide guidelines for evaluating a reverse mortgage, and Chapter 7 discusses independent advisers. The following section examines decision making, including what specific pitfalls to avoid.

Buyer Beware

The responsibilities associated with maintaining a home have made many older homeowners astute and experienced consumers. However, unsuspecting, illiterate, or isolated homeowners may be at risk when they enter the reverse mortgage marketplace. Exploitation, deception, and fraud are particularly destructive, almost evil, when the elderly are targeted. They have little opportunity to rebuild lost finances and may be particularly susceptible to physical and emotional stress.

Homeowners who are looking for easy answers or who are embarrassed to reveal that they do not understand financial concepts or terminology can be "sold" a product too easily. **When salespeople, financial consultants, or managers promise the "best financial solution," the "best financial product," or the "best buy," beware of hidden agendas, biased information, and slick, superficial treatment of complex issues.**

Most lenders have a staff of representatives who may have impressive-sounding titles, but, whatever their titles, these individuals should be considered salespeople. Also, keep in mind that the product a salesperson suggests is "best for you" depends on the salesperson's perspective. For example, if the salesperson has only two products on which to earn a commission, the product that is "best for you" will be one of these. Be wary of variations on one product that may be presented as separate alternatives. You may feel as if you have "shopped around" if you have seen two or three computer simulations of variations on the product, but in fact you may merely have seen one product from different perspectives. The fewer the number of products that generate a commission for the salesperson, the more the word "best" translates as, "best in terms of what the salesperson gets paid to offer," not "best of all that is available to you in the open market." Ask for clear, written disclosure of all sources of fees and commissions, and attempt to discover biases on the part of the sales staff, *before* you sign up for a reverse mortgage or pay any nonrefundable fees. Remember that your peace of mind and your future are at stake, so stay in control.

Read Before You Leap

Read *everything* carefully before you sign. If you are not completely sure what you and the lender are promising each other, ask more questions. Take nothing for granted. Contract law binds you to what you sign, even if you do not read the document or understand its terms.

For example, you read earlier that one common covenant (a legally binding promise) made by a borrower to a lender, allows the lender the right to inspect the property to ensure the house is in good repair. If your reverse mortgage contract gives the lender the right to inspection, the lender can enter your home, with the appropriate prior notice. A lender cannot exercise this right every day or when you are not at home. But a lender could have access when there is reason to believe something is wrong, or according to the frequency of inspection as set out in the contract, which may be once a year. Most lenders include this right in traditional mortgages as well, although it is rarely exercised. The important point is that the lender can give you all sorts of verbal assurances, but if policy or circumstances change, the contract gives the lender the authority to inspect the house to determine the state of repair.

Do not lose sleep over such clauses, but remember that if something is in writing, it could happen. Be sure you fully understand the promises and obligations that you and the lender are agreeing to in the contract. Independent legal advice will help you understand the implications of the clauses. Chapters 5, 6, and 7 provide the background information necessary to understand a reverse mortgage contract.

If a reverse mortgage contract includes a "cooling-off" period, you could void or cancel the contract *after* signing it but *before* the cooling-off period ends, without losing anything or being penalized (unless the contract states otherwise). As this type of clause is not common, however, signing the contract must, in most cases, be taken seriously. After the cooling-off period ends, you are committed to the terms and conditions of the contract. One variation of the cooling-off period involves a delay in the sign-up process. This version gives you time to reflect *before* signing; *after* signing, however, you are committed to the terms and conditions of the contract. (For more on cooling-off periods, see Chapter 6, page 122.)

To make sure the lender is committed to fulfilling all the promises made by staff and salespeople, get everything in writing in the contract. Later on, "I said" and "You said" are very hard to prove. Also, years down the road, many staff and salespeople may have left the organization, or they may not even remember having met you.

THE SAVVY CONSUMER

- **Knowledge is power**. Find out as much as possible about reverse mortgages. The lenders, their managers, and sales staff are not responsible for educating you about home equity conversion and reverse mortgages. Their job is to promote their products. *You* must know which questions *you* need to ask.

- **Keep up to date**. New housing alternatives and financial options are evolving constantly. Join a seniors' advocacy group and get involved with their housing committee. Ask friends, neighbours, and advisers to keep an eye out for books, magazine articles, and other sources of information on housing. Tune into seniors' programming on radio and television.

- **Reach out**. Isolation inhibits inspiration and can make you vulnerable. Join a seniors' organization to develop a network of friends and acquaintances who can serve as a sounding board when you are facing a major decision. In turn, if you know someone who is isolated or is at a disadvantage in handling financial matters, you can lend a friendly hand.

- **Pace yourself**. Beware of looking for fast answers when investigating reverse mortgages. Avoid rushing to "get things done" simply because you have "more important" things to do. What could be more important than peace of mind and security for the future? Use time to your advantage. Slow down and reflect before making a decision. You will have to live with your choice for a long time.

- **Acknowledge your weaknesses and rely on your strengths**. Take the initiative to overcome any disadvantages. If you have trouble understanding English or if you have problems hearing, ask a trusted friend or family member to accompany you when you are negotiating a financial decision. Get everything in writing before you spend a cent!

- **Be realistic**. There are no free lunches. If something sounds too good to be true, it probably is. Needs and fears are the target of advertising and marketing campaigns. You may wish all your problems and pains would disappear, but there are no "miracle cures." Verify that all verbal promises and assurances are accurately represented in the document *before* you spend any money or sign a contract.

How Do You Decide?

Everyone makes decisions differently. And we make different kinds of decisions differently. We take great care when shopping for a new stereo system or a set of golf clubs. That degree of care is rarely matched, however, when we select an RRSP or buy a house! When making a major decision, many people prefer to keep their business to themselves. Others tell everyone and listen to no one. Some people rely on feedback from family members and/or professional advisers. A few look for someone else to make the decision for them. Many others procrastinate until an emergency or a deadline destroys choice and drives them to action.

Relationship Selling

Although many of us do not realize it, when making buying decisions we are tremendously influenced by the salespeople involved. The average person's fears of having to make decisions, combined with an inherent resistance to change are tendencies that create selling opportunities for salespeople, as well as for those who advertise and market products. Advertising, marketing, and sales campaigns succeed by hitting consumers' "hot buttons," that is, targeting needs, addressing fears, and making things appear easier than they should appear. Also, if potential customers live a fairly isolated life, the selling opportunity is amplified for businesses. The factors mentioned here that cause us to be both cautious and nervous combine to make us most comfortable when dealing with friends.

IT'S YOUR DECISION

If you have lived in Canada for a while, you have probably had to get into cold water. How did you do it? Did you take a breath and plunge in? Did you Inch In, letting each body part adjust gradually to the shock? Did you creep in slowly at first, then suddenly grow impatient and dunk yourself to get it over with? Or, did you just accept someone's word that the water was cold and sit on the beach? These varying approaches to cold water are analogous to the reactions people have to the revolutionary concepts of home equity conversion and reverse mortgages. Also, the same approach may be used for different reasons. Some people "plunge in" and make decisions quickly, to get the painful process over with. Others "plunge in" to pursue what sounds like a dream come true. How are you "testing the waters" of home equity conversion and reverse mortgages?

Friends, after all, will look after us and make sure things turn out all right; friends know what to do and how to do it; friends are always happy to see us, and listen carefully to all we say; and friends can be trusted. If you substitute the word "salespeople" for the word "friends" in the previous sentence, you will have described *relationship selling,* a powerful sales approach with high-intensity, trust-building techniques. In fact, to distance themselves from sales, with its negative image for consumers, businesses now talk about "building relationships" or "marketing to clients," instead of "selling to customers."

Studies have shown that more than 80 percent of a buying decision rests with how we feel about the salesperson. If we like and trust the salesperson, the result is a sale. Conversely, unless we are pressured by time constraints, there is no sale if we do not like or trust this individual. Because we know there are many more salespeople "out there," we will usually search for a friendly one. Relationship selling is based on the trust building that is the spark of friendship. For this reason, it can be mistaken for a "low pressure" sales approach—this is what makes relationship selling potentially more dangerous for the consumer than other sales techniques. When this sales approach matches a sincere, deeply felt respect and interest in the well-being of the client, all is as it should be. If the client's interests were placed first, the client could feel comfortable in trusting a lender and the lender's managers, administrative staff, and salespeople. However, these professionals are in business to make money. Lenders and their managers, staff, and salespeople are biased in favour of business agendas, sales commissions, sales quotas, and sales incentives. However, if all the commissions, quotas, incentives, referral fees, and biases are disclosed to the client in full and in writing, the client has a better opportunity to make an informed decision. When clients believe that in speaking with a salesperson they are talking to a friend, it may be that clients' best interests are not being served. As mentioned previously, Chapter 7 discusses how to get objective professional advice.

Relationship selling is not a technique used to trick or defraud the consumer. It is a method of communication designed to reach out to potential clients, to build trust relatively quickly, and to convince the consumer to become a client. It is not the technique itself but the motives of the user that must be examined. If the salesperson is focused on sales and is working with reckless disregard for the interests of the client or with fraudulent intent, relationship selling can be dangerous for unsophisticated or unsuspecting consumers of any age.

You **must be comfortable with your decision.** You can never be 100 percent sure, that degree of confidence comes only with hindsight. However, you can use the "51 Percent Rule," by which you will at least be more "sure" than "not sure." While others may express doubts about your decision concerning a reverse mortgage, only those directly affected by your decision need to be convinced. But having the courage of your convictions is not to be confused with merely being stubborn. On the other hand, waiting until everyone, including your entire family, agrees with you may be exhausting. Accept all the help you can get! Enlist the aid of an independent professional adviser. For example, most lenders encourage or require borrowers to hire a lawyer to read through the contract with them. (Chapter 7 explores the challenges of making the most of the advice given by professional advisers and other resource people.) However, when "the dust settles," the decision is yours, and the only person or people who really need to be content with the choice are you, or you and your spouse.

"How Can I Be Sure?"

This question gnaws at everyone contemplating any kind of important decision. In reality, only hindsight can tell you whether a decision has been good or bad. However, an important aspect of gaining confidence in your decision is to be able to ask yourself the right questions. For example, when homeowners ask: "Should I get a reverse mortgage?" they are really asking the fundamental question: "Is arranging a reverse mortgage the best way to satisfy my financial, housing, personal, and family's needs?" This is a huge question—certainly a larger question than most of us want to answer or feel capable of answering. This unmanageable question should be broken down into separate issues; such as:

- Is arranging a reverse mortgage the best way to satisfy my financial needs?

- Is arranging a reverse mortgage the best way to satisfy my housing needs?

- Is arranging a reverse mortgage the best way to satisfy my personal needs?

- Is arranging a reverse mortgage the best way to satisfy my family's needs?

In turn, answering these questions will be easier if you break each one down further to determine your specific needs in every category. For instance, your personal needs may range from privacy, so you can get up in the night without having to put on a housecoat, to the layout of your house, for example, the importance of having a bathroom on the main floor. In assessing your financial needs, simply reviewing your daily budget may not be enough. If you have lived in the house for many years, you may soon be faced with major repairs, for instance, a new furnace, a new roof, or new plumbing. Price out these repairs and modernizations, even if you do not need them today. Creating short- and long-term budgets will be essential to getting a clear picture of your financial needs. Write everything down. Doing so may remind you of someone or something you had overlooked. As you clarify your needs and concerns, and define the problem or problems, you will create criteria for decision making.

Defining your needs and wants is an important first step in decision making. By first identifying the problems that must be solved when researching alternatives, you will know exactly what questions to ask and how to evaluate the answers in light of your particular situation. While "Buyer Beware" must set the tone, your restraint should be an educated caution, not one that brings on the paralysis of either indecision or fear of the unknown. Instead of looking for excuses to eliminate an alternative, approach every new idea with an open mind and an eye to the opportunities it holds for you. Explore both the advantages and the disadvantages of each housing option, each reverse mortgage product, and each financial solution.

Just because someone asks you to decide does not mean you must. Make decisions only when it suits you, and make them for your own good.

STATUS QUO OR PACK AND GO?

"Home" is a word we all understand, although this word has a multitude of individual interpretations. The common theme? Home is, above all else, the place where you belong.

Linked with the sense of belonging is the complex and energizing characteristic of independence. Independence goes beyond the ability to act for yourself or to live on your own. Independence begins inside; it is an attitude towards your existence, a perspective on living, and a view of the future. Independence is not a function of walls and doors, but of how we view ourselves, how we interact with others, and how we contribute to the community. For many people, "home" becomes the outward symbol of independence. Therefore, moving can be perceived as a threat to self-determination, autonomy, and personal freedom.

The degree of independence essential to an individual is determined by many factors: knowledge, skills, abilities, cultural patterns, resources, income, informal service networks, and attitudes—the individual's, the family's, and society's. Whether we realize it or not, our personal definition of independence is at the heart of our decisions concerning whether to stay in our own home and where to move to when selecting new housing. In order to make lifestyle changes that truly work, it is vital to identify the factors that define independence for you, before you make a decision about where you will live.

Caring Pressure

Although we talk of "earning" independence, no one can give you independence—you must take it and you must maintain it. Your independence can be undermined by those who deliberately, unconsciously, or unknowingly erode your self-confidence. For example, imposing more services on people than they need can violate their rights and erode their independence. An older homeowner may find that well-meaning friends and relatives—reacting to their own fears—are exerting pressure, gentle or otherwise, to sell the home and to move. While the homeowner wishes to continue to live alone, these helpful people want the homeowner to move in with them or into retirement housing. Their "but we worry about you" approach can compel the older homeowner to make premature decisions.

By overriding the individual's right to evaluate risk and to live with risk, friends and relatives can jeopardize your personal independence. Others will try to make decisions for you if you cannot convince them that you are in control of your life. The solution? Face tomorrow head on. Be prepared. Remember: there is more personal satisfaction in being *independent* than in becoming dependent.

Aging in Place

To stay or not to stay? Many homeowners find this question difficult to answer. While the decision is complex at any stage of life, many additional factors arise as one ages, and the margin for error narrows. "They'll have to carry me out!" may express your private feelings about living in your home. However, sheer stubbornness and resistance to change are not the best motives for staying. Nor is the fear of clearing out 20-plus years of "stuff." Ensure that your decision to stay in your home and to age in place is based on positive motives and a clear understanding of how independence and quality of life overlap for you.

"Aging in place" and "staying put" are terms that describe staying in your own home as you grow older, rather than moving into an institutional setting. Whether as a tenant in your apartment of many years or as a homeowner in the house you have grown to love, you have become an integral part of your neighbourhood, just as the neighbourhood has become an integral part of your life. Aging in place reinforces the sense of belonging that is at the heart of our concept of "home."

Aging in place is an attractive alternative for many people, even if it merely delays the dreaded task of sorting through the flotsam and jetsam that most of us accumulate in drawers, closets, and basements over a lifetime. What you must examine carefully is whether the decision to stay put is practical and feasible. The availability of accessible community support services and the physical layout of your home are two important factors in analyzing whether this is the right place to age in place. Community support services should be carefully researched to determine, not only the types of programs available, but also whether you would qualify for these programs and any other support benefits. If you would not currently qualify, what changes would have to occur, particularly financially, to make you eligible?

A question such as, "What do I consider irreplaceable about this home?" can be extremely useful if you take the time to write down specific ideas. For example, in answering this question, think about each season, time of day, and day of the week when you make your list. "I love the summer" is too vague. What do you specifically love about the summer in your home? How many days of this pleasure do you have in a year? Could you experience the same thing in another place? How might the experience be even better elsewhere?

The Foundation of Your Decision

Once you make a decision about aging in place you may think you will be able to sit back and relax, with no more ideas to mull over. Wrong! Things change—in your life and in the world. Any housing choice you make should be what I call a "flexible decision." This involves making a "decision," which I call plan A, but also acknowledging that the circumstances under which you decided on Plan A may change. Therefore, built into your decision are one or two alternatives: Plan B and Plan C. You have worked out the details of Plan A; the other plans may be only rough outlines, but are strong possibilities nonetheless. Having back-up plans takes the pressure off you, while giving you the flexibility that is so vital in life planning. For instance, Plan B might come into play if the stairs in the home must be modified and if live-in attendant care is necessary.

Take the following factors into account when making your flexible decision to age in place:

♠ **Caring community.** Interdependence promotes independence. "Doing it alone" may be a habit, stubbornness, false pride, or martyrdom, but it is not independence. Independence and autonomy mean "being responsible for yourself," not "being alone." We need human contact to feel connected to the community and to the world. How will you ensure that your contact with the community will have the intensity, frequency, quality, and diversity necessary to reinforce your autonomy? In short, how will you get your hugs?

♠ **Anticipate change.** Plan for change—it's the only constant in life. Anticipating change involves planning for change "while the sun shines," that is, before you are forced into a corner. Develop strategies for adapting to changes in income, in physical health, and in the seasons. Look at all the "what ifs." Anticipation reinforces independence. What modifications would be necessary if you were to develop physical limitations, for example? Canada Mortgage and Housing Corporation has a number of excellent booklets on home modification. You can contact your local office to order these free guides for independent living.

Do you believe that you can achieve the future of your dreams by accident or by wishing on a star? Too often people wander into the future with a "hope it turns out alright" sigh or an apathetic shrug. Anticipating changes fosters an "If it is to be, it's up to me" attitude. Take action to make your home safe so that accidents become unlikely. At the same time, keep yourself physically fit so that you can bounce back from any problem that might arise.

♠ **Services plus.** As we age, community services become more important. You should assess the community and the services it offers when analyzing whether to age in place. Health services are an obvious priority, but more important are the day-to-day services that can mean the difference between staying in your home and being forced to move. These services include: home delivery by grocery stores, drugstores, hardware stores, and clothing shops, as well as at-home service by hairdressers, libraries, doctors, and house cleaners. Accessible public transportation is also vital to independent living. What community services exist to support your plans to age in place, especially if you require home care? Will you qualify? If the age-in-place support systems are minimal or non-existent, what are you going to do about it?

♠ **Be realistic.** Is your home a good site for aging in place? Are there too many stairs to the bathroom? Does it take all week to get the lawn mowed? Are you actually living in only two rooms? Have all of your friends moved away? Do you enjoy the neighbourhood, or have all the familiar landmarks disappeared?

♠ **Home safe home.** Where home safety is concerned, anticipation is the best defence. Here are a few ideas:

- Throw out those sloppy knitted slippers.
- Stop using the staircase as a storage area.
- Select non-slip flooring, especially in wet areas.
- Choose broadloom rather than scatter rugs.
- Buy fire-resistant nightclothes.
- Make sure stairways, entrances, and working areas are well-lit.

♠ **Take care of details.** You can do little things to adapt your home for independent, barrier-free living:

- Install accessible shelving.
- Lower kitchen cabinets.
- Add bathroom grab bars.
- Redo stairs and steps in contrasting colours.
- Remove obstacles, especially on the night route from bedroom to bathroom.
- Install lever-style handles on doors and taps.
- Lower the mailbox, light switches, and closet rods.
- Raise electrical outlets.
- Collect gadgets that make life easier such as jar openers and zipper hooks.
- Install technical devices to enhance safety and security.

♠ **Embrace wellness.** Independence goes hand in hand with physical fitness. Regardless of your current degree of mobility, wellness is important. Most daily activities require some degree of physical fitness: walking to the mailbox, sitting down to read, getting up to answer the door, reaching for a frying pan, getting into the shower, lifting the teapot, and climbing the front steps. Incorporate simple exercises into your routine to reinforce flexibility, cardio-respiratory efficiency, stamina, and muscle tone. Eat a balanced diet. Laugh at least once a day. If your doctor has a "don't be silly" attitude and always prescribes medication, look for a more empathetic doctor. Taking responsibility for your well-being means gaining self-awareness, exercising self-discipline, and acquiring self-care skills. A wellness attitude allows you to reach out to the challenges of life with a balanced perspective.

♠ **Keep an open mind.** In our constantly changing world, new housing alternatives are becoming commonplace. Regularly re-evaluate the decision to stay in your home against new opportunities. Because we cannot see the future, "I could never" should be rephrased as, "I have never, but perhaps I could." Keep up to date on innovations. Stay informed.

Benefits Must Outweigh Burdens

Having arranged a reverse mortgage, the homeowner continues to be responsible for all aspects of property maintenance. Carefully evaluate the time, energy, and stress involved in the annual maintenance tasks. Try to assess the future major repairs or modernizations that could become necessary over the next ten or more years. For instance, after twenty years a roof is living on borrowed time. How old are the furnace, the electrical wiring, and the plumbing? Upgrades of these kinds of equipment and material, and any resulting increases in property taxes, must be factored into your budget when you are deciding whether to stay or to move. Owning a home is a responsiblity that requires time, energy, and money. Be sure that investing these resources in your home is a reasonable choice, and not just a habit.

Ask yourself many questions about the physical practicality of the house and of your plans to stay in it. As you age, so does the house. Will it age well? What do you really love about living there? Make a list of your needs and desires. Could you satisfy these needs and desires, and perhaps others as well, with other housing?

Too often what appears to be a decision to stay or to avoid change is really inertia, fuelled by fear. Whether it is the fear of uncertainty or the dread of having to sort through and pack up

GOVERNMENT PROGRAMS

In exploring the potential of your home as an age-in-place site, investigate current government programs to see what is available to support your efforts. Municipal and provincial governments, as well as the federal government, often sponsor programs for homeowners that range from property tax deferral plans and property tax grant programs to renovation loans, emergency repair programs, and snow removal services. These programs may offer the solution to one or all of your home ownership concerns. However, government at all levels is undergoing budgetary reviews, so always check directly with the office administering the program to determine the latest qualification requirements and program guidelines. Many programs are designed to assist moderate to low income homeowners, and some are restricted to those over 65.

A number of programs cover all construction costs in a renovation; others may only pay for labour. Read the literature carefully to determine the application procedure, since your request may be rejected or delayed if you file incorrectly. Do not begin any construction work until you have been approved for a renovation grant or loan. It is also worth asking whether assistance is available to fill out the required paperwork. However, be careful if a contractor offers to do repairs, modernizations, or renovations with a "Don't worry, the government will pay for everything later." assurance. Investigate the government program yourself before signing anything or paying any deposits.

Between the municipal building, housing and taxation departments, the provincial housing ministry, and the federal Canada Mortgage and Housing Corporation, you should be able to locate the programs available in your area. Community information centres, public libraries, and local seniors' organizations are also excellent resources; your local politicians, MP, and MPP may also be helpful.

more than twenty years worth of belongings, such fears can compel you to stay in your current home. Sadness at the prospect of leaving a home and neighbourhood you know and love is natural. Staying because you don't know what else to do or where you could go may mean that you are shortchanging yourself permanently.

If you decide to stay, the costs of maintenance, repairs, and general upkeep will increase, as will property taxes, utilities, and insurance. When calculating how much money you need each month to stay in your home, be sure to factor in these costs, as well as those of inflation.

Isolation can immobilize you. Do you really enjoy your neighbourhood? Or are you housebound by necessity or choice much of the time? Reflect on the past two weeks. How much time did you spend in your house, in the neighbourhood, or outside of either? Examining the patterns of your life will help you see whether staying is a function of love or of habit.

By planning ahead, you can build a series of contingency plans that will take the worry out of tomorrow. If your home does not lend itself to modification, you should develop a plan to move to another home. If you shop for housing alternatives before you really need them, the transition will be less traumatic and will guarantee your independence. In the meantime, if you decide to stay, enjoy yourself—comfortably secure that you have the future in focus.

If You Go, Where Could You Go?

What can you do if you have no idea what housing alternatives exist in your area? Get the local papers and the community weeklies, and start reading the housing sections. Get a map of your chosen area and start plotting sites for your possible relocation.

Innovative Housing Options

Until recently, few retirement housing options were available to those faced with the "to stay or not to stay" housing decision. Now, older consumers have an increasing range of innovative housing options, real estate retirement concepts, and related financial products to consider. The best alternatives focus on independence: preserving it, enhancing it, protecting it.

Today's term, "retirement housing," is a catchall for everything from mobile home communities, waterfront condominiums, and hotel-style luxury complexes, to nonprofit co-operatives and continuum-of-care communities, which offer a range of alternatives from traditional houses to chronic-care hospitals. New housing concepts and innovative approaches are becoming more and more commonplace. The Canada Mortgage and Housing

Corporation office nearest you is a good place to begin your research. (See Appendix on page 287.)

The following suggestions will put things in perspective and provide a foundation for your research, regardless of the type of retirement housing you are investigating:

♠ **Begin with you.** Know what you and, perhaps, your spouse really want and need in a home. Ask your family and close friends too, as they often think of things you take for granted. Make a list of "must haves" and "like to haves" and refer to it when visiting a community or complex.

♠ **Invest time.** Last-minute thinking may leave you with few housing alternatives. Start exploring housing options today—in your community, province, Canada, and other countries. Write letters requesting literature; plan a trip or two to investigate first hand; subscribe to local papers to get to know the area. Slowly building a life around the move will make it a much more enjoyable experience.

♠ **More than once.** Although buildings are important, in all cases, people make the difference between "a facility" and "your home." A quick visit cannot give you a clear picture of all of the factors to consider: management policies; personalities, and atmosphere are only the beginning. Be prepared to tour, chat, eat, play, and explore the premises on several occasions, over a period of time. Developers, salespeople, and managers of retirement housing know that mature consumers like to get to know a facility, often over a number of years, before making a decision.

♠ **Take care of business.** Understanding the legal and financial complexities is your responsibility. If you are married, both you and your spouse should get involved to ensure peace of mind. Reliable, knowledgeable advisers will be valuable assets to your search.

♠ **Questions, Questions.** Ask questions and keep asking. Take notes. Assume nothing.

CHAPTER 5

Where Do I Start?

REVERSE MORTGAGE BASICS

For the best results, reverse mortgage features should correspond to the homeowner's individual requirements for income, security, and estate planning. Compare products carefully and thoroughly before deciding which, if any, would suit most or all of your needs. Again, "buyer beware" must be your operative attitude. Focus on getting clear, detailed answers, as well as written responses to key points.

Product comparison centres on three basic questions:

- How much will the reverse mortgage pay?
- What will the total cost be, including interest?
- What equity will be left at the end of the reverse mortgage?

In less formal terms, these questions can be translated as:

- What do I get?
- What will it cost?
- What will be left?

The first two questions are commonly asked when considering any new product. The third, an important question when comparing reverse mortgages, reflects the unique perspective necessary for eval-uating home equity conversion products. The diagram on page 99 represents the division of home equity brought about through a reverse mortgage and illustrates the answers to these three questions:

What do I get?

Equity advances

- the amount of equity released to the homeowner(s) by the reverse mortgage, while ownership and possession are retained by the homeowner; and,
- the amount paid to the homeowner by the lender.

What will it cost?

Loan costs

- the expenses, including interest, incurred by the homeown-er(s) in arranging a reverse mortgage; and,
- the amount the lender collects to cover profit and costs for providing the homeowner's reverse mortgage.

What will be left?

Residual equity

- the amount of equity remaining for the homeowner after the equity advances and the loan costs, including interest, have been withdrawn; and,
- the amount of equity that is not part of the reverse mortgage and is, therefore, not available to the lender.
  (*Note:* **There may not be any residual equity left by the time the reverse mortgage terminates.**)

To properly evaluate a reverse mortgage product, you must be prepared to ask questions concerning the equity advances, the loan costs, and the residual equity. This chapter discusses the "So what?" and "What should I do about it?" aspects of a number of important questions. If necessary, consult a financial, housing, and/or legal adviser for help in evaluating the relevance of each question to your personal circumstances.

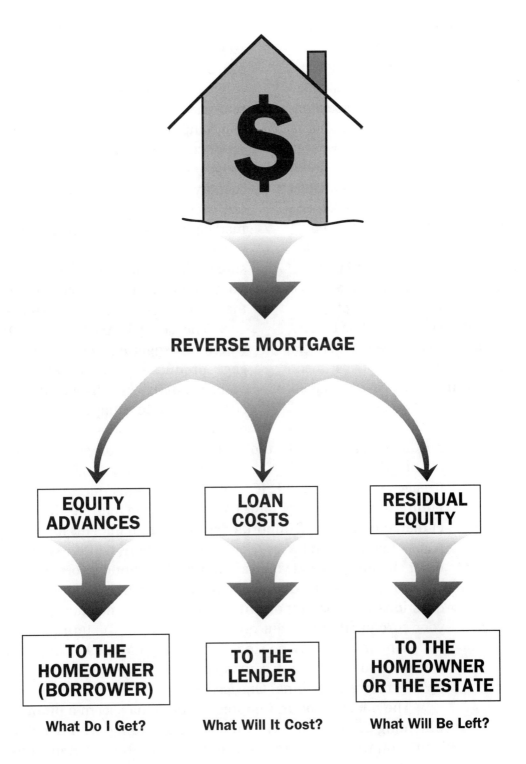

REVERSE MORTGAGE

EQUITY ADVANCES	LOAN COSTS	RESIDUAL EQUITY
TO THE HOMEOWNER (BORROWER)	TO THE LENDER	TO THE HOMEOWNER OR THE ESTATE
What Do I Get?	What Will It Cost?	What Will Be Left?

For Those Readers Who Turned Directly to Chapter 5:
As this book is a reference guide, flipping from chapter to chapter is quite acceptable. The Glossary and the Quick Question Index on pages 291–301 are designed to give you the greatest possible flexibility in using the book. **However, I caution you to base your decisions on *all* the information in the book, not just on one section, especially if your immediate reaction is, "A reverse mortgage is for me."** Once you understand the concepts presented here, you will be better prepared to make the most of home equity conversion, if not now, then perhaps at some time in the future.

Knowing what questions to ask, and why to ask them, characterizes a savvy consumer, whether you are buying a house, a car, a self-improvement course, or a registered retirement savings plan (RRSP). When shopping for any type of financial product, consumers are generally attracted to those that offer value and security with a degree of flexibility for the user. While competition in the marketplace usually increases value, security, and flexibility for the consumer, the resulting increase in the number of choices can complicate the buying decision for the consumer.

The critical questions to ask when investigating reverse mortgage products for value, security, and flexibility are listed in this chapter and in Chapter 6. These questions are organized under headings that represent the four stages of the process: "Before Signing Up" (Chapter 5, page 101), "What Am I Signing?" (Chapter 6, page 119), "Signing Off" (Chapter 6, page 145), and "Signs of the Future"(Chapter 6, page 148). This final section reminds the reader that *tomorrow* is an important consideration in plans for today. (Cross-references in italics relate these questions to discussions in other chapters, should you want more background information.)

Your unique needs and circumstances will determine which questions are most important. Some questions may not relate to your current situation, but no one knows what the future holds. For example, you may be single now, but what might happen if you were to marry and your spouse were to move into your reverse-mortgaged home? Or, vice versa?

The information in Chapters 5 and 6 may seem a bit overwhelming at first. However, on a second reading, with pencil in hand, you will be able to list or to highlight, the questions most relevant to you in arranging a reverse mortgage to meet your needs. Ideally, you should clarify these points with a professional and/or a personal adviser, before talking to a salesperson. If you take the time to read carefully and to think things through—either alone or with competent assistance—you will be rewarded with the peace of mind and the personal satisfaction of a decision well made. Further, the questions posed in Chapters 5 and 6 are designed to overcome the paralysis of indecision and empower you to be your own agent for change.

BEFORE SIGNING UP

All of the topics listed below and discussed in the pages that follow are equally important. Each should be carefully evaluated by you, and your advisers, before you consider signing up for a reverse mortgage. In Chapter 6, issues relevant to the reverse mortgage contract will be examined in detail to reveal the implications of various contract terms and conditions to the consumer.

- **Lender Credibility**
- **Qualifying for a Reverse Mortgage**
- **Appraised Value of the Property**
- **Total Cost of Set-up and Administration**
- **Equity Preservation**
- **The Annuity**
- **Lender Service Programs**

Getting off to a good start is vital in home equity conversion. Thoroughly addressing the topics raised in the following question-by-question expansion ensures that you, the consumer, start out on the right foot when selecting a reverse mortgage lender and a reverse mortgage product. (*Note:* "Consumer" is used here in the singular; please substitute the plural for couples or joint owners, to suit your personal situation.)

Lender Credibility

♠ **What is the lender's track record to date?**

Your interest in the stability of the lender is twofold. First, you wish to protect the stream of regular equity advance payments. (Unless you have chosen a lump sum reverse mortgage.) Second, you want to understand the management style and policies of the lender with whom you have signed the reverse mortgage contract.

🏠 **What characteristics of the lender and its principals reassure the borrower that the relationship between the lender and the homeowner will be financially stable?**

Remember—this is a long-term relationship between you and one, or two *companies*. What is it about the company, or companies, and the principals/owners that makes you feel secure? Do not base your trust in the organization solely on the personalities of its salespeople. Get answers to basic questions, including, "How long have you been in business?" "Are reverse mortgages your only product?" and "Who are the principals/owners of the company?" You could request a copy of the company's financial statements or annual report, if you know how to evaluate them. To get a sense of the company's follow-up procedures, as well as its customer service policies, asking for references and talking with some of the lender's earliest clients would be ideal. Also, put out a call to your "information" network of friends and contacts to see what you can find out. Since your reverse mortgage may run for 20 or 30 years, it is worth some effort to get a few answers now to start you off on the right foot. Although no one can really foresee the future, independent financial advice may be useful here.

🏠 **If the annuity offered to you is provided by another organization, what is the relationship between the lender and that corporation? What is the track record and long-term credibility of this company?**

In other words, learn as much as you can about the company responsible for paying you. Not even insurance companies are immune to financial setbacks or insolvency.

For further discussion of this issue, see "The Annuity," page 115.

🏠 **Will the lender provide full written disclosure of all charges, commissions, fees, and benefits to be received by the lender, the lender's staff, and related companies?**

To assist the borrower in making an informed decision, the lender should provide a clearly written disclosure statement of all the costs involved for the borrower. Borrowers are entitled to know how much sales commission is hanging on their decision to sign up for a reverse mortgage. Understanding the motives of those involved helps homeowners distance themselves from the sales pitch, thus making an objective decision more likely.

Relationship selling techniques can lead a borrower into a (perhaps inappropriate) trusting relationship with the sales staff. The implications of this are discussed in Chapter 4, page 83. Also see Chapter 6, "Lender Bankruptcy," on page 130.

Qualifying for a Reverse Mortgage

🏠 **Product availability: Does the lender offer products in your area?**

All other questions become academic if the reverse mortgage lender does not offer reverse mortgages in your area. However, if the product is not available, continue your inquiry to educate yourself for future reference, or to establish a point of comparison for evaluating the available reverse mortgage(s). It is possible that the lender might eventually offer reverse mortgages in your location. Also, your next house-buying decision could take into account the availability of reverse mortgages in a specific area. Theoretically, a private reverse mortgage may be possible, so do not give up on your research.

QUALIFICATION CRITERIA

- 🏠 Product availability
- 🏠 Property values
- 🏠 Minimum reverse mortgage principal
- 🏠 Timeframe and payment plan options
- 🏠 Age requirements
- 🏠 Type of home ownership
- 🏠 Existing mortgages
- 🏠 Joint borrowers
- 🏠 Uses of equity advances
- 🏠 Income verification

For more information on the lenders' area selection criteria, see Chapter 3, page 55. For qualification criteria, see Chapter 2, page 20.

⬥ **Property value: Does the lender set a minimum or a maximum acceptable property value?**

The lender may further limit eligibility by setting a minimum and/or maximum value for homes eligible for its reverse mortgage. For example, does the lender insist that only properties worth $100,000 or more are eligible?

See "Appraised Value of the Property," page 107, for details and a discussion of maximum reverse mortgage limits.

⬥ **Minimum reverse mortgage principal: Is there a minimum amount or percentage of equity that must be mortgaged?**

The reverse mortgage lender may set a minimum borrowing limit as well.

For details on maximum limits, see "Appraised Value of the Property," page 107.

⬥ **Timeframe and payment plan options: What timeframe options and payment plan alternatives are available?**

As mentioned earlier, only homeowners in a few locations across Canada have a choice of reverse mortgage products. At best, you may be able to choose between a fixed-term reverse annuity mortgage and a tenure-plan reverse annuity mortgage, or perhaps the latter type and a reverse mortgage line of credit. Avoid snap decisions! Investigate each option to evaluate its impact on your lifestyle and standard of living. Carefully assess which option gives you the benefits you need today, along with security and flexibility for the future.

The contract between the lender and the borrower specifies the design or type of reverse mortgage. The basic types of reverse mortgages discussed in Chapter 3 can be modified in any way that is mutually satisfactory to the lender and the borrower. A commercial lender may be less flexible in negotiating modifications than a private lender, as the latter may not be restricted by corporate lending policies.

To clarify your needs and values as a frame of reference, see Chapter 4. For more on the different reverse mortgage design variables, see Chapter 3, page 36.

⌂ Age requirements: What are the minimum age requirements?

The lender has designed its reverse mortgage products to give satisfactory returns for both lender and borrower. For reverse mortgages, the minimum age for eligibility is usually between 60 and 65. While the minimum for fixed-term reverse mortgages may be lower, the minimum for tenure-plan reverse mortgages may be higher. For couples, the lender may base eligibility on the age of the younger spouse, or on the average of the two ages. On the other hand, the lender may not set age requirements. There is no upper age limit for reverse mortgages; even at 100 you would qualify.

The size of reverse mortgage equity advances is based on life expectancy projections; therefore, older homeowners earn the greatest returns. Reverse mortgages work best for those aged 70 and older. For a more detailed explanation, see Chapter 3, page 33. Also see Chapter 4, page 71.

⌂ Type of home ownership: Does my type of home ownership qualify?

Lenders want the highest level of security for their investment. They prefer to lend on detached houses, semi-detached homes, and townhouses held in fee simple estate; most also offer reverse mortgages on condominiums. A lender may consider a duplex eligible, provided at least one of the two units is owner-occupied. However, co-operatives (co-ops) do not qualify, as the co-op owner is not a homeowner. Instead, each posseses shares in a corporation that owns and manages the property; the co-op owner has the right to occupy one unit or apartment.

Mobile home and other retirement properties, where the land is leased—not owned—by the homeowner, are not eligible at this stage.

For further details, see Chapter 4, page 72, and the Glossary on page 291.

♠ **Existing mortgages: What is the lender's policy if there is an existing traditional mortgage?**

As previously discussed, the lender wants maximum security for the reverse mortgage, and so prefers that the reverse mortgage is the first mortgage registered against the property. Lenders usually insist that existing debts be paid off to give the reverse mortgage first-claim priority. Some lenders may, in fact, demand the reverse mortgage be the only mortgage or debt against the property. However, others may allow a property tax deferral plan (a type of home equity conversion program discussed in Chapter 8) to be registered against the property before, or after, a reverse mortgage has been arranged.

The proceeds of the reverse mortgage may be used to pay off an existing traditional mortgage, thus relieving the homeowner of the financial strain of regular repayment of the traditional mortgage.

To review the ideas expressed in this section, see Chapter 4, page 77. See also Chapter 6, "Property Tax Deferral Plans," page 141, to continue this examination. Go on to Chapter 8, page 178, if you wish to learn more about property tax deferral plans themselves.

♠ **Joint borrowers: If the property is owned by more than one person and if the owners are not married to one another, does the property qualify?**
Must unrelated owners hold the home in joint tenancy so that the surviving owner automatically gains ownership through the right of survivorship?

Properties owned by common-law couples or unrelated people living together as families may not meet the lender's criteria. Also, if one of the homeowners is under the age minimum, the lender may require that the entire property ownership be transferred to the qualifying owner—the lender will not place a reverse mortgage on "half" a property. You may live alone now, but if you acquire a housemate, what are the possible repercussions? Suppose a relative or friend moved in to become a full-time, primary caregiver. Could a reverse mortgage be arranged to cover both the caregiver and the homeowner?

Long-range planning is an important part of the decision-making process. For an exploration of this topic, see Chapter 4, page 85. For more information, see "Spousal and Joint Borrower Rights," in Chapter 6, page 143. Chapter 12 explores joint ownership, right of survivorship, and joint tenancy further, beginning on page 277.

♠ **Uses of equity advances: Does the lender place restrictions on the use of the equity advances? If so, must each expenditure be approved?**

Lenders generally allow homeowners to use the equity advances in any way they feel is suitable. However, an individual lender may restrict the reverse mortgage payments to uses such as home improvement, taxes, medical costs, funeral expenses, or other "worthwhile" needs, the lender deciding which uses are worthwhile.

For further discussion of the uses of equity advances, see Chapter 4, page 75.

♠ **Income verification: Does the lender require income verification or a credit check on the homeowner(s)?**

The home equity conversion is based on the principle that the lender makes the homeowner an equity advance that is secured against the property, not against the homeowner's income, as is the case with traditional mortgages. However, lenders are free to include any criteria they feel are important in the rules of qualification. For example, a lender offering reverse mortgages to younger homeowners, that is, those under 60, may take the borrower's income into consideration when assessing eligibility.

Appraised Value of the Property

The appraised value of a property is an unbiased estimate based on analysis and interpretation carried out by a professional appraiser hired by the lender. If you want or need the maximum equity advance possible, you may have to make some improvements to your property before having it appraised. Obviously, if you are cash-poor, this is not a realistic option. Since an appraisal establishes lending value, not market value, check with an appraiser before spending any money on repairs or renovations. Ideally, lending value represents the amount the property would sell for in any market in a short period of time, for example, four months. When estimating lending value, the appraiser looks at the location of the property, the land value, and the style of the house, for example, whether it is detached or semi-detached. The general condition of the building, or buildings, is also considered; however, in determining lending value, the appraiser may not even see the interior.

For a discussion of lending value and market value, see Chapter 2, page 17, or the Glossary on page 291.

The cost of the appraisal is charged back to the mortgage applicant—the homeowner. This can be done either directly, as an appraisal fee, or indirectly, as an expense built in to the overall cost of the homeowner's reverse mortgage. An appraisal to establish lending value usually costs approximately two hundred dollars. The lender may decide the appraisal is confidential, that is, not to be shared with the homeowner.

See "Total Cost of Set-up and Administration," page 109, for more details.

⌂ What is the maximum percentage of the appraised value that the reverse mortgage lender will give the homeowner?

The maximum borrowing limit, called the loan-to-value ratio or percentage, that a reverse mortgage lender imposes will probably fall between 25 and 60 percent of the property's appraised lending value. Individual lenders may be willing to advance more equity. The location of the property and the stability of the real estate market in that area affect the borrowing limit set for each reverse mortgage.

Lenders tend to be conservative, and, therefore, usually like to keep the accumulated loan value of the reverse mortgage below 75 percent of the value of the property. For further explanation, see Chapter 2, page 16. Also see Chapter 6, "Limited Liability or Nonrecourse Provision," on page 132.

Total Cost of Set-up and Administration

The greater the cost of the reverse mortgage, the less equity there is available for the homeowner to use as equity advances or to preserve as residual equity. (See the diagram on page 99.) The set-up and administration costs for the borrower include (1) origination charges, including application and appraisal fees, and (2) the interest that accumulates against the reverse mortgage balance.

Full disclosure of all costs by the lender is important for the borrower who wishes to make an informed decision when comparing reverse mortgage products. The disclosure of total costs should be made before the application process begins and well before the homeowner is swept up in the "sales machine." If this information is released after the homeowner has committed a great deal of time and energy to the search for a lender, even unfavourable total cost figures may not be enough to overcome the pressure on the homeowner—internal and external—to continue with a particular lender. By then, the prospect of beginning a new search may be too exhausting. The older homeowner may be intimidated by an aggressive salesperson, may have been drawn into a "trusting" relationship with a salesperson, or may simply be too embarrassed to withdraw at this stage. (Note that lenders may use a variety of terms to describe the borrower's costs, so avoid assumptions. Ask questions to get down to the basics.)

SET-UP AND ADMINISTRATION COSTS

- Administration charges
- Interest
- Shared Appreciation and other features
- Upgrades
- Counselling

Administration Charges:

What application, appraisal, and legal fees are involved?

Set-up and administration costs may include costs for the following: application processing, appraisal, credit check/income verification, title search to verify home ownership status, property survey, registration of the reverse mortgage, banking charges for payment administration, sales commissions, referral or finder's fees, preparation of documentation, and legal fees for preparing and registering the reverse mortgage. The total of these costs may range from a few hundred dollars to well over a thousand. Getting information about costs in writing is always best, since it minimizes opportunities for misunderstanding.

⌂ Can these costs be financed as part of the transaction?

If the homeowner did not have the cash to pay these expenses at the time of arranging the reverse mortgage, they could perhaps be "financed," that is, added to the mortgage debt. The homeowner would then be paying interest on these costs for many years. Paying expenses by adding this amount to the balance of the reverse mortgage should only occur when cash is a serious problem. The lender may also deduct costs from the total amount of cash generated by a reverse annuity mortgage. The remaining balance could be used to purchase an annuity, and perhaps to provide the homeowner with a cash lump sum.

⌂ Is an up-to-date survey required?

The lender will determine whether an existing property survey is considered acceptable or not. If a new survey is required, this may add another few hundred dollars, perhaps even more than a thousand, to the total cost of the reverse mortgage.

⌂ Are any or all of the fees mentioned above refundable if the homeowner decides not to sign the reverse mortgage contract?

Identifying the point or points of no return is important in any purchase. A nonrefundable deposit or fee becomes a problem only if the homeowner does not completely understand the conditions before making the deposit or paying the fee. To avoid unpleasant surprises, ask about the lender's refund policies before you spend any money.

⌂ Does the reverse mortgage involve any additional monthly or periodic servicing fees?

If so, how are they calculated?

How frequently will they be increased, and by how much?

Are they to be paid outright or will they be added to the balance of the reverse mortgage?

Clarifying the total cost of the reverse mortgage involves determining not only the application costs, but also all the costs or payments, such as ongoing administration expenses, that are part of arranging a reverse mortgage with a particular lender.

Interest

♠ **What will the *effective*, or actual, interest rate on the reverse mortgage be?**

How frequently will the interest be compounded?

If appropriate, what will the interest rate for the annuity be?

Interest paid to the lender is one of the main reverse mortgage costs for the homeowner. As with all mortgages, most applicants will naturally ask about the interest rates. However, few people realize the importance of clarifying exactly what the effective interest rate is and how frequently the interest is compounded. The more frequent the compounding, the greater the cost to the homeowner.

Compounding involves paying interest on the interest. For more information on compounding, see Chapter 2, page 22. The effective interest rate is discussed in Chapter 3, page 51. Also, see Chapter 6, "Interest," on page 129.

♠ **Is the interest rate fixed over the life of the reverse mortgage, or is it adjusted periodically?**

What standard is used to establish the reverse mortgage interest rate when adjustments are made?

Is there a limit on how much the rate can be increased between adjustment periods or over the life of the reverse mortgage?

Will the homeowner be notified of every rate change and the impact on the outstanding reverse mortgage balance?

Fluctuations in interest rates occur constantly, and as often as weekly. A reverse mortgage with a fixed rate of interest would be advantageous to you in a market in which the interest rates are going up, but would be less attractive if the rates are headed down. A comparison of reverse mortgage rates with those for traditional mortgages provides insight into the actual cost of a particular product. Lenders often charge rates of $1/2$ percent and more above comparable traditional mortgage rates. *See "Interest," on page 129, in Chapter 6.*

🏠 **Will the lender disclose the total interest cost for a fixed-term reverse mortgage and estimates of the total interest cost for a tenure-plan reverse mortgage in advance of signing?**

Computers allow lenders to make quick, accurate calculations of even the most complex mathematical concepts. A lender should be able to provide you with a number of possible payout period totals for a tenure-plan reverse mortgage, or the total interest for a fixed-term.

Shared Appreciation and Other Features

🏠 **In a shared appreciation reverse mortgage, what amount or percentage of the appreciation will go to the lender?**

Special features such as shared appreciation (see Chapter 3, page 51) and equity preservation (see Chapter 6, page 125) may increase flexibility or security for a homeowner, but they also increase the cost of a reverse mortgage. Although they are an additional expense, some, such as shared appreciation, usually increase the size of the payments. However, others, for example, equity preservation, reduce them.
See "Shared Appreciation" on page 143 of Chapter 6, for a complete discussion of this reverse mortgage feature and the cost implications for the homeowner.

Upgrades

🏠 **Will repairs or renovations to the property be necessary to bring the property up to the lender's standards?**

Should the lender require repairs or renovations, clearly establish the cost of these upgrades before signing the reverse mortgage contract. The homeowner should be able to select the construction contractor or renovator, if one is necessary. Before making a commitment to the lender or the contractor, the homeowner would be well advised to get an independent opinion. In the United States, renovation scams have been linked to financial products including a few reverse mortgage cases.

Counselling

♠ **What costs should be estimated for professional legal, housing, or financial counselling?**

The lender will provide an estimate for "independent legal advice," that is, the cost of having a lawyer read over the contract with you. The lender may also offer financial planning advice. Find out the lender's costs so that you can compare them with those of an independent financial or legal adviser. Seeking independent advice is vital.

Choosing an adviser can be challenging. For some suggestions, see Chapter 7, page 154.

♠ **What size of mortgage would be ideal?**

What type of repayment plan will suit you now and in the future?

The answers to these questions are up to you. The lender will tell you how much you can borrow and whether you can increase the size of the equity advance later. You do not have to arrange a reverse mortgage for the full amount. Once again, base your decision on a careful consideration of your needs and wants. An adviser will help you explore present and future options and explain the flexibility and the restrictions of the reverse mortgage you have chosen.

To review the decision-making process, see Chapter 4, page 79.

Note that additional costs incurred during the reverse mortgage and on its termination are discussed on the following page, including property insurance premiums, renewal fees, maintenance costs, property taxes, and annuity costs, as well as the possibility of reverse mortgage lender insurance premiums.

Equity Preservation

⌂ **Does the reverse mortgage product guarantee that a set percentage or a dollar amount of the equity (i.e., the residual equity) will be preserved for the estate?**

If so, what is the cost and the impact of this feature?

It is possible to stipulate that a set amount, for example 20 percent of the equity in the property (that is, 20 percent of the appraised lending value), be preserved when the reverse mortgage terminates.

Whether this stipulation is set up as an item in the contract or as a type of mortgage insurance, including this feature will reduce the size of the equity advances made to the borrower. Ask the lender to show you, by simulating the figures on a computer, exactly what the additional costs will be for the equity preservation feature. If you have accepted a modest equity advance, are over 70, and live in an area where real estate values traditionally appreciate steadily, you will probably be able to preserve some equity for your estate without arranging a special feature. If you feel you *must* preserve some equity for yourself or your heirs, a written guarantee in the reverse mortgage contract would be necessary.

Balancing a need to use the equity now with a need to preserve equity for the estate can be challenging. Check the borrower profile in Chapter 4, page 69, to determine whether preserving equity would be the best strategy for you. For more details on equity preservation, see also Chapter 6, page 125.

⌂ **What system of notification will inform the homeowner, at least annually, about the size of the mortgage and the amount of equity remaining?**

Knowing "where you stand" regarding your reverse mortgage is important. You should always be able to weigh the advantages of staying in your home against the benefits of moving. Even though homeowners are told that the reverse mortgage debt will accumulate fairly quickly, and are sometimes shown as much via computer simulations, it is not until a biannual or an annual statement arrives that the reality of rising debt hits home.

The Annuity

♠ **How many of the features available in annuities are available with the annuity offered with the reverse mortgage you are considering?**

If the reverse mortgage involves an annuity, the usual criteria for evaluating annuities apply. Many types of annuities with a wide range of features, such as indexing for inflation, are available in the open market. To compare annuities, a number of questions should be answered. For example, in arranging a reverse annuity mortgage, what guaranteed annuity payment periods are available to protect the income for the surviving spouse or for the estate, in the event of the homeowner's premature death? Without a guaranteed payment period, if the homeowner died the day after the $50,000 annuity became effective, the homeowner's estate would receive nothing. However, the estate would still be responsible for paying off the $50,000 reverse annuity mortgage debt and the accumulated interest. A guaranteed period of 10 or 15 years would give the estate a sum of money representing the total payments that would have been paid to the homeowner over this period of time. Also ask whether you can have the annuity indexed for inflation. (See "Inflation," Chapter 6, page 149.) What rights are built into the annuity to protect a surviving spouse?

Your insurance broker can explain the ins and outs of annuities, as well as the features that are relevant to your needs and those of your family. Your choice of features may be limited, however, to the annuity options offered by the reverse mortgage lender you have selected. Since each feature affects the size of the payments, make sure that the annuity income will still be large enough to make arranging a reverse mortgage worthwhile.

♠ **Are the annuity rate and the terms competitive?**

Again, you will probably be restricted to the annuity rate and the terms offered by the insurance company or companies that the lender uses. But at least you can compare the total cost of the reverse mortgage against the cost of selling your home and buying an annuity yourself. Annuity rates are published in major newspapers. You can also ask your insurance broker for an up-to-date quote. Independent financial advice would be useful here.

♠ What percentage of the principal of the reverse mortgage will be used to purchase the annuity for the homeowner?

Is all of the money from the reverse mortgage, less any lump sum amounts paid to the homeowner, being used to buy the annuity? Or are some of the funds paid to the lender going towards administration charges? Once again, get everything in writing. Ask for full disclosure of all reverse mortgage borrowing costs, including those associated with the annuity.

♠ How stable is the insurance company that will provide the annuity, and how secure, therefore, is the annuity income?

Is the company that is providing the annuity a member of CompCorp?

With a reverse annuity mortgage, your future is tied to the insurance company providing the annuity income, and not to the reverse mortgage lender. Therefore, the security of your future income is directly linked to the stability of the insurance company. Canadian life and health insurance companies banded together and formed the Canadian Life & Health Insurance Compensation Corporation, known as CompCorp, a private company established to administer the insurance industry's Consumer Protection Plan. CompCorp is funded by assessments against its members. This protection plan is not a fund or a reserve. If one of the member insurance companies becomes insolvent, CompCorp will request contributions from the other members to pay the claims of the defaulting insurance company. Remember, although annuity incomes of up to $2000 per month per person are covered by CompCorp, payments would be disrupted until CompCorp sorted out all the claims. Caution may direct you to ensure your annuity is placed with the most stable insurance companies, usually the largest.

Since no legislation exists and CompCorp is not a government agency, consumers have no guarantee that the Consumer Protection Plan will continue or that CompCorp would be financially able to meet its obligations if a major default were to occur.

🏠 **Who is earning the sales commission or referral (finder's) fee on your purchase of an annuity and how much commission is involved?**

These sales commissions and referral fees represent additional costs for the borrower in arranging a reverse mortgage.

Lender Service Programs

🏠 **How will you know where you stand with your reverse mortgage, once it has been in place for a few months or a few years?**

The reverse mortgage lender should keep the homeowner up to date, at least annually, on the status of the equity in their home, especially if the interest rate will be reviewed and adjusted regularly. The lender should provide information on the exact balance of the reverse mortgage as of a certain date.

To estimate the amount of equity remaining, the homeowner will need an estimate of the property's current market value. The difference between the property's market value and the reverse mortgage balance is an estimate of the equity remaining in the home. For a fee of a hundred or so dollars, an appraiser will appraise your property to determine its market value as of the same date the lender used in calculating the current reverse mortgage debt. However, local real estate professionals, whose work revolves around market values, can provide you with an estimate at no cost. Check your mailbox for offers of free market evaluations.

A property is worth exactly what someone will pay for it on a given date, not what you want your home to be worth. Therefore, the actual value of the home can only be determined by selling it. For this reason, take care to get conservative estimates of value, or to calculate the average of two or three estimates. Real estate practitioners may be optimistic in their pricing when they give a complimentary market evaluation.

Lenders providing fixed-term reverse mortgages should also provide regular (at least annual) reports on the accumulated total debt of the reverse mortgage. Ask for status reports so that you can update your plans, prepare for the discharge of your fixed-term mortgage, or budget for alternative housing should a move become necessary.

♠ **What other long-term services does the lender provide for clients?**

Does the lender publish financial statements or hold annual meetings to keep clients up-to-date with the most recent developments in the company and in the reverse mortgage industry?

Communication is the most valuable service of all. Knowing what the reverse mortgage lender and the annuity-providing insurance company, if one is involved, are doing is your business. What style of management is in force? Have they acquired other businesses or are they being bought out by another corporation themselves? Use your information sources, including business publications, to monitor how the financial community rates their stability. Your independent financial adviser may be able to help you keep an eye on things.

CHAPTER 6

What Am I Signing?

D o you read everything before you sign? Do you understand everything you sign? If your answer is "no" to one or both of these questions, my question is "Why?" What do you gain by not reading or understanding the documents you sign? Why would you be too trusting, too embarrassed, or too busy to read— or to have your lawyer read—an agreement important enough to have been put on paper in the first place? If you are considering home equity conversion, you might ask yourself, "Why am I willing to spend decades of my life earning, maintaining, and cherishing my home but not to spend a few hours understanding exactly what I am agreeing to do to my home when I sign a reverse mortgage contract?"

The consumer's goal in reading a contract should be to understand what the reverse mortgage lender is specifically agreeing to do for the borrower, now and in the future, as well as precisely what will happen if the lender's obligations to the borrower are not fulfilled. The consumer must also be careful to determine exactly what the borrower will be responsible for and what will happen if these responsibilities are not met. If you are not clear on these issues even after asking the lender or the sales representatives to explain the contract to you, or if you find reading the contract difficult, have your legal adviser explain the

For those readers who turned directly to Chapter 6:
To get the most out of this chapter, the reader should be equipped with an understanding of the concepts, issues, and terminology presented in Chapters 2 through 5. In many respects, Chapter 6 is a distillation of the information discussed in these earlier chapters. Although the Glossary and the Quick Question Index, beginning on pages 291 and 297, may assist you with this section, they are not a substitute for reading the material in sequence. **Once more, I caution you to base your decisions on *all* the information in the book whatever your immediate reaction to reverse mortgages is.** Carefully examine the potential and the pitfalls of home equity conversion, both for the present and the future, whether you initially feel a reverse mortgage is ideal for you or not.

details to you. Even if you feel you understand what the contract says, have an independent legal adviser read the contract over to be sure you are right and have not missed anything.

This reference guide is designed to support the consumer in dealing with financial institutions and businesses offering reverse mortgages commercially, or with an individual investor interested in arranging a reverse mortgage privately. Keep the three questions introduced in Chapter 5 in mind at all times: (1) What do I get? (2) What will it cost? and (3) What will be left?

You will find some lenders very flexible and ready to custom design a reverse mortgage for you. Others have developed a product they feel can be matched with common homeowner needs, so they are less ready, or able, to make changes to individual contracts. Go over the terms and conditions in the contract with the help of your personal and professional advisers. You may want to make some changes and additions. Some lenders will negotiate, others will not. But you won't know what can be changed until you ask.

The reverse mortgage contract should contain provisions covering the issues discussed in Chapter 5, and those listed on page 122, beginning with "Cooling-Off Period." A provision may be contained in one clause or be expressed over a number of pages. Lenders usually each have their own contract standards, but document formats and wording differ from lender to lender.

If the issues explored in Chapter 5 and to be introduced in Chapter 6 are not clearly addressed in the reverse mortgage contract, you should ask yourself whether you understand why the topic is not included and you should feel comfortable with its absence. Verbal promises are difficult, if not impossible, to enforce in law. Remember it's what's in writing that counts. Your independent legal adviser will read the contract with you to ensure the appropriate terms and conditions are present, add any missing provisions, and eliminate any imprecise wording that could cause problems later.

Topics are presented in alphabetical order, for ease of reference. Even though all of these issues are important, some will be more relevant to your situation than others. When you are faced with the decision of whether to sign a reverse mortgage contract or not, read through all of the issues here, even if they do not immediately appear significant. Clarify any concerns or questions with your personal and professional advisers.

GETTING AT THE MEANING BEHIND THE WORDS

If consumers keep up the pressure, eventually all contracts and legal documents will be in plain English, not legal jargon, and, therefore, more readily translated into a number of languages. In the meantime, consumers are faced with the often daunting task of reading and understanding a contract written in *legalese*, the standard language of legal documents. This chapter explores the concepts and obligations that may be hidden by legalese in a reverse mortgage document. Remember, you do not have to become an expert on reverse mortgages or on contract law to make an informed decision. However, you should become an expert at *asking* questions and at not settling for less

INVESTIGATING THE TERMS AND CONDITIONS OF A REVERSE MORTGAGE CONTRACT

- Cooling-off period
- Covenants
- Default remedies
- Equity preservation
- Heirs' options
- Increasing the principal
- Insurance (property)
- Interest
- Legal compliance
- Lender bankruptcy
- Limited liability or nonrecourse provision
- Maintenance standards and inspections
- Occupancy requirements
- Portability
- Prepayment privilege
- Property tax deferral programs
- Renewal of fixed-term reverse mortgages
- Shared appreciation
- Spousal and joint borrower rights

than clear answers. The questions presented in this chapter are designed to be asked by you (where relevant to your personal situation) and to be answered by your legal, housing, and financial advisers, as well as by a lender and any salespeople involved. Keep asking until everything makes sense. Doing so will help you keep your "cents," your home, and your peace of mind.

Cooling-Off Period

Is there a realistic cooling-off period in the agreement that allows for cancellations or revisions of the reverse mortgage contract after the borrower signs?

If there is a cooling-off period, its duration must be stipulated in the contract, for example, 60 days from the date of signing. Otherwise, once the contract is signed, the homeowner is bound by its terms and conditions. The period usually begins when the contract is signed, however, ask exactly when the period begins and ends. A cooling-off period gives the homeowner time to think things through again after the exact terms, conditions, and costs of the contract have been understood, without paying a penalty. To use the cooling-off period effectively, before it begins, the homeowner should have all the facts at hand: full disclosure of all reverse mortgage costs, as well as projections of the reverse mortgage balance for a variety of time spans, interest rates (if the rate is adjusted during the reverse mortgage), and real estate appreciation rates. It would also be wise to know exactly how to notify the lender of your intention to cancel—just in case.

Once the cooling-off period ends, the contract is automatically legally binding, unless the homeowner has given written notice to the lender, before that point, of the intention to end the contract at that point. The lender is bound to the terms and conditions from the date of signing the contract.

If the borrower does elect to cancel the agreement during the cooling-off period, the reverse mortgage contract is considered null and void. The homeowner is not liable for any fees or charges unless the lender stipulates in the contract that some fees are non-refundable fees. To cancel a reverse mortgage contract during a cooling-off period, carefully follow every detail of the notification procedure set out in the contract, otherwise the contract may not be considered null and void. Independent legal advice may be useful to guarantee the legalities are handled properly.

Covenants

The basic covenants, legal promises made by the borrower (the mortgagor) to the lender (the mortgagee), are commitments to: pay property taxes, maintain the property in good repair, keep the property insured (fire and casualty insurance), pay condominium fees (if applicable), and, upon termination of the reverse mortgage, pay off the principal as well as the accumulated interest. The reverse mortgage contract may include one or all of these covenants.

♠ **What specific conditions for inspection and remedy by the lender does each covenant set forth?**

Must the borrower make any other legally binding promises?

When you sign a contract, you agree to do and to accept what is specified in it. For example, it is quite common for the lender to receive the right to inspect the property in order to make sure it is in good repair and therefore, ensure that the value of the property is maintained and the lender's investment is protected. If the property is run down, the lender has the right to order repairs. The cost of these repairs may be added to the mortgage debt, and interest will be charged on the cost of the repairs from then on. This covenant also restricts the homeowner from making renovations that decrease the value of the property. Find out exactly what you are promising when you sign a reverse mortgage contract. While lenders do not always enforce the covenants, they can exercise their rights should the need arise or the lender's policies change.

See "Insurance (Property)," page 128, and "Maintenance Standards and Inspections," page 136.

Default Remedies

A more complex problem arises on default. Once a covenant has been broken, the reverse mortgage is in default and the lender can call the entire reverse mortgage balance due. If necessary, the lender can take legal action to recover the debt. The lender's corporate policy will dictate the remedy or remedies chosen when the borrower defaults. For example, credit unions usually take a more lenient attitude towards the default of a member, compared with that of trust companies and financial organizations towards the default of a customer.

For more about the lender's remedies to default, see Chapter 2, page 22.

♠ **What rights and options does the contract give the lender, should the borrower default on the reverse mortgage, that is, break one of the mortgage covenants?**

Can the lender apply to the courts for an order to sell the property, or for an order of foreclosure that would transfer ownership to the lender?

As discussed previously, although the remedies for default on traditional and reverse mortgages are similar, details and procedures may vary from one province to another.

♠ **How can the borrower end the default situation and put the mortgage in good standing again?**

Is the borrower given a period of grace to rectify the default before action is initiated by the lender?

The contract should explain exactly what the borrower can do to correct each type of default situation. Ideally, for reverse mortgages, the default should have to exist for a reasonable period of time—a grace period—before the lender can deliver notice that legal action will begin against the borrower. Also, the length of time provided by law for the borrower to have the opportunity to reverse the default situation should be as long as is reasonably possible. For instance, if under the legal requirements for foreclosure of traditional mortgages the homeowner had 60 days to respond, with reverse mortgages perhaps the homeowner should be given 120 days or longer. The lender's legal power to sell the home to pay off the debt should also be delayed, for instance, 6 months or more, to give the homeowner time to rectify the situation or make alternative housing arrangements. Provincial laws currently only dictate the default remedy procedures for traditional mortgages, but they are applied to reverse mortgages.

🏠 **Does the mortgage contract give the lender the right to demand repayment of all money, including interest and costs, even if this amount exceeds the value of the property?**

Is the lender given the right to sue the homeowner personally for the outstanding debt when the reverse mortgage goes into default?

The lender's remedies for default may include the lender having recourse against the homeowner's other assets and/or being able to sue the homeowner personally to recover the debt. In other words, liability may not be limited to the value of the property in default situations. Your independent legal adviser will clarify your rights and those of the lender in default conditions. Understanding your rights here is vital—with this knowledge you can protect your interest should problems arise in the future, for instance, in paying the taxes or in keeping the property in good repair. For a fee, the lender may provide services to protect the borrower from default, for instance, property maintenance services. If this is the case, be sure the charge for these services is competitive with those available from other sources.

See "Limited Liability or Nonrecourse Provision," page 132, to contrast default with the lender's and the borrower's rights when the mortgage is in good standing.

Equity Preservation

Can the homeowner preserve part of the home equity in an equity guarantee program offered by the lender?

The lender may allow the homeowner to preserve a set amount or percentage of the equity for the homeowner or the heirs. If so, the contract must state exactly how this amount is to be calculated and what fees, if any, the homeowner would have to pay.

See Chapter 5, "Equity Preservation," page 114.

Heirs' Options

🏠 If the homeowner dies and the reverse mortgage debt becomes due, will the heirs have the option of repaying the reverse mortgage debt and keeping the home?

How much time will they be given to act? Are extensions possible?

Could they refinance the debt, rather than selling the house to pay off the reverse mortgage?

What would the qualification process for refinancing involve?

What fees would be charged to the heirs for refinancing?

The house does not automatically belong to the lender when the homeowner dies, unless a clause in the contract gives the lender the right to the property at the end of the reverse mortgage. Without this clause, even if the debt is greater than the value of the house, ownership of the property transfers to the estate, not the lender. If any residual equity should exist, it would become part of the homeowner's estate.

Reverse mortgage lenders will probably not be able to arrange to refinance the reverse mortgage for the heirs unless the lenders normally deal in traditional mortgages. Therefore, the heirs would have to find another source for their financing. The reverse mortgage contract will stipulate how much time they have to act and what the procedure would be.

A problem might arise if the reverse mortgage debt equalled the value of the property, since qualifying for 100 percent financing could be difficult for most heirs. They would probably need at least 10 percent cash as a downpayment, as well as sufficient income to qualify for a traditional mortgage for the balance. The cost of arranging a traditional mortgage to repay the reverse mortgage may be a few hundred dollars, or more than a thousand, depending on who arranges the new mortgage and on the legal costs.

🏠 Can a reverse mortgage be transferred to another person: that is, could an heir take over or *assume* your reverse mortgage?

Probably not. Traditional mortgages can be carried on, or assumed, by someone else when a house is sold. But because reverse mortgages are based on your age and life expectancy projections, the reverse mortgage link with the property is broken when you move or sell. Assuming a reverse mortgage would be like taking over someone else's life insurance policy. Since most things are possible if both parties are willing, conceivably a fixed-term lender might allow an assumption if the term were short, the gender were the same, and the age match were a good one. More likely, though, the reverse mortgage would be converted to a traditional mortgage, for which the new borrower would have to qualify based on income.

Increasing the Principal

⌂ **Does the reverse mortgage contract include a provision to reduce the size or number of equity advances if the homeowner requires less income in the future?**

What happens if larger or more frequent payments are required by the borrower in the future?

Does the contract specify when changes may be made or can they take place at any time that suits the homeowner?

What penalties or service charges would the homeowner have to pay?

Always ask whether you can increase the principal at a later date. If you can, ask when, by how much, and whether doing so would mean additional charges. Things may change so that you will need more money later. Finding out what it would cost to increase the reverse mortgage will help you weigh that cost against other options as they arise.

⌂ **What if the home has not appreciated in value as quickly as the lender projected?**

Knowing the degree of flexibility you will have to adjust payments will help you create a budget to calculate the ideal size of your reverse mortgage. The main obstacle may be how quickly the home appreciates in value. If it does not keep pace with the lender's projected increases, you may not be able to increase the principal, even if the lender originally offered you a larger amount than what you now want.

⌂ **If the borrower originally took the maximum equity advance and the property has since appreciated in value, can the borrower increase the reverse mortgage, provided there is sufficient equity, according to the lender's lending criteria?**

Would the same conditions and costs apply as above?

Always play the "What if" game when exploring your options. Find out what all the variations and costs are so that you will be free to plan wisely. Understanding your options should circumstances change will help you make a good choice in the first place.

If you want the payment flexibility discussed above, reverse mortgage lines of credit may interest you. See Chapter 3, page 49, for details on lines of credit. The homeowner's aim is to take the right amount of money—not too much and not too little. Also in Chapter 3, see page 32, and in Chapter 4, page 85, for suggestions on deciding how much is enough.

⌂ **If a portion of the balance has been prepaid, can the borrower "reborrow" this amount?**

Will there be any charges or penalties for increasing the principal in this situation?

Flexibility is the operative word. Always consider change in the future. Remember, asking what you can do does not commit you to actually doing anything.

Insurance (Property)

Will the current amount and type of property insurance carried on the home meet the lender's requirements?

Reverse mortgages contain a covenant made by the borrower to keep the property insured. During the reverse mortgage, the lender is the beneficiary of the insurance policy, even though the borrower pays the premiums. The insurance is usually required to cover the full replacement value of all buildings on the property, so that the structures can be repaired or rebuilt in case of fire, to protect the value of the property.

See Chapter 2, page 17, for more details on covenants.

Interest

As discussed in Chapter 5, the interest rate and the frequency of compounding must be spelt out in the reverse mortgage contract.

- ♠ **Does the lender fix the interest rate over the life of the reverse mortgage, or adjust the interest rate at intervals throughout the reverse mortgage?**

  If the rate is adjusted, at what intervals will it be reset, and against what standards?

  Is there a ceiling on the annual adjustment to the interest rate and/or on the interest rate adjustment over the life of the mortgage?

  The interest rate could be set for the entire term or for the life of the mortgage. For example, over the 10 years of a fixed-term reverse mortgage, or over the 25 years that a tenure-plan reverse annuity mortgage may run, the interest rate would stay the same, even if the market rate drops dramatically. Alternatively, the rate may be adjusted at intervals—annually or at set periods. For instance, every 5 years the rate could be adjusted to a rate $3/4$ percent above the average of the 5-year interest rates set by the top three banks. Or, the rate could be reset annually against a recognized financial standard, such as Treasury Bond rates or the prime lending rate. Reverse mortgage rates are usually higher than equivalent rates for traditional mortgages since the lender's risk is higher.

- ♠ **If the rate is to be adjusted, what annual or periodic charges will the homeowner have to pay when the interest rate is reviewed?**

  The annual review fee for adjusting the interest rate may be approximately a hundred dollars or more.

- ♠ **Will adjustments in the interest rate affect the equity advance amounts?**

  Even if the interest rate is adjusted over the life of the reverse mortgage, the equity advance amounts will not change, since they were set at the beginning of the reverse mortgage. Instead, the change in interest rate results in the balance of the reverse mortgage growing at a faster or a slower rate. As a result, the final balance could be more or less than the amount that would have accumulated if the interest rate had been fixed over the life of the mortgage.

For more information on interest, see the previous section on page 129.

Legal Compliance

Are you asked to guarantee full compliance with all federal, provincial, and municipal laws?

If so and you run a business from your home that violates zoning by-laws, how would this affect the standing of the reverse mortgage?

Or, if you rent out the home in violation of local zoning laws, have you jeopardized the status of the reverse mortgage?

As ignorance of the law is not considered an excuse, clarify these details before you sign the contract. Contact your local municipal government to get the zoning information you require. Your independent legal adviser should be able to assist you with any other issues that arise.

Also see Chapter 12, page 268, for a discussion of renting out all or part of your home.

Lender Bankruptcy

♠ **What provisions does the contract contain to protect the homeowner if the equity advances are late or if they cease?**

Most lenders are uncomfortable with discussions of their own financial demise. The organizations offering reverse mortgages range from huge corporations and insurance companies to mortgage companies and credit unions. (Remember, no banks yet.) It is hard to imagine most of these companies going bankrupt. And yet, the nineties have been full of surprises.

Find out what legal recourse you have if the lender becomes insolvent or goes bankrupt. The following questions highlight the issues involved here. Your advisers may also have suggestions to make for your particular situation.

See "Lender Credibility," page 101 in Chapter 5 for background on this topic.

Are there any industry-wide or government-backed consumer programs to protect your payments?

For instance, with reverse annuity mortgages, up to $2000 of annuity income per month, per person, is protected by CompCorp. If there is an external consumer protection plan, the lender will be eager to tell you about it as it reinforces your security. However, check directly with the program administration, or have your adviser do so, to be sure your reverse mortgage payments would qualify for their program.
See Chapter 5, "The Annuity," page 115, for details on CompCorp and Chapter 3, page 45, for background on annuities.

What legal recourse will the homeowner have in these circumstances?

How does the contract require that the homeowner notify the lender if equity advances are late or if they cease?

Determine exactly what rights you have if payments are occasionally or frequently late. Also ask what administrative safeguards the lender has in place to ensure payments are not late.

Will the homeowner remain responsible for paying interest that is compounding throughout the period in which the equity advances are late or have stopped?

Does the contract mention loan forgiveness or limited homeowner liability, if the lender were to go bankrupt?

If the lender defaults on payments to the homeowner, can the borrower stay in the home and not have to repay the principal until death, the sale of the property, or a permanent move, even if the reverse mortgage was for a fixed term?

These questions should be addressed in the reverse mortgage contract. Be sure you are comfortable with the lender's answers. Remember, if this is a long-term contract—a tenure-plan reverse mortgage for example—changes are bound to happen in Canada and in the world during the reverse mortgage. With a 5-year term reverse mortgage, you will probably feel less vulnerable.

If the lender fails to make the equity advances, is the home-owner bound to keep contractual responsibilities? The answer lies in the contract terms and conditions. Find out exactly what would happen if the payments were to stop, for a while or permanently.

To review the Canadian lender profile, see Chapter 2, page 30.

⌂ **If the homeowner cannot meet contractual obligations (for example, payment of property taxes) because the equity advances are late or cease, will the lender, or the organization that takes over the reverse mortgage contract, forfeit the default right to seek repayment of the reverse mortgage debt, until after the homeowner's death or until the sale of the property?**

Details matter. Explore the issues of nonpayment of the equity advances and of lender insolvency with both the lender and your adviser(s).

Chapter 2, page 22, outlines the details of borrower default.

Limited Liability or Nonrecourse Provision

⌂ **Does the reverse mortgage contract contain a limited liability or nonrecourse provision, which sets the value of the property as the financial limit for debt recovery by the lender?**

A limited liability, or nonrecourse, provision is neither legally required nor automatically inserted in a reverse mortgage contract. A vital consumer safeguard in tenure-plan reverse mortgages, this provision offers financial protection for the homeowner by limiting debt recovery by the lender to the value of the property. In other words, the lender has no recourse against the homeowner or the estate above the value of the home. Therefore, this clause offers limited liability to the homeowner or the estate. Without a limited liability provision, the homeowner or the estate would be responsible for full repayment of the mortgage debt even if the amount exceeded the value of the property.

A limited liability provision is of particular significance if the property does not achieve the appreciation, or increase, in value estimated by the lender, or if the borrower outlives the lender's projections of the homeowner's life expectancy. These circumstances may also occur simultaneously. If one or both of these situations arise, by the time the homeowner moves permanently, sells the property, or dies, the reverse mortgage debt may be greater than the value of the property. A limited liability provision restricts debt recovery by the lender to the proceeds from the sale of the property, that is, the homeowner or the estate is liable for repayment of the debt only to an amount equal to the value of the property. The lender would be prevented from seeking recovery of the loss from the homeowner's other assets, from the estate, including life insurance, or from the homeowner's family, and would have to absorb the financial loss.

If the mortgage debt exceeds the property value, does the lender have any right to sue the homeowner to recover any debt that will not be covered by the sale of the property?

Provided the borrower has not made a personal promise to repay the debt in the reverse mortgage contract, the lender has no legal right to sue the borrower personally for any deficiency in debt recovery. The lender must absorb the loss—the difference between what was paid out as equity advances and the actual amount of equity remaining in the property. If the lender has the right to look to other assets to recover the debt, the lender's debt recovery alternatives should be clearly described in the reverse mortgage contract and recovery limits set. Clarify the lender's rights for debt recovery when the contract is being drawn up, not after it is signed or when the executor of the homeowner's estate inquires on behalf of the surviving spouse.

Will the heirs owe anything to the reverse mortgage lender if the mortgage balance exceeds the value of the property on the death of the homeowner(s)?

No, provided the mortgage contract limits the estate's liability to the value of the property.

With tenure-plan reverse mortgages, can the homeowner be forced to sell or vacate the property when the value of the loan exceeds the value of the property?

No, provided the contract does not contain provisions that give the lender special rights to the property if the reverse mortgage debt exceeds the property value. The lender cannot evict the homeowner or turn to the family or estate to recoup losses, unless the contract gives the lender these rights. Otherwise, the tenure-plan or lifetime reverse mortgage allows the homeowner to live in the home as long as they wish or as long as they live, providing the home is occupied by the borrower as a principal residence and the mortgage covenants are upheld by the homeowner. Tenure-plan reverse annuity mortgages can allow homeowners to stay in their homes and continue to receive payments for as long as they live, even if that period stretches beyond the point at which all the equity has been exhausted.

How does the contract define the maximum limit for debt recovery, that is, the limit of the homeowner's financial liability?

Lenders use lending value, a deliberately conservative estimate of the value of the property, when determining how much to lend the homeowner in the first place. However, they usually set the upper limit of debt recovery at or near the market value of the property (the highest price a buyer would pay in an open competitive market).

For instance, the limit could be set at the "net proceeds of the sale at market value," which means the proceeds of the sale after the costs of the sale, including real estate fees, have been deducted. The limit may be set by using an appraisal, or the average of two or three appraisals, to establish market value. In this case, the homeowner would be responsible for the costs of the sale. The limit could also be set at a percentage of the sale price that would exclude the real estate commission, that is, at 94 percent of the sale price. Once again, knowing what you have agreed to in the contract is important.

See Chapter 2, page 16, for a review of the difference between these types of value. Or check the Glossary, which begins on page 291.

Does the lender retain the first right of refusal to purchase the property at the sale price, in order to prevent the sale to a third party at less than market value?

This provision protects the lender against the homeowner selling to a family member or friend at less than market value. One or more appraisals would probably be used to establish fair market value.

See the previous discussion about establishing the maximum debt recovery limit.

Lines of Credit

Can the homeowner combine a lump sum equity advance with the line of credit?

Does the contract restrict how often in one month or in one year withdrawals can be made?

Is there a ceiling on the amount that can be withdrawn each month or each year?

Will the lender automatically deposit regular payments in the line of credit account?

Can the homeowner repay some of the balance during the line of credit?

What charges or penalties, if any, will there be for this prepayment privilege?

Is the term line of credit renewable? How often?

Is there a maximum debt limit? If so, what happens when it is reached?

Use your own wants and needs to decide what the "best" answers to these questions might be. For instance, if the answer to first question is yes for one lender and no for another, this does not necessarily make one product better than the other. However, one of these products may be better *for you* than the other. For instance, if you want $5,000 for a new furnace and an air conditioner, plus the option to withdraw up to $500 per month, the yes product may be worth a closer look. You may, however, consider talking to the lender of the no product before you turn this product down completely. There may be other features belonging to the latter that are very attractive. The lender may even have a suggestion for arranging for a new furnace and air conditioner that will cost you less than a lump sum equity advance would over the next few years.

See Chapter 3, page 49, for background information on reverse mortgage lines of credit.

Maintenance Standards and Inspections

⌂ Does the reverse mortgage include a covenant by the home-owner to keep the property in good repair?

What requirements and standards are set for maintenance of the property?

Evaluate your home to determine what will need repairing or replacing over the next few years and over the next decades. If your roof has only a few good years left, calculate the differ-ence in cost between a patch job and a new roof. If your plumbing and heating systems are more than twenty years old, consider what costs you could be facing. When calculating how much in equity advances you will need, include estimates for repair and maintenance that reflect inflation.

See Chapter 4, page 89, for suggestions on how to decide whether this home is the right one for aging in place with a reverse mortgage.

⌂ If the homeowner allows the property to fall into disrepair, does the reverse mortgage include a clause permitting the lender to perform maintenance and repairs to the home and to add these costs to the mortgage balance?

Will the lender monitor the condition of the property by reg-ular inspections?

How frequently will these inspections occur?

How much notice before an inspection visit will the home-owner be given?

Remember, while the lender may say that the maintenance and repair requirements are just formalities, company policies can and may change over the 10, 20, or even 30 years of a reverse mortgage. The lender can exercise any rights described in the contract.

See Chapter 2, page 17 for more on covenants.

🏠 **Does the homeowner retain the right to make improvements or changes to the property without obtaining prior approval from the lender?**

If so, what limitations or restrictions apply to this right?

If you have plans for major renovations in the future, perhaps an addition, an accessory apartment, or modifications for wheel-chair accessibility, you may wish to have these changes specified as being acceptable in the contract.
See page 123, "Covenants."

Occupancy Requirements

🏠 **How long might the homeowner be absent from the property, without jeopardizing owner-occupied status?**

According to the terms of the reverse mortgage contract, the homeowner's absence from the home could be grounds for legal action by the lender. The requirement for owner occupancy may be drawn up as a covenant. The lender wants to be sure the house is occupied for two reasons. First, the insurance coverage that protects the lender's investment in the home may be void if the property is vacant or abandoned. (What does your insurance policy say?) Second, the risk of vandalism or damage increases when the home is unoccupied. As the home is security for repayment of the reverse mortgage, the lender wants to protect the investment and the property.

🏠 **Can the homeowner meet the occupancy requirements by having a family member live in the home until the homeowner returns?**

Are there any allowable exceptions to the occupancy requirement?

For example, would an extended holiday be possible?

Would a prolonged stay in hospital be an allowable exception?

These questions relate to the flexibility valued by many homeowners who wish to travel or to maintain two homes. For instance, if the period of allowable absence were three months, would that force you to turn down an attractive opportunity to trade houses with a family in Switzerland for six months? Would you still be able to invite a close friend or family member to move in and house-sit while you are in Florida? Even if you expect no lengthy absences, inquire about occupancy requirements to be completely aware of what you have agreed to in the mortgage contract. Again, life is full of surprises, so be prepared.

⌂ **By signing a reverse mortgage, does the homeowner lose the right to rent the house or part of it, or to take in a boarder?**

Would having a primary caregiver—a family member or a professional—move in to share the home affect the status of the reverse mortgage?

Find out whether sharing your home to generate additional income and/or to receive the support necessary to stay in your home will violate the reverse mortgage contract in any way. *See Chapter 12, page 268, for details on renting out your home.*

⌂ **If the homeowner loses owner-occupied status for the property, what period of time does the lender allow the homeowner to pay off the reverse mortgage, before the lender can exercise the legal right to take action to sell the homeowner's property?**

Knowing where you stand will reduce the possibility of unpleasant surprises or unnecessary stress.

Portability

⌂ **Is the reverse mortgage portable, that is, can it be moved to another property?**

If so, what restrictions apply, for example, as to location or type of home ownership?

What charges, fees, or penalties will be levied against the homeowner for activating this option?

If you want to sell your current home in a few years and buy another property while maintaining the reverse mortgage, portability is the answer. A portability provision allows the reverse mortgage—balance, interest rate, and equity advance plan—to be transferred to another property. In this way, the homeowner has the flexibility of moving to a new home during the reverse mortgage. This option is more practical for tenure-plan reverse mortgages or long-term reverse mortgage lines of credit.

Obviously, since the reverse mortgage was designed for a property with a specific value, moving to a home of similar or greater value will mean that the transfer process will be straightforward. Portability may not be possible if you move to a less expensive property or to an area that has traditionally lower rates of appreciation, as the lender wants to keep the reverse mortgage balance down to less than 75 percent of the appraised value. For example, if you want to move from a $300,000 home to a $100,000 property and your reverse mortgage balance is $85,000, the lender may say no, as the reverse mortgage would represent 85 percent of the value of the property. In this case, the risk of loss, should the reverse mortgage balance exceed the value of the property, may be too great for the lender.

♠ **Are there any restrictions on the length of time that may elapse between selling the original home and taking ownership of the new property?**

How many times could the reverse mortgage be transferred during the life of this mortgage?

Once again, think ahead.

Prepayment Privilege

♠ **Does the reverse mortgage contract contain a prepayment privilege, permitting the homeowner to pay down some of the balance of the reverse mortgage during the term?**

What costs or penalties are attached to exercising a prepayment privilege?

Suppose a lender arranges a 5-year term reverse mortgage for you. In the reverse mortgage contract you agreed that in return for having the use of the money you will pay a certain amount of interest on the balance, over 5 years. The lender has borrowed

the money for the equity advance from an investor at a specified interest rate for the 5-year term. In other words, the lender
has made a commitment to pay the investor a certain return
on this investment. If you decide you would like to prepay
some of the reverse mortgage debt, the reduction in the balance also means a reduction in the amount of interest the
lender will earn. The lender may allow you pay off some of the
balance, but the lender's commitment to the investor still
exists. The lender may ask that a few months' interest or the
interest differential be paid by the borrower.

This penalty reimburses the lender for losses and costs
associated with the prepayment. The penalty, designed to
compensate the lender for lost interest, may represent a portion of the interest that the lender would have earned over a
few months; for instance, the penalty may be three or six
months' worth of interest.

Exercising the prepayment privilege may carry a stiffer
penalty—the *interest differential*. This is the amount of interest
equivalent to the lender's loss if the funds have to be reinvested and the current interest rates are lower than the reverse
mortgage rate. The interest differential is a formula based on
the difference between (1) the amount of interest that the
lender would have earned based on the interest rate originally
agreed to in the reverse mortgage contract, and (2) the amount
of interest that the lender could earn if the sum prepaid were
reinvested at current interest rates. Formulas for calculating
interest differential vary from lender to lender.

♠ If the mortgage does not specifically describe the prepay-ment penalty, how is it determined?

A reverse mortgage would be considered *fully open*, that is,
able to be completely prepaid without any penalties, provided
a clause in the mortgage describes this possibility. If this
option is not set out specifically in the reverse mortgage, the
homeowner may have to pay an interest penalty on the
amount being prepaid.

The prepayment provision in the reverse mortgage contract
may state that the penalty will be 3 months' interest or the
interest rate differential, whichever is greater. If no prepayment

penalty is described in the contract and the reverse mortgage is not described as fully open, lenders can charge any penalty they like—including all the interest owing on the remaining term of the reverse mortgage.

♠ **Do the penalties for this provision remain the same throughout the term of the mortgage, or do they decrease after an initial period of, for instance, 5 to 10 years?**

Are there any circumstances, for instance the homeowner's ill health, under which the lender would waive the prepayment penalty for the homeowner?

The prepayment penalty for the borrower is often described as a bonus for the lender. Your discussion with an independent legal adviser should cover all aspects of prepayment and default, as described in the contract and as set out in provincial legislation.
See "Reversing the Reverse Mortgage," on page 146, for a discussion of premature termination of a reverse mortgage.

Property Tax Deferral Programs

If property taxes are not paid, payment of these taxes takes priority over any other debt or mortgage registered against the ownership of a property. The debt incurred through a property tax deferral program, therefore, would take first priority.
See Chapter 5, page oo, for further information on the priority of registration. Property tax deferral plans are discussed in Chapter 8, page 178.

♠ **If the homeowner is currently enrolled in a property tax deferral program, can a reverse mortgage be arranged?**

Once the reverse mortgage is in effect, can the homeowner sign up for a property tax deferral program?

In order to have the option of entering into an existing or future property tax deferral plan, a provision in the reverse mortgage must acknowledge that the reverse mortgage will take second priority to this plan, even if the homeowner signs up for the plan after the reverse mortgage is in place.

See Chapter 2, page 17, and Chapter 5, page 106, for information on registration priorities. While province-wide property tax deferral plans are currently available only in British Columbia and Prince Edward Island, homeowners can expect more plans to appear elsewhere in Canada in the future. See Chapter 8, page 178.

Renewal of Fixed-Term Reverse Mortgages

⌂ **Does the contract include a renewal privilege for the home-owner?**

What renewal restrictions apply to the term, the interest rate, and the amount of the reverse mortgage?

Even with traditional mortgages, renewal is not an automatic right of the borrower but must be set out as a provision in the mortgage contract. Otherwise, renewal is solely the lender's prerogative; the lender is under no legal obligation to renew the mortgage. Unless the reverse mortgage contains a provision giving the borrower the option of renewal at the end of the term, the reverse mortgage will be payable in full at the end of the term.

A lender may allow renewal but set restrictions on the renewal rate, on the new term, or on the amount of the reverse mortgage debt that can be renewed.

A reverse mortgage lender may agree to renew a fixed-term reverse mortgage if there is sufficient equity left in the home to meet the lender's criteria for reverse mortgages. The lender will probably refer to the general maximum loan percentage that is defined by company policy. Sufficient equity may be left, for example, if the value of the home increased during an upswing in the real estate market, or if the initial term reverse mortgage used up only a small percentage of the equity. If renewal is feasible, the homeowner could extend the reverse mortgage without all of the set-up costs associated with a brand new reverse mortgage. But eventually, the fixed-term reverse mortgage will be due without the option of renewal. *See "Increasing the Principal," page 127.*

⌂ **What will exercising a renewal privilege cost the homeowner?**

The cost of renewal may be one hundred dollars or more.

Shared Appreciation

♠ In a shared appreciation reverse mortgage, what amount or percentage of the appreciation will go to the lender?

Is there an upper limit on the amount of appreciation to be shared with the lender?

Will the homeowner receive a statement that quotes the effective rate of interest, which includes the cost of the shared appreciation to the homeowner?

This amount can be estimated by the lender, using projections of appreciation. However, the exact amount of the lender's share of the appreciation cannot be determined until the property is sold. The lender could establish a maximum projected amount of appreciation and quote this as a cost to the borrower. If the actual appreciation is less, the lender would get the agreed upon percentage of the real increase in value of the property. For example, a lender might agree to a 20 percent share of the appreciation and may estimate that the property will increase in value by 7 percent over the life of the reverse mortgage. However, if the property increases in value by only 4 percent, the lender would still take 20 percent of the appreciation, even though it is a smaller amount of money.

♠ If the homeowner significantly improves the property using the equity advances, would the homeowner receive additional credit for any resulting increase in appreciation?

How would this improvement credit be calculated?

These are also important issues that should be determined before signing.
Details on shared appreciation appear in Chapter 3, page 51.

Spousal and Joint Borrower Rights

Be realistic when arranging a reverse mortgage. Find out exactly what is going to happen to the reverse mortgage, to the equity advances, and to your property if you die first or if you are the surviving owner. The following questions provide a framework for exploring the options and limitations that must be considered in the terms and conditions of your reverse mortgage contract. Provincial laws and the details of your relationship with the joint borrower must also be taken into account. If there is an annuity involved, similar questions must be asked to determine the impact on the annuity income.

♠ **Does the reverse mortgage contract comply with the restrictions and responsibilities set out in provincial laws that relate to real estate owned by a married couple?**

For example, in Ontario, each spouse owns half of the family home even if the property is registered only in the name of one spouse. In this case, the reverse mortgage contract must cover both legal owners, that is, both spouses.

♠ **If one spouse or joint borrower predeceases the other, will the survivor retain all the original rights, including ownership of the home?**

If the equity advances paid to the survivor are to be reduced, how will the size, frequency, and total number of payments be affected?

What impact, if any, would the marriage of the surviving spouse or borrower have on the reverse mortgage?

Insist that your spouse or joint borrower go through the entire investigation process with you. They may pick up on something you have overlooked. I believe that we are each other's raw material. Having someone who knows you and the situation and whom you can bounce ideas off is invaluable. If you are a joint owner, you have a joint responsibility. Do not leave everything to the other person. Complaining about things you thought of but did not share before signing will be a hollow victory if the worst happens after the reverse mortgage contract is signed.

♠ **What happens if a new spouse does not meet the age requirements of the reverse mortgage lender?**

If the spouse does not qualify for the reverse mortgage, the reverse mortgage may have to be converted into a traditional mortgage. Spousal rights of property ownership are complex and differ from province to province. Contact an independent legal adviser with experience in family law if you are in this situation or foresee its occurring.

🏠 **To whom will the cheques be made out?**

Will payments be deposited in a joint chequing account automatically?

How many signatures will be required for withdrawal?

In the case of a couple with a reverse mortgage line of credit, will withdrawals require one signature or two?

The following case study highlights an important issue: personal empowerment. A friend told me that her marriage of thirty years had been in trouble for a long time when, about ten years ago, she and her husband sold the family home, which had been in her name. My friend hired the lawyer who handled the details of the sale. Since she was the client, the lawyer complied when my friend requested that the cheque for the sale be made out to her. Her husband was upset about this, but only for a while. Not having to ask for money has changed my friend's life. And, although the couple had intended to separate, they have reconsidered. She says, "After a bitter marriage, we have a love affair." She now has money of her own in an account in her name, and her husband has access to the rest of the family money. She sums up her experience this way: "While I wouldn't recommend this for everyone, it led me on the road of independence—independence is *very* sweet."

SIGNING OFF

A reverse mortgage terminates and becomes due and payable: when the homeowner sells; when the homeowner moves permanently; when the term—perhaps 5 or 10 years—ends; or when the homeowner dies. With a married couple, termination of the reverse mortgage will occur when the surviving spouse sells, moves, or dies.

On termination of the reverse mortgage, all of the money advanced to the homeowner(s) plus all interest charges and any penalties must be repaid. If a nonrecourse provision exists in the contract, the total amount to be repaid will not be greater than the value of the home. The income from a lifetime annuity will end on the death of the surviving recipient, or include a payment representing the guaranteed period, if one exists.

For further information on the termination of reverse mortgages see Chapter 3, page 52.

Premature Death

What provisions does the reverse mortgage contract contain to cover the death of the homeowner soon after the reverse mortgage takes effect?

Would the set-up and administration fees, or a portion of these charges, be refunded to the estate?

If you die just after the reverse mortgage has been arranged, your reverse mortgage may become very expensive. For example, if the lender holds your estate to the reverse annuity mortgage contract, as is the lender's right, the estate would be responsible for repaying the entire balance of the reverse mortgage. The income from the annuity would be lost on the death of the homeowner, unless a guaranteed period had been purchased—then, at least a portion of the money spent on the annuity could be recovered. Once again, get the details on the costs and responsibilities for the estate should you die prematurely, without a spouse or joint owner.

See Chapter 3, page 45, and Chapter 5, page 115, for more on annuities.

Reversing the Reverse Mortgage

⌂ **What options exist should you wish to end the reverse mortgage before the termination date originally agreed upon by you and the lender?**

What fees or penalties are charged on termination of the reverse mortgage contract, through death or early withdrawal?

Will there be a penalty or an additional fee to set up the reverse mortgage for the surviving homeowner when the other dies?

The explanation presented in "Prepayment Privileges" on page 139 holds true here as well. The lender has made a commitment to an investor to give a specific return, or profit, on the money invested in your reverse mortgage. If you wish to break the original reverse mortgage contract, the lender must still satisfy the investor, which means you will have to pay the interest. The penalties are set by the lender. Understand what they mean before you sign the contract. For instance, ask the lender to translate the penalties into dollar figures for a date a year or so in the future and for another, further away, just to give you an idea of how the balance will grow. For example, ask for the figures for the third and the eighth year of the mortgage. This lets you know where you stand and how much equity will be left, should you need to end the reverse mortgage contract. There may a period following the signing of the contract when the reverse mortgage cannot be terminated for any reason. ***This is not mean, this is simply business. Above all else, reverse mortgage lending is a business.***

A cooling-off period allows the homeowner to rethink the terms and conditions of the contract. During this period, the homeowner can cancel the contract without any penalties, making the reverse mortgage null and void. See "Cooling-Off Period," page 122. Also, see the second case study in Chapter 7, page 163.

🏠 **Can the homeowner sell the property to the children and continue to live in the home?**

The reverse mortgage becomes due if the property is sold, regardless of who the buyers are. If the loan is refinanced as a traditional mortgage and if the reverse mortgage is paid off with the proceeds of this mortgage, you would be able to continue to live in the home, provided you and/or your children make the traditional mortgage repayments.

🏠 **How long after the death of the homeowner(s) or after the end of a fixed term does the reverse mortgage become due and payable?**

What will happen to children or relatives living in the home if they cannot afford to pay off the mortgage without selling the home?

Reverse mortgages become due and payable upon the death of the homeowner(s) or at the end of the term, unless the reverse mortgage contract states otherwise. The reverse mortgage contract should allow a reasonable period of time for the borrower or the heirs to be able to arrange to pay off the mortgage without selling the home. For example, the contract could define the end of the reverse mortgage not as the homeowner's date of death but as taking place a number of days after that date. For instance, the reverse mortgage could terminate 120 days after the death of a single, unmarried homeowner or 120 days after the death of the surviving homeowner, for a couple.

And then, what would the other members of the family living in the home do? Your plans should include ideas for their future, either to ensure they can pay off or refinance the debt, or affort alternative living accommodation.

If you live alone and have no close family, you may think this issue is irrelevant to you. But suppose things change and you acquire a housemate, or decide to take in a boarder. Perhaps you may need a personal attendant. If a relative or friend were to move in to help you, that person would probably be sacrificing earning power. Upon your death, the reverse mortgage terminates. What will happen to your primary caregiver? If the caregiver is a relative, what compensation will the individual receive for lost earnings and lost retirement-building years? The lender may permit the person to reside in the home only until the property is sold. In a strong real estate market, that might be only a month or so. If they are an heir to your estate, will there be enough cash in the estate to pay off the reverse mortgage or will the home have to be sold.

SIGNS OF THE FUTURE

The following factors add another degree of complexity to the reverse mortgage market, as each is constantly in flux or subject to ongoing review.

Income Tax Implications

♠ Has Revenue Canada ruled that the equity advanced by a particular reverse mortgage product is not taxable?

Does it matter whether the equity advances are in a lump sum or in monthly payments, or how they are used?

Revenue Canada has not made a general ruling on reverse mortgages; each reverse mortgage product must be considered separately.

Currently, the equity advance payments from simple reverse mortgages and lines of credit are not taxable, as they are equivalent to loan advances from a traditional mortgage. Although annuity income is taxable, the income generated by a reverse annuity mortgage is not. This is because the mortgage costs are tax-deductible creating a "negative income" and, therefore, a "tax-neutral" situation. "Tax neutral" means that the cost of the investment, that is, the interest costs of borrowing the money, is equal to or greater than the income earned on the investment.

In Chapter 10, see "Keeping the Tax Collector from the Door," page 229, for more details on taxation.

Inflation

♠ Has the impact of inflation been considered in all future projections of benefits and costs associated with the reverse mortgage?

For instance, can equity advances or annuity payments be indexed against inflation, so that they grow at the same rate as inflation?

Have calculations concerning property maintenance and property taxes taken inflation into account?

As inflation erodes consumers' purchasing power, inflation can have considerable impact on homeowners with long-term reverse mortgages. Inflation is a progressive increase in prices and, therefore, affects the cost of buying services and products. For example, an item that cost $20 ten years ago may cost over $35 today.

While economists can predict inflation rates for the next quarter, the next year, and the next decade, long-range projections are largely guesswork. When inflation is at a low, predictable rate, its impact can be incorporated into contracts, interest rates, and payments. Consumers can budget for increased service and maintenance costs. If the economy shifts to double-digit inflation, however, people on fixed incomes, including those receiving regular reverse mortgage payments, can find their purchasing power severely undermined. With rising inflation, increasing costs may erode the monthly payments so that the homeowner is once again "cash-poor." At the same time, the homeowner is not as "house-rich," because the reverse mortgage balance has grown and has reduced the remaining equity in the home.

Deciding on an anti-inflation strategy may require some professional input. Diversification, that is, not putting all your money into one type of investment, is one of the best defences against the ravages of inflation. Homeowners who are using reverse mortgages as a money-management tool will have options here, as they have other assets and income sources to counterbalance the reverse mortgage payments. Those who are using their one and only asset in a reverse mortgage have less flexibility. Rising inflation can erode the purchasing power of the equity advances and the annuity income, as well as the residual equity itself .

Public Benefits Support Programs

Will the reverse mortgage payments reduce the benefits available from public benefits support programs now, or as you age? Health and Welfare Canada has ruled that the annuity payments from a reverse annuity mortgage are not considered to be income, as the reverse annuity mortgage costs result in "negative income." Therefore, a reverse annuity mortgage does not disqualify an older homeowner from receiving Guaranteed Income Supplement (GIS) payments. The GIS is an income-tested benefit that ensures an Old Age Security (OAS) pensioner's income does not fall below a specified level. This benefit program was designed for those who have little or no income besides the OAS pension.

Qualification for the GIS takes income from all sources into account, as calculated according to the Income Tax Act in that year. If the reverse mortgage equity advance is reinvested in an annuity, payments to the homeowner will be tax-neutral according to the Income Tax Act, as long as the home is owned by that homeowner. If the annuity income exceeds the cost of borrowing the money, that excess income would be considered income for tax and GIS purposes. As the interest paid on the reverse mortgage by the homeowner is greater than the interest the homeowner receives on the annuity, the taxable income will be nullified by these costs. The excess expense of borrowing the money cannot be used to reduce other income. If the house is sold, the continuing annuity income will then be taxable. This income would be included in the GIS income calculations and may affect eligibility for the Supplement.

As yet, no across-the-board rulings exist among government agencies in Canada. The lender must apply for a separate decision for each program, and each reverse mortgage product offered. When a homeowner checks directly with the local benefits office, confusion may result. In clarifying GIS eligibility, the assistance of an independent financial or legal adviser would be useful. Homeowners may also contact their MP, MPP, or local politicians for information.

The equity advances of a simple reverse mortgage or a reverse mortgage line of credit are considered to be the proceeds of a loan. Therefore, these advances are not taxable, nor do they upset GIS eligibility. Reverse mortgages also do not have any impact on Canada Pension Plan (CPP) eligibility.

The social safety net will undergo many changes in the coming years. Eventually we may see even equity advances considered as available resources in determining eligibility for benefits programs. Restrictions related to use may also appear; for example, homeowners may be required to spend the advances in the month they are issued in order not to jeopardize their eligibility for a benefit program.

For further discussion of the future of home equity conversion, see Chapter 9, page 220.

Reverse Mortgage Lender Insurance Program

There will be more questions than answers here until a lender insurance program is in place.

- ♠ Will Canada Mortgage and Housing Corporation administer a reverse mortgage lender insurance program?

- ♠ Will the program encourage lenders to offer reverse mortgages outside the main urban centres—in rural areas and locations with unstable real estate markets?

- ♠ Will the program also protect borrowers from defaulting lenders?

- ♠ Will nonrecourse provisions become mandatory?

- ♠ Will lenders be required to provide full, written disclosure of all of the costs of the reverse mortgage before the homeowner signs?

- ♠ How much will insurance premiums cost the homeowner?

- ♠ Will independent counselling be available?

- ♠ Will independent counsellors be trained and monitored through this program?

- ♠ Will reverse mortgage forms, documents, and calculations be standardized?

- ♠ If lenders default, will they lose the right to collect interest on the equity advanced?

- ♠ Will restrictions be placed on who can borrow, how much can be borrowed, and how the funds can be used?

- ♠ Will reverse mortgages that exist when the insurance program is introduced be affected by the insurance program?

As you can see from the questions, an insurance program will introduce features that are advantageous to borrowers, as well as some restrictions.

For more about lender insurance, see Chapter 3, page 64, and Chapter 9, page 219.

CHAPTER 7

Getting Good Advice

Even the best advice and the best adviser available to you may not be adequate when faced with making a decision concerning home equity conversion. The responsibility for protecting a homeowner's rights and for making a good decision rests squarely on the consumer's shoulders. While this may not be a comforting thought for a consumer, consider the alternative: living with the consequences of a bad decision made by others the consumer unwisely deferred to or a bad one based on flawed information. Maturity in decision making means realizing that while family, friends, and professionals may provide assistance, individuals must take responsibility for their own lives. Once you let go of the idea that someone else will look after you, you are on the right road—the road to sound decision making.

Advice is not magic. It does not appear out of thin air or at the blink of an eye. Finding someone who understands you, your needs, and your options well enough to offer suggestions, counselling, or encouragement is only part of the challenge. So that you can make a good decision, this individual must also have the necessary skills and knowledge, as well as offer services that are both affordable and accessible for you.

Reverse mortgages should not be sold; homeowners should buy them.

Where do you start your search for good advice? With yourself. Determine what type of advice you need. Do you need suggestions in order to determine the financial implications of a reverse mortgage product or to explore your financial options? Do you want guidance in investigating housing alternatives, assistance in evaluating personal tax implications, or clarifications of legal considerations? Do you need help determining what type of advice you need? Or do you need counselling in regards to elder abuse, isolation, eligibility for public benefits programs, or marital problems at the same time as you examine your housing options?

Professional advisers, such as chartered accountants, insurance brokers, stock brokers, real estate agents, lawyers, financial planners, and retirement counsellors, can offer ideas and opinions, but no one of them has all the answers. Often you can gain valuable insight into an opportunity or situation through an informal discussion of the personal experiences of family, friends, and acquaintances. On the other hand, people occasionally ask for advice when what they really want is someone to make their decision for them. In my years as a creative life planner, I have also found that when people feel they need advice, often what they really require is information. A lack of information can leave normally capable individuals feeling helpless, disoriented, or unsure of their decision-making abilities. Once people understand a concept and the issues involved, they gain the confidence and the ability to make their own decisions. When you ask for advice, what do you mean?

HOW IS GETTING ADVICE USEFUL?

Everyone, at some stage in analyzing housing and/or financial problems, can benefit from advice for a number of reasons, including the fact that being too close to the problem or isolated from others can limit an individual's thinking. Some people are good at applying ideas and information to their personal circumstances, others are not and rely on help to do so.

The complexities of home equity conversion, coupled with the newness of the concept, make seeking other perspectives on home equity conversion advantageous. Taking a holistic approach is also vital. You will need a variety of advisers: housing, financial, legal, and perhaps, medical, community services, or construction as well.

Furthermore, this innovation, or any other housing or financial solution that you select, must be integrated into your whole financial picture, including personal income tax and estate planning. A reverse mortgage is one element of a financial plan not a replacement for financial planning.

This book is designed to provide the information you need to assist you in making an informed decision about home equity conversion, reverse mortgages, or other housing options. However, you may seek professional or informal support in analyzing your personal situation, applying the concepts discussed here, identifying all your options, and/or evaluating the alternatives to determine where your best choice lies. You may also need assistance in determining which public benefits programs would be available to you as a consequence of your decision and which are available now. Professional advisers may also be able to assist you in qualifying for a home equity conversion product, or any other alternative that you select, because, with the exception of government-sponsored support programs, qualification is not based on need but on a number of external factors. For example, to qualify for a reverse annuity mortgage product your home must be of a certain value, located in a certain area, and you must be of a specific age. Advisers may also be able to match you with a private reverse mortgage lender—one of their clients or a private investor who is the client of an associate.

As well as direct questions on home equity conversion or the other options discussed in this book, related issues must also be discussed with advisers. For example, you should ask your lawyer whether your will may have to be adjusted to cover the possibility of the equity in the home being exhausted. If you have a medical problem, you might be wise to discuss the progress of

INDEPENDENT LEGAL ADVICE

Current reverse mortgage lenders suggest or require borrowers to seek independent legal advice before they sign a reverse mortgage contract. A lawyer, paid by the borrower, will read through the reverse mortgage documents with the borrower to ensure the homeowner has been fairly dealt with in the contract. Ideally, the lawyer should also make the homeowner completely aware of the implications and responsibilities, for both parties, that are attached to the terms of the contract. However, a few hundred dollars, the usual fee quoted for this service, allows little time to be spent on any in-depth personal analysis with a new client.

your condition with your doctor relative to your housing needs. If you decide to delay arranging a reverse mortgage until you are older because the payments will be larger, you should have your financial adviser calculate the cost of delay, as well as measuring the increase in payments against rising costs.

The following exercise represents one of the first steps in seeking advice—assessing what you want and what you value. The list below outlines the direct benefits of arranging a reverse mortgage. These are, in fact, the guarantees that lenders give home-owners arranging tenure-plan reverse mortgages (most are also appropriate for other types of reverse mortgages). Each home-owner may derive additional benefits particular to their situation.

THE DIRECT BENEFITS OF REVERSE MORTGAGES

Run through this checklist and rank the following 10 benefits from 1, for that with the greatest benefit to you, to 10, for that with the least.

- [ ] continue to enjoy an independent lifestyle
- [ ] receive the equity advances or annuity payments for life
- [ ] not have to make repayments during my lifetime as long as I live in my home*
- [ ] retain full ownership of my home
- [ ] live in my home as long as I wish**
- [ ] delay or avoid the trauma of moving
- [ ] protect my other assets and the assets of my family through a nonrecourse clause in the contract
- [ ] have residual equity to finance my next move or to leave to my estate
- [ ] receive tax-free money from my home while retaining owner-ship
- [ ] have the choice of keeping the home in the family by paying off the reverse mortgage using other resources

* With fixed-term reverse mortgages, no repayments are necessary until the term ends, when the entire balance is due.

** With fixed-term reverse mortgages, the home may have to be sold to settle the reverse mortgage debt at the end of the term.

Perhaps an adviser will be helpful as a sounding board or a resource in helping you determine whether a reverse mortgage is the best method of achieving the benefits that you have given highest priority. Professional or informal support may also be useful in integrating your other goals with those that appear on this list.

It's a Question of Risk

Another important step in getting good advice is identifying which risks concern you the most. While I am very "pro" home equity conversion and the choices it provides, I know that the homeowner who arranges a reverse mortgage faces certain risks. In exploring home equity conversion, a homeowner

THERE'S MORE THAN ONE WAY

If you decide against arranging a reverse mortgage but still want many of the items mentioned in the above list, the other alternatives presented in Chapters 8 through 12 will be of interest to you.

must take these risks into account. The issues and information discussed in Chapters 5 and 6 have revealed the risks underlying each of the statements in the exercise above.

The checklist on page 158 summarizes the main risks consumers face in arranging a reverse mortgage. This exercise can also be used as an acid test for your final decision regarding a reverse mortgage. Once you have definitely decided to arrange a reverse mortgage, but before you sign up, read through this list of negatives to see if you have been able to make yourself comfortable with the risks involved.

DO YOU BUY GREEN BANANAS?

Your outlook on life will bias the weight you place on the negative information you collect and the risks you face. Are you optimistic, that is, buy green bananas believing you will be around to see them ripen? If so you will find ways to overcome problems, roadblocks, and snags instead of being defeated by them.

Our attitude is often the only real barrier we face. Our view of life can undermine or energize us faster than anything you can name. With a strong positive attitude, risks become challenges and problems become opportunities.

THE DISADVANTAGES OF REVERSE MORTGAGES

In this exercise, rank the following 9 risks, in order of which seems most and least overwhelming to you (most = 1; least = 9).

☐ use up all the equity in my home

☐ have to sell my home

☐ need to move before I am ready (an important concern with fixed-term reverse mortgages)

☐ not be able to leave my home, or its cash equivalent, to my heirs

☐ find the buying power of the payments eroded by inflation

☐ not receive my payments if the lender defaults

☐ live with steadily increasing debt

☐ no longer be eligible for public benefits or other support programs

☐ not be able to find reliable, independent advice

Think of your list of risks as your "to do" list. Tackle the biggest risk first. Strategies for minimizing these risks have been presented in Chapters 2 to 6. Your search for the ideal reverse mortgage is an investigation into risk reduction or at least risk management. If you can not find a way to eliminate a risk, try to find a way to minimize it and to live with the possible consequences. The plan-A/plan-B suggestion in Chapter 4, page 89, is a good backup approach to risk management. Create a strategy to control the outcome, either by yourself, with the help of friends, or with professional advice.

How can you use advisers to the greatest advantage and get the most out the advice you are given? Regardless of the source of the advice, there are a number of points to keep in mind to make getting the advice a worthwhile exercise:

⌂ **This is a two way relationship.**

You should not be a passive vessel into which experts pour knowledge or information to be accepted without question. There should be a meeting of the minds.

♠ Don't be your own worst enemy.

One of the greatest obstacles can be your own perception of aging. If you perpetuate the stereotype that age means a loss of mental abilities, you will begin to discount the importance of your own questions and undervalue your opinions. You will not get good service or the right advice because you undervalue your own role in the process. Or you may feel that anything mathematical is beyond you and stop listening at the first mention of numbers. While you may not be a "math whiz," you can contribute ideas and questions. "Experts," used to dealing with complexities, have been known to overlook simple or non-fee-generating alternatives.

♠ Be prepared.

Know what you want to ask and why. Write out a list of questions. You may even want to tape discussions so that you can go over them again later.

♠ Apples with apples.

Take care always to compare similar things, not apples with oranges. Each reverse mortgage product has distinct features and options, so that direct comparison can be difficult. If you get a quote on one reverse mortgage product, use the same criteria to compare a quote on another. Lenders usually provide rough estimates of equity advances, costs, and residual equity in the introductory stages. If you change your criteria, you may need to get new quotes.

♠ Invest well.

If you worked 20 years to pay off your traditional mortgage, you have at least 40,000 income-earning hours and thousands of dollars invested in your home. How many hours and how much money are you willing to invest to keep it?

♠ Give yourself a chance.

If you have trouble seeing or hearing, let your adviser know. Most advisers use computers that can easily produce printed material in larger type to make things easier for you. In the case of hearing problems, tell your adviser exactly how to help you compensate.

♠ **Keep things in perspective.**

Remember if you get financial advice, the adviser will make suggestions that are based on financial criteria. You may have to balance this advice with your own evaluation of the suggestion. For example, selling your home may make financial sense, but it may still be a bad idea because of the value you place on staying in your home.

♠ **Speak up.**

When something does not make sense, speak up. Ask a question and get the point settled before you go on, or the confusion will just get worse. Your advisers are paid to help you; let them do their job by insisting they find a way to help you understand. If an adviser cannot or will not, find another adviser.

♠ **Let go of yesterday.**

Stop trying to please others. Stop basing decisions on what you think your deceased spouse would have wanted or on what you believe friends and family will think appropriate. Live your own life. Explore ideas that at first glance may not be your customary way of doing things.

♠ **Listen.**

What is the point of asking for suggestions and then telling the adviser or friend why each of the ideas will not work before a suggestion has been fully explained to you? Listen. Listen to the whole idea. Ask questions so you see why it has been suggested and what you would gain. Look at the positive aspects and then at the negative before you decide.

CONSIDER THE SOURCE
You

Educate yourself about the issues and concepts. You have years of experience looking after yourself and your family. Draw on your own expertise. See Chapter 4, page 82, for ideas on how to help yourself.

Your Family

With families it is necessary to distinguish between caring inter-vention and outright interference. Family members can offer wonderful support to the older homeowner faced with major housing and financial decisions, or they can undermine the homeowner's confidence. Sometimes they do both at the same time. How would you characterize your relationship with your family? If you ask family members for ideas, for example, can you detach yourself from your history with a family member long enough to really listen to the points that are being made? Do you react to the relationship rather than to the advice? Also, whose interests are your relatives really serving in the suggestions they make? In the nasty nineties, some "children" have been hit hard by the recession. Before dipping into the equity in your home to help them out, see whether the suggestions in Chapters 8 through 12 may not offer them a short-term solution. Using a reverse mort-gage to stave off bankruptcy can be dangerous. Converting home equity for short-term reasons can be an expensive approach to problem solving. Independent financial and housing advice will be useful in enabling you to say no to your children when conver-sion will hurt you in the long run. It will also assist you in coming up with alternatives for your children.

Does a family member have access to retirement counselling through work? They may be able to get information for you or may know someone who can answer your questions. A grandchild in high school or university may be a valuable researcher for your project. (Chapter 4, page 87, discusses the role of the family in the homeowner's decision-making process.)

If you are recently widowed, the sudden responsibility for every aspect of life, on top of coping with personal loss, can be overwhelming. Support groups and community services exist in most communities. Ask your friends to help you find one. To head this problem off, couples should start teaching each other how to take care of everything from starting the lawn mower, balancing the chequebook, and winterizing the car to using the washing machine, planning a week of meals, and managing long-term investments.

Your Social Circle and Your Community

Isolation is more than having no one to talk to. It includes a lack of stimulation, reduced exposure to new ideas, and being unaware of new options. Ask questions, attend seminars, reach out to friends and neighbours, and find the information you need. If learning about reverse mortgages and other housing options proves tough going alone, get a group together and pool your findings/expertise. You could also invite a series of advisers and salespeople to talk to your group (most welcome an opportunity to speak to potential clients and charge no fees). Join a local seniors' group that has ongoing educational programs, or start your own self-help financial information committee within a seniors' group.

The Government

Provincial and federal governments publish a great deal of general literature offering consumer advice. Many municipal and community support agencies offer housing and financial information or advisory services for older consumers. Canada Mortgage and Housing Corporation, the federal housing agency, offers a wide selection of housing publications. See the Appendix for the telephone number of your regional office, or check the telephone book for the office nearest you.

**Case Study:
Your Best Friend...**

Mrs. L. has lived in her small bungalow in a community outside Vancouver since 1959—first with her family and then alone. Retired from a career in interior decorating, Mrs. L., now 84, found she could manage on her pension income but just barely. After payment for basic or essential home repairs, no money remained for "extras."

In 1989, she heard about reverse mortgages and investigated the product with the help of her lawyer, a long-time friend. Mrs. L. decided to purchase a reverse annuity mortgage. Although not involved in the decision, Mrs. L's son and daughter were "much in approval" of her choice to arrange a reverse mortgage.

Mrs. L. now receives just over $300 per month and now feels she has "financial freedom." "I'm free. I can do things I couldn't do before. I have gotten a lot of enjoyment from improvements to my home. Now I can use my interior design ideas as I have some money." Mrs. L. has taken great pleasure from refurbishing her home. Aluminum siding, new living room furniture, and wall-to-wall carpeting to replace the linoleum were a few of her expenditures.

"I am released from having to count the nickles...I know how to save and make it stretch but now I do not have to think about it. I am free to spend money on books and music or just go out for lunch. Not big amounts really, but I'm free to do it...the reverse mortgage has been a happiness thing for me..."

Case Study: Or Your Worst Enemy...

Excerpts from a December 1993 letter written by a retired school teacher who lives in a small community near Hamilton, Ontario:

"Less than three years ago, I owned my home free and clear, and didn't owe a cent to anyone. Today my home is heavily mortgaged, I owe money to a lawyer, I may be involved in litigation, and have had other heavy expenses. I lost the chance of buying a beautiful country property, where I planned to move. My health has suffered, and I have nothing to show for this disastrous state of affairs, except perhaps a diminished trust in the integrity of my fellow man.

Why am I being penalized so severely? For being unbusinesslike and trusting. For believing propaganda about reverse mortgages....

I became involved when my car was stolen, and I found that the insurance didn't begin to cover its replacement. My income had until then seemed adequate for a pleasant if unostentatious lifestyle. But prices were rising inexorably, the cost of utilities increased steadily, and taxes soared. Suddenly I felt poor. A reverse mortgage sounded like a good idea.

It cost considerably more to get into than I had anticipated, and I had not been warned about an appraiser's fee, legal fees, etc. By the time I'd spent the up-front money, the only way I could recover my costs was to go ahead with the plan. If I'd had any business know-how, I'd have cut my losses and got out then....

The [reverse annuity] mortgage was set at $28,000, which seemed low. But somehow I received the impression that if I decided to get out, all I had to do was repay the annuity payments, plus interest, and a penalty of three months' interest, which was reasonable. I'm not sure where I got this idea, but I suspect it was intimated by the agent, if not in so many words. I certainly had no hint of the real penalty.

I was, no doubt, a sitting duck for a con artist. I'm a widow, living alone, my family grown, no close relatives in the vicinity, and absolutely no business skills or experience...my brain turns off at the sight of contracts and balance sheets....

My home represented the only real asset I had, apart from a few RRSPs. Now I have to start paying for it all over again.... That's one reason I'm writing...to prevent the same thing happening to others like me.

Thirty-odd months after I made the mortgage arrangement, my personal circumstances changed, and I decided to sell the house; I'd found a lovely little place in the country...I wasn't worried about my ability to pay [the mortgage off]; I'd received just over $9,000, which I hadn't spent....

To my horror, I discovered that the [reverse annuity] mortgage had increased by about 70%, from $28,000 to $48,000, including a penalty of $8,000 for early withdrawal from the contract. So I had gained $9,000 and lost $48,000...I didn't understand what I was getting into, and *they knew it*....

I should add that the salesman told me I must see a lawyer before completing the deal. The lawyer I had always dealt with had retired, and I didn't know any others. The one I picked was worse than useless...he explained nothing. Not a word on paper. He thought the [reverse annuity mortgage] "looked okay." No warnings about the difficulties of getting out...or the penalty of $8,000 for early termination. He didn't warn me that the interest rate of 13.75% was for *thirty years*...with no opportunity for negotiation, even though the rate dropped to unprecedented lows, as it has....The lawyer did not explain that the note "Life

Plan—No Guarantee" meant that the annuity died with me…He told me it was all in order, and I believed him.…

It was March when I notified the [reverse] mortgage firm that I proposed to sell my property; the mortgage was then about $39,000 plus the $8,000 penalty. It was August before I was clear of them, and the mortgage had increased to about $42,000, plus the penalty: $50,000.

To make a long story short: I found a new lawyer.…He advised me to re-mortgage the house since the rate of interest has now decreased considerably, and pay off the [reverse annuity mortgage] while I still haven't lost all equity in my home. The income from the annuity goes into the monthly mortgage payments.…I used the $9,000 to reduce the mortgage to $33,000. However, since I haven't paid the $8,000 penalty the company refuses to give a release.…This solution was only made possible because my new lawyer arranged a mortgage for me. I was turned down by other institutions.…

I've learned some lessons: never to assume integrity in any salesperson; never to sign anything unless I completely understand it.…Well, it's never too late to learn. Unfortunately, I can't afford such costly lessons.…Obviously, I'm stuck, but I'd feel better if my experience could save other seniors from falling into the same trap."

Professional Advisers

Older homeowners can afford little margin for error in housing or financial decisions. Professional financial, housing, and legal counsellors should assist with the research and decision making. A clear view of the "big picture" may be difficult to achieve alone. Personal financial planning is a rapidly growing area and offers business opportunities to many professional advisers, including those who are attached to a range of industries such as banks, insurance companies, trust companies, and credit unions. These advisers can be accountants, financial or retirement planners, independents, lawyers, and paralegal counsellors. Free legal or financial services may also be available through community groups. With this growing amount of choice, consumers must shop for professional support the way they shop for any service or product.

Professional advisers are not magicians or psychics. In a half-hour meeting, advisers are not going to transform you into a wealthy person or solve all of your problems. At best, they can offer sound financial advice based on a fair assessment of your means and objectives. *You* must live with the consequences of your decisions. Accept the fact that you are the one with something to lose and that the responsibility for your future rests with you.

Knowledge is your weapon against unfair, incompetent, or insensitive professional advisers and salespeople. Make an effort to understand what your advisers suggest, why they suggest it, and what your alternatives are. If you do not understand what they are saying or why they are saying it, let them know immediately. Your job is to ask questions, theirs is to answer them. "Stupid questions" are the ones you do *not* ask and that come back to haunt you later in the form of self-reproach ("If only I had").

The advisers you select must be a source of accurate information, but supplying information is not enough. The professionals should also have the knowledge, the imagination, and the creativity to apply the information to your situation and your needs. In addition, they require the communication skills to make everything clear to you so you can make an informed decision.

Find out how the adviser gets paid. Sometimes telling the difference between a salesperson and an adviser is not easy, as many advisers earn sales commissions on the products they suggest you buy. This conflict of interest is one of the biggest issues for the professional advisers and their industries to resolve. Full disclosure of all fees and biases should be a basic requirement for all financial, housing, retirement, and other professionals offering advisory services.

As the consumer, you must discover the adviser's biases and hidden agendas to be able to evaluate their advice. For example, some financial planners and consultants work on a fee-for-service basis, charging an hourly rate or a set fee, with no ties to particular products or types of investment. Costs can run from a hundred dollars to a few thousand, depending on the amount of time and work involved. You are their client and the law makes them responsible to you. However, the majority of financial advisers do not have this completely independent perspective.

In most advisory relationships, the consumer buys products from the adviser and so "Buyer Beware" is in force. Some financial planners and consultants speak in general terms about retirement planning, but are paid commissions on sales of a narrow range of mutual fund, insurance, or financial products they represent and, therefore, advise the consumer to buy. Other "no charge" financial advisers work for one corporation and concentrate their efforts on selling that company's products to earn their living. Commission-based financial advisers often use free seminars and workshops to promote their businesses and sell their products. Still other financial advisers combine a fee-for-service approach with commissions from the products they advise you to buy. In either case, the amount of commission and, therefore, the cost to the consumer, can again run from a few hundred to a few thousand dollars. However, here the cost is based on the size of the reverse mortgage or financial product that is sold, not on time spent with or work done for the client. One way or the other the consumer pays for the advice.

Commissions can be earned for either selling a financial product or referring a potential consumer to a company who sells the product directly. For example, an adviser may earn a referral or finder's fee of a small percentage of the total value of the reverse mortgage for providing your name to a company that sells reverse mortgages.

One way or another, advisers are selling their services, so the ideas on relationship selling presented in Chapter 4, page 83, also apply here. Also see Chapter 9, page 212, for a discussion of the problems some British homeowners had when salspeople were confused with advisers.

Professional associations or organizations to which professionals belong, including trade associations, and real estate boards, as well as many bureaus and institutes, are advocates for their members—the professionals. Since promoting a good public image is usually an important role for the organization, they may be a useful resource for consumers looking for information.

These organizations may even provide referrals or free consultations for consumers looking for particular expertise. However, do not assume any additional protection when dealing with a member of a professional group. Instead, contact the organization and find out exactly what benefits or protection, if any, the consumer gains in dealing with one of their members. Once again, asking for written confirmation would be prudent. You may also inquire what updating and ongoing education requirements members must meet. Further, some organizations monitor their members' activities and maintain special committees to regulate unprofessional business practices and unethical behaviour. Find out how rigorously these safeguards are enforced and what recourse, if any, a dissatisfied consumer might have.

When selecting a professional adviser, remember that for many new products and options, little unbiased, practical, non-technical information is readily available. Therefore, professional advice may be a necessity. At the very least, you would be wise to arrange independent legal advice before you sign any contracts. However, consulting a professional can be an expensive and often unsatisfying experience. Many consumers complain about the inconsistency of the quality of service offered by many profession-als. Too often, even when paying the same fees, one client is given better service than another, or initially good service becomes inad-equate over time. As you are building an ongoing relationship with the adviser, ask what precautions they take to maintain the quality of their services and advice. The following ideas may also prove useful in selecting an adviser:

- ♠ **Expect more than "looks good to me."** Look for an adviser who will explain the possible positive and negative repercussions of a decision, instead of one that believes in the "just trust me" or "looks good to me" approach to consulting.

- ♠ **Find out exactly who will work on your file.** Will the adviser handle your business personally or transfer the file to an assis-tant? If it is being transferred, you may want to talk to that per-son to make sure there are no misunderstandings.

- ♠ **Ask about additional charges.** As well as any fees discussed, ask if there will be administrative charges or *disbursements*, including photocopying and processing fees.

- ♠ **Get things in writing.** Even if you feel the services and fees have been fully explained to you, get everything in writing.

- ♠ **Full written disclosure.** All affiliations and compensation should be made very clear to you from the beginning so that you know where the adviser's loyalties lie. For instance, sharing a reverse mortgage lender's lawyer to keep fees to a minimum may not be wise. If advisers have read this book, they will be prepared for your questions and ready to provide you with the information you request.

- **References please.** Even if an adviser has been recommended by a knowledgeable friend or a trusted professional, ask for references. Ideally, you should speak to at least two clients who are in a similar situation to yours. You may even want to ask for the name(s) of one or two professionals who would vouch for the adviser's credentials and expertise.

- **Background information helps.** What qualifies the adviser to assist you? What training have they had? What are their goals in building their practice? Also, pay attention to what they ask you. Do they get a clear picture of your circumstances before offering suggestions, or do they offer ideas too soon. (Obviously, if you have paid to get as many ideas in one consultation as possible, this would not apply.)

Key Characteristics of the Best Professional Advisers

Remember "expert" and "professional" are not legally regulated terms; many business people use these labels to describe themselves or their business services. Also, keep in mind that all experts and professionals may not be in tune with the needs of older homeowners. Many advisers spend their careers assisting clients to accumulate and keep wealth. These "wealth managers" may not be able to relate to home equity conversion or to your wish to stay in the home you love.

Over the years, I have interviewed or worked with many professional advisers, including retirement planners, real estate agents, lawyers, estate planners, tax specialists, chartered accountants, financial planners, placement coordinators, and other consultants and counsellors. Having been in business a long time is not automatically the mark of a more accomplished adviser. If they have been doing the same thing in the same way for the past ten years instead of updating their skills and keeping up with what's new, they will be of little use to you. From my experience, the best advisers, regardless of their profession, exhibit the following characteristics in their dealings with the client—the person who pays them:

♠ **A genuine respect for others.** These advisers value the client's point of view. They support an individual's autonomy and right to decide. They are courteous and well-mannered. These professionals take the time to get in tune with you and your needs so that they can use *your* criteria to help you decide, not theirs.

♠ **Empathetic, but practical.** Your values become their values, and your concerns their concerns. If it matters to *you*, these advisers believe it matters. They make an effort to understand the client's definitions of value and quality, as well as the client's priorities.

♠ **A flexible workstyle.** They have the ability to quickly adapt their counselling style and method of information delivery to suit both the personality and needs of an individual client.

♠ **A thirst for knowledge.** These advisers have a strict professional regime that includes ongoing professional and personal development. Keeping one step ahead for the sake of the client is vital to this group. They love the challenge and share their enthusiasm with their clients.

♠ **Skilled listeners.** Listening is an art to these professionals. They are active listeners—asking questions, taking notes, getting the client's opinions on various topics.

♠ **Committed to communication.** They reject the "just trust me" approach, and instead work hard both to understand the client's needs and to be understood by the client. These advisers do not patronize clients. They avoid jargon and speak the client's language. They realize that many clients want to understand the financial issues and make decisions for themselves, using the adviser to gain confidence in their own abilities.

♠ **Open-minded.** They embrace change. These professionals are receptive to new concepts and look for the potential in each new idea, even if the new product requires a complete shift in their perspective, such as home equity conversion does for "wealth managers." In this way, these advisers also assist you in keeping *your* mind open to emerging concepts.

♠ **Ethical practices.** These professionals do not put personal interest or gain ahead of the client's interest. When they refer you to another professional, for example, you can be sure that the person recommended is the best person at the best price, not just an acquaintance or a friend who needs clients. These advisers have verified the quality of the services they refer clients to and will follow up with the client afterwards. They disclose, in writing, all fees, commissions, incentives, and benefits that they could or do receive in the course of working for the client. They also explain, in advance and in writing, all fees and charges, so that the client will not have an unpleasant surprise when the bill arrives.

♠ **Long-term commitment.** These advisers are in business "for the long haul." They are building long-term relationships with their clients and realize that the success of their business is linked to the satisfaction of their clients, now and in the future. For this reason, they believe in providing references from existing clients to prospective clients.

PART THREE

The Evolution of Home Equity Conversion

AGING IN PLACE: HAVING THE CHOICE

The determination to stay in your home as you grow older is vital to successful aging in place, but it is not enough. Another important consideration is the feasibility of adapting your home to changing physical needs. However, without the financial resources to stay put, the homeowner will be deprived of the choice of aging in place—at least in that particular house or condominium.

Property taxes and major home repairs put the greatest strain on an older homeowner's financial resources. In most areas, property taxes increase steadily. Tax rates are based on property values and municipal spending. As one or both of these financial factors increase, property taxes are bound to go up as well. Many older homeowners find that property taxes are eating up more and more of their total retirement income.

Since many retired homeowners live in older houses, major home maintenance expenses—such as new roofs, plumbing upgrades and heating modernizations—can add thousands of dollars to the growing financial burden of home ownership. If the homeowner does not have sufficient income or savings to cover rising taxes and home maintenance costs, overwhelming debt or the necessity of moving may result.

Home equity conversion allows homeowners to have their home and money too. Conversion offers homeowners financial alternatives when their incomes are no longer sufficent to meet housing expenses. You read about reverse mortgages, the most common conversion technique, in Chapters 1 through 6. Other home equity conversion methods offer homeowners different approaches to financial liberation. These options can allow a homeowner to stay in the home, despite rising maintenance costs and property taxes.

In Chapter 8, "Other Types of Home Equity Conversion," you will see that there is more than one way to have your home and money too. Property tax deferral plans promise relief for many older homeowners faced with dramatic increases in property taxes. The home equity conversion market still has a long way to go, however, as the discussion of deferral plans will reveal. The section of the chapter entitled, "Sale Plans: Selling and Staying," examines conversion plans through which the homeowner sells the property, but retains possession. There are two types of sale plans: sale lease-back *arrangements, in which the seller becomes a tenant on the property; and* life estate *in which the seller retains ownership for life. Then, a discussion of joint ownership explores the potential of selling a share in your property while you remain in residence.*

Anticipation is a powerful strategy for mastering change. In Chapter 9, "Right from the Beginning," an overview of the evolving home equity conversion market will answer the question, "Where do we go from here?"

CHAPTER 8

Other Types of Home Equity Conversion

The only limit to the number of potential variations on the home equity conversion theme is our imagination. Any technique or agreement that allows a homeowner to use the equity that has accumulated in a property—either a part or all of it—would qualify as a method of home equity conversion.

As you read this chapter, give free rein to your imagination. In Canada, the home equity conversion market in still in its infancy. While possibilities are limitless, the types of home equity conversion programs discussed in this chapter are: (1) available in only a few geographic areas; (2) only arranged privately—usually between family members; or (3) are still at the theoretical stage. However, when older homeowners clarify and publicize their needs and desires, lenders will react. In other words, response will come when the voices of consumers can be clearly heard by lenders, businesses, and governments alike.

If no home equity conversion programs exist in your community, find out which seniors' groups might be interested in seeing these options developed for older homeowners in the area. Since government support is an important factor, identify those elected government representatives for your area who would be most responsive to the needs of older homeowners. Think about potential arrangements within your family that might offer relief from some of the expenses of home ownership. Also, investigate the long-range potential of investing your money in home equity conversion for others.

After weighing the alternatives, decide on the best plan for you. In the process, you might even end up with more ideas on how to use a reverse mortgage. For example, you could use a reverse mortgage line of credit as an emergency fund for home maintenance expenses. Or, you could "top up" your tax payments by making the bulk of the payment yourself then paying for the increase in your annual property tax through your reverse mortgage line of credit. (See Chapter 3, page 49, "Types of Reverse Mortgages," for an explanation of reverse mortgage lines of credit.)

In comparing one deferral program with another or with a reverse mortgage, be careful to project the total cost of each, as well as the total benefits from each, over similar periods of time. In other words, compare apples and apples, not apples and oranges.

PROPERTY TAX DEFERRAL AND OTHER PLANS

For homeowners across Canada, steadily increasing property taxes have become one of the realities of life. As the social safety net develops gaping holes, older homeowners are searching for innovative programs to help them stay in their homes as they age. Those who live on pensions and other fixed-income plans find that rising property taxes make aging in place increasingly difficult. If they do not have sufficient income or savings to offset increasing taxes and maintenance costs, these homeowners may face growing debt or be forced to sell their homes. Property tax deferral programs offer a solution that allows the homeowner to stay in the home, while resolving the problem of the tax bill.

Typically, deferred payment programs convert less of the equity in a home than reverse mortgages. Also, while a reverse mortgage releases equity as cash to the homeowner, deferred payment plans merely allow the homeowner to delay or postpone payment of an expense. Deferral offers a reprieve from payment. Through deferral, cash flow is enhanced: more of your current income is available for your use today.

Payment is put off until a time in the future—usually when the home changes ownership. In the meantime, the homeowner's payment is not considered overdue, nor is the account labelled in arrears. However, interest may be charged on the total deferred payments. Deferral programs are ideal for covering property taxes and other periodic payments. These programs are also useful for subsidizing large cash outlays, such as major home repairs or renovations.

Property Tax Deferral

Property tax deferral plans allow seniors to postpone payment of property taxes until a future date, leaving more current income available for daily living.

REAL PROPERTY, IMPROVEMENTS, AND TAXES

Property taxes are actually known as "real property taxes," since it is real property that is being taxed. In law, there are two types of *property: real property* and *personal property*. "Real property" is land plus anything added to, on, or under the land (known in law as *improvements*, where even a garbage dump would be an improvement in this context). Houses, garages, sewers, and sidewalks are all improvements and are, therefore, part of real property. Real property also includes the complete rights of ownership—the rights, within the restrictions of law, to use your real property as you wish. "Personal property" is a catchall definition that describes moveable property, including stocks and bonds, furniture, cars, appliances, boats, clothing—in short, your "stuff." Personal property is not taxed under real property tax programs.

For the sake of simplicity, real property taxes will be referred to as property taxes in this book. I will continue to use "property" to mean a house plus land, or a condominium, including the rights of ownership, and to consider "property" equivalent to "home."

Provincial governments establish property taxation policies and procedures. Individual municipalities—counties, towns, cities—usually establish taxation rates and collect the taxes. Property tax rates are usually set *ad valorem*, that is according to the value of the property. In this way, the owner of a $250,000 property should pay more taxes than the owner of a $100,000 property, and less than the owner of a $500,000 home, even if all three homeowners earned the same income. Property taxation systems can be based on other criteria including the income of the homeowner.

Governments at the provincial or municipal level in a number of Canadian provinces sponsor property tax deferral programs. These deferral programs allow homeowners to enjoy the benefits and the rights of home ownership, along with the peace of mind that comes from not having to worry about property taxes. The deferral of property taxes can free up hundreds or thousands of dollars of a homeowner's income. Homeowners can improve their standard of living today, while using their home equity to pay property taxes tomorrow. Since these government-run programs allow property taxes to accumulate interest-free or at a low rate of interest, property tax deferral may also offer money-management opportunities for older homeowners. There are usually no additional fees or charges to the homeowner. Financial institutions or private lenders could offer similar deferral programs, although probably at greater cost to the consumer.

How Do Property Tax Deferral Plans Work?

Deferred property taxes are registered against the home as a *lien*, a legal claim that usually becomes payable when the property is sold or the homeowner dies. Ownership cannot be transferred until the deferred taxes are paid off. Payment is due when the property is sold or when ownership is transferred either by the homeowner or by the estate (in the event of the homeowner's death). If the property is sold by the homeowner or by the estate, the deferred taxes would probably be paid from the proceeds of the sale. Any leftover money would go to repaying existing mortgages, and funds remaining after that would go to the seller or the estate, depending on the circumstances of the sale. The lawyers acting for both parties in the change of ownership would handle the technicalities involved in the payment of the deferred taxes.

However, it is essential to understand that the house would not necessarily have to be sold. If the heirs want to keep the property as their own residence, they may be able to use part of their inheritance or their own savings to pay off the debt. Alternatively, they could refinance the amount owing to pay off the deferred taxes, by arranging a traditional mortgage or a personal loan. Since the tax office provides regular financial statements giving the current total of the tax deferred plus interest, if applicable, the homeowner—alone or with potential heirs—can plan for eventual transfer of ownership.

Homeowners can feel secure in the fact that the government considers a tax account with deferred taxes to be an account in good standing. You are still a tax-paying citizen if you defer your taxes and are not considered delinquent in your taxes. Remedies for taxes in arrears, or nonpayment of taxes, do not apply here. When the property finally changes owners, the total accumulation of deferred payments, plus any interest charged, would fall due. The government knows the debt is secure, because the transfer of property ownership could not be completed legally until the deferred balance is settled in full.

Since occupancy is normally a condition of eligibility, renting out some or all of the property may jeopardize your right to continue to defer taxes. Once again, even if this were the case, the amount outstanding would not usually become due until the property changed hands.

Tax deferral programs are designed to provide homeowners with tax relief, not to correct or delay an action in a delinquent tax payment situation. Usually payment of taxes must be up to date before a homeowner can apply for a deferral program. The programs are not retroactive; homeowners cannot claim credit for taxes that have already been paid in full. The deferral applies to property taxes due in the year of application. In addition, limits may be set on the amount deferred. For example, the annual maximum deferral amount may be less than the taxes due or it may be set at a percentage of the value of the home.

Property tax deferral programs can make aging in place an achievable and comfortable reality for many older homeowners. However, it is important to keep this opportunity in perspective. **When you defer all of your annual tax bill each year, without making any repayments along the way, the balance of the deferral will increase, for three reasons.** Each year, additional taxes are postponed, so the balance will grow. Add to this any increase in property taxes over the years, and you have rising debt against your home. Finally, if interest is charged on the outstanding balance, the debt rises even more quickly. If compound interest, that is, interest on the interest, is accumulating, the balance could grow at an alarming rate. While increases in property values over the years will dilute the impact of the rising debt to some degree, be careful not to count too heavily on the unpredictable real estate market to save you. Like all types of home equity conversion, property tax deferral plans should be approached with caution and long-range thinking. Nongovernment plans should be treated with the same caution a wise consumer uses when investigating a reverse mortgage.

To ensure you are not restricting your home equity conversion options in the future, do some long-range planning before you sign up for a property tax deferral program. Compare the returns from an equivalent reverse mortgage—both a reverse annuity and a reverse line of credit—to see where your greatest benefits would lie. For example, a life tenure reverse annuity mortgage would provide you with income and the right to stay in your home long after the equity is exhausted. A reverse mortgage line of credit would allow you to pay back the tax bill gradually over the course of the year, so that the debt would be greatly reduced or eliminated each year. On the other hand, property tax deferral programs are usually government-backed, low- or no-interest programs. This is in sharp contrast to the private, compound-interest reverse mortgage programs currently available. Some reverse mortgage lenders may be prepared to give you the numbers from their plan so that you can compare them with a tax deferral plan. Your financial adviser can help you with the number crunching.

The Impact on Mortgages

To ensure that the government has maximum security, property tax claims are always given first priority over any mortgages or other debts registered against a property. If a traditional or reverse mortgage exists, the property tax deferral balance would jump ahead of the mortgage in priority and would be the first claim settled if ownership were transferred. For this reason, the existence of a mortgage may not concern program administrators, provided all other qualification requirements are met.

However, the size of a traditional or reverse mortgage may be affected if the property tax deferral program sets limitations on the residual equity (the amount of equity that must remain available in the property throughout the plan). For example, the British Columbia Land Tax Deferment Program requires that homeowners maintain a minimum residual equity of 25 percent of the assessed value of the property (a value defined by the government's evaluation procedures). Once this equity limit is exceeded, no additional taxes may be deferred. However, the outstanding amount does not come due at this point, but may be carried until ownership is transferred or until the homeowner dies.

When you arrange a mortgage—traditional or reverse—on your home, you would be wise to include a clause in the mortgage contract that would allow you to take part in any property tax deferral program that is available now, or that might be established in the future. Without a clause in the traditional or reverse mortgage contract giving the borrower this privilege, the lender would have the right to stop you from taking advantage of a deferral program in the future. Since the lender's degree of risk increases if the priority of its claim decreases, lenders (especially reverse mortgage lenders) may not volunteer to give up the security of their current claim priority.

As a participant in a property tax deferral program, you may not qualify for a reverse mortgage. Even if you do, the lender may insist that you use a lump sum portion of the reverse mortgage to pay off the deferred taxes. This would leave less money to generate a reasonable monthly income from the reverse mortgage.

Property Tax Deferral Programs: A Comparison

British Columbia and Prince Edward Island offer province-wide property tax deferral programs.* The two programs in these provinces illustrate the potential and the diversity of this type of home equity conversion plan. While the conversion principles are the same, the programs differ in many respects:

🏠 *Interest charged*: The B.C. program charges simple interest on the outstanding taxes at a rate that is set twice a year and is not more than 2 percent below the prime borrowing rate available to the provincial government. The P.E.I. program is interest-free, even if the homeowner becomes ineligible for future property tax deferrals.

---

* Government programs are constantly changing; verify the details before you proceed.

⌂ *Residual equity:* As mentioned above, the B.C. program allows deferral only when the residual equity exceeds 25 percent. The P.E.I. program sets no limit on the deferral of taxes. This provincial government will forgive those shortages that result when the value of the homeowner's estate does not cover the amount of taxes outstanding.

⌂ *Eligibility:* In B.C., the program covers homeowners aged 60 and over, and homeowners who are widowed or those who are handicapped, as defined in the Guaranteed Available Income for Need Act (GAIN). (Application for the provincial home-owner's grant is an eligibility requirement for the program.) The minimum residency period needed to qualify for deferral is one year. In P.E.I., eligibility for the program is limited to the principal residence of homeowners aged 65 and over, whose total annual household income does not exceed $15,000. The minimum residency period prior to application is six months. Neither plan has an application fee.

⌂ *Renewal procedures:* Under the B.C. program, the homeowner must return a Notice to Collector form and a signed home-owner grant application annually in order to continue in the program. The P.E.I. program is automatically renewed each year.

⌂ *Government's role:* In B.C., the Ministry of Finance and Corporate Relations pays the property taxes, and then registers a lien or claim against the property for repayment of the amount paid on the homeowner's behalf. The P.E.I. provincial government keeps a running record of taxes owing.

In 1993, the B.C. program serviced approximately 7400 accounts, including approximately 600 new applicants, while the P.E.I. program had 40 accounts in total. B.C. administrators attributed the steadily growing interest in the tax deferral program to increased publicity, the discontinuation of government home grant plan, and increased property taxes. However, in both provinces the user numbers represented only a fraction of those eligible. For example, in the city of Vancouver, in 1993, approximately 30,000 residents were eligible, but only 1100 applications, including renewals, were processed. Vancouver program administrators sensed there was a reluctance to go into debt, especially to the government. They also felt that a belief in the importance of leaving the property debt-free for heirs kept many older homeowners from applying for the program. Other eligible residents may not even have been aware that the program existed. Language may also have been a barrier for some potential applicants.

At the time of this writing, all provincial and territorial governments have been surveyed for tax deferral plans; but still only British Columbia and Prince Edward Island offer such programs. However, things change. Check with your local tax department, or provincial office for senior citizens' affairs, if there is one. Or, you could contact your Member of Parliment, or call your provincial government's information number to verify whether a tax deferral program exists in your province. (Addresses and phone numbers for the provincial programs mentioned here are included in the Appendix on page 287.)

The tremendous administrative workload and legal costs of these programs (specifically, registration for the program and removal of the tax debt for individual properties) make them more feasible to initiate at the provincial level, although, a few municipalities do offer property tax deferral programs. To find out if a municipal program is available to you, contact your local tax office, seniors' information line, community information centre, or local elected representative.

Each municipal program is unique to the needs of the community it services and to the administrative structure of the department managing the program. For instance, in Nova Scotia, the city of Halifax allows resident homeowners who earn less than $25,000 a year to defer 50 percent of their annual property taxes. The plan has no age restrictions, nor residency requirements; the only stipulation is that the property be a principal residence. The property tax deferral program in Edmonton, Alberta, focuses on tax increases that arose in 1993 as a result of adjustments to the method of property assessment. Any homeowners aged 65 or over whose 1993 property taxes increased by 10 percent or more, or by at least $100, qualified for deferral of a portion of their taxes. Those widowed or handicapped were also eligible if they suffered the same degree of increase. The municipality charges interest at a rate that is equivalent to the city's borrowing rate; for example, the program rate was 6 percent in 1993. The city of Edmonton received applications from only a fraction of the estimated 1000 eligible homeowners.

If you decide against the property tax deferral program available to you *only* because you do not want to leave your property to your heirs with taxes owing, I would suggest that you ask your heirs how they feel before you discard this opportunity. Most family and heirs would prefer to see you living as comfortably as possible. A financial gift from you on your death will not compensate them if they feel that they have gained something at the expense of your health, happiness, or peace of mind. If you are really intent on doing something for your heirs, talk to them about your plans. Times are changing: most "children" are going to be over 65 themselves by the time their parents die. At that stage in their lives, knowing that you are comfortable should be more important to them than a reduction in the amount of money they would get. If the property tax deferral program in your area charges no interest or uses a nominal rate, opting for it may even be viewed as a money management opportunity.

No one home equity conversion program will appeal to every homeowner. Property tax deferral programs are no exception. The important issue here is always choice. If older homeowners see the advantage of deferring property taxes until they want to move or in order to stay in their home, these programs have an important role to play. Governments that support aging in place should make this option, or an alternative program, available to homeowners. If you agree, let your provincial and municipal politicians know your views.

If taxation systems shift away from the property base system (see page 179), the need for tax deferral may lessen. Under systems that tie payment to income, those with higher incomes would pay more. But, since most older homeowners fall at the low end of the income spectrum, an adjustment such as this would reduce their tax burden considerably. Removal of the education tax would also take a weight off their shoulders. As a homeowner, you have a stake in the outcome of changing government economic policies. At the very least, support your local ratepayers association; it will keep you up to date on local issues.

Listed on page 188–192, in "Signing up for a Deferral Program," are the questions you should ask when applying for a property tax deferral. This summary should give you a practical start on most of the issues discussed above. To apply for a property tax deferral program, provincial or municipal, start with your local property tax collection office. The staff there will either be administering the program or know how to direct you. These questions can also be of use in designing a tax deferral program should your ratepayers' or seniors' group want to submit a proposal to your municipal or provincial government.

Are you eligible for property tax relief?

Many provinces, territories, and communities have tax relief, tax reduction, or tax credit programs. These plans reduce the amount of taxes to be paid each year. Most of these programs reduce property taxes, through grants or credits, by at least a few hundred dollars, and there is nothing to pay back at a later date. However, these programs are not designed to remove the entire property tax burden from the older homeowner.

Are you benefiting from the plans available to homeowners in your area? For information on the property tax relief programs applicable to you, contact your local municipal tax office, your seniors' information line, or your elected provincial or municipal government representative. There may be a provincial and a municipal program for which you are eligible.

Home Rehabilitation Deferral Plans

Home rehabilitation deferral plans postpone repayment of a home renovation or modernization loan until the homeowner moves permanently, the property is sold, or the homeowner dies. In this way, a homeowner would be able to enjoy improved living conditions without draining current income. The rehabilitation may include replacing a furnace or modernizing the plumbing, but not merely redecorating or beautifying the home. In government-sponsored programs, costs would be kept to a minimum and interest may or may not be charged against the loan until it is repaid in full. Nongovernment plans would probably prove to be more expensive.

If you were to arrange a reverse mortgage after deferring a home rehabilitation loan, the lender would probably insist you use some of the proceeds of the reverse mortgage to pay off the deferred loan. However, if the deferred loan program were a government-sponsored plan, it may be possible to arrange for this debt to take second priority to the reverse mortgage, so repayment could continue to be postponed. The other cautions expressed for property tax deferral plans on page 180 also apply to these deferral programs.

The home equity conversion basics hold true for these plans as well. Homeowners are responsible for property maintenance and taxes. They are entitled to the full benefits of the sale of the house, including any increase in value attributable to the home rehabilitation, after the loan and the interest on it are repaid.

At the time of writing this book, the home renovation and maintenance programs available in Canada are either grant or loan programs. As governments look for ways to assist those interested in aging in place, deferral plans may be developed. Such programs are not a drain on public funds, as the money, and perhaps interest, will eventually be repaid. If you would like to see this type of program made available in your area, let your provincial and municipal politicians know. According to "the-squeaky-wheel-gets-the-oil" principle, if enough people ask, the government will respond.

Given the tremendous changes being made to social programs in all provinces, readers should check carefully to see what home repair programs are still available before making any definite plans. Check with your municipal housing department, seniors' information line, local Canada Mortgage and Housing Corporation office, or elected representatives to find out about programs available in your area.

Signing Up for a Deferral Program

This section covers the issues you will need to be clear on when you sign up for a property tax or home rehabilitation program. In Canada, deferral programs have traditionally been government-run. However, be sure you know who or what you are dealing with before you sign up for anything. When applying, read the rules carefully to ensure you do not get "stuck" on a technicality.

Knowing what questions to ask can be quite a challenge. **Your goals in asking should be to find out exactly what to expect as well as what is expected of you. At the same time as you are finding out how to get into the program, you should also be asking how to get out.** The questions listed below will provide an excellent basis for your investigation.

Program Eligibility

- ♠ What communities or areas are covered by the plan?

- ♠ Must you claim other homeowner grants before you can be eligible for the deferral program?

- ♠ Is eligibility linked to a provincial income assistance program?

- ♠ Is income a consideration? If so, how is "income" defined and determined?

- ♠ What are the age limits for individuals, couples, and widows/widowers?

- ♠ Are people with disabilities eligible? What criteria are used to determine eligibility?

- ♠ Is eligibility based on where you lived on January 1 of that tax year?

- ♠ Is the length of time you have lived in the province a relevant factor?

- ♠ What occupancy requirements are there? Is there a minimum number of days you must reside in the home each year?

- ♠ Would you be eligible if you owned more than one property?

- ♠ Are there any citizenship requirements: Canadian citizen? Landed immigrant?

- ♠ Are you still eligible for the entire plan deferral if one of the homeowners qualifies but the other does not?

- ♠ What if there are existing mortgages or debts against the property? What if there is already a reverse mortgage on the property?

- ♠ Must the taxes be paid up in full for the previous tax years?

Qualifying Properties

- ⌂ What types of properties are eligible?

- ⌂ Do mobile homes and manufactured houses qualify?

- ⌂ For farm properties, is tax deferral limited to the property taxes on the house and its lot?

- ⌂ If you own a duplex or a multiple family residence and live in one of its units, will you be eligible to defer property taxes only on that portion of the property?

- ⌂ Do individuals who hold a registered life estate in their principal residence qualify? (See "life estate" in the Glossary on page 291.)

- ⌂ If you own and use more than one residential property, do you have a choice regarding which property to defer on?

The Application Process

- ⌂ Where can you get an application? Can you return it by mail?

- ⌂ Are there any application fees?

- ⌂ Is assistance available to help prepare the application?

- ⌂ Is there a deadline for filing an application?

- ⌂ Once an application is filed, how long will it be before the plan takes effect?

- ⌂ Are the application form and literature available in languages other than English?

Other Factors to Consider

- ⌂ What exactly does the program cover?

- ⌂ Can a portion of the annual tax bill, rather than the entire amount be deferred?

- ⌂ During a tax year, when are that year's unpaid taxes added to the balance, in the case of property tax deferral programs?

- ⌂ What interest rate, if any, will be charged? How is the rate established? How often is the rate adjusted? How frequently will the interest be compounded?

- If the homeowner rents out a portion of the home, can the program be applied to the portion of the home the homeowner lives in?

- If the home were rented out, how would this affect participation in the program?

- Can the deferred debt be repaid at any time? Can partial repayments be made? If so, is there any restriction on the minimum size of the repayments? What portion of the repayment will be applied to the principal, and what portion to the interest? Are there any penalties for partial repayment?

- What procedure must be followed when making a full or partial repayment?

Ongoing Requirements

- Does the program automatically renew itself, or must an application or notice be filed each year by the homeowner? Are there renewal or administration charges?

- Must surviving spouses refile on the death of their spouse?

- Are there annual equity or property value checks made on the property by the administrators or their representatives? If so, is there any charge to the homeowner?

- How long may the homeowner be absent from the home before the debt becomes due?

- Can the program be used intermittently over the years, a year at a time, without adversely affecting the position of the homeowner or causing the debt to fall due?

- If the deferment is no longer necessary, but the homeowner cannot afford to repay the debt until the house is sold, may the deferral continue? What interest, if any, would be charged in this case?

- Will the homeowner receive an annual statement showing the full balance of the deferred amount and any interest owing?

- Are there any personal tax considerations that would increase the seller's benefit from the deferral plan?

- Will the participation in the deferral plan affect a homeowner's eligibility for, or benefits from, any social benefits programs?

Termination of the Program

- ♠ Other than the sale of the property by the homeowner, the transfer of ownership, or the death of the homeowner, what circumstances could make the full deferred amount due and payable?

- ♠ Is there a cutoff limit on the size of the deferral, including accumulated interest, or a minimum amount of equity that must always be available? If so, how is the limit or the minimum equity established? How much notice is the homeowner given?

- ♠ Must the deferred amount and all the interest be repaid before a transport permit for moving mobile or manufactured homes out of the province can be approved?

- ♠ If a widow or widower who is eligible for deferral only because the deceased spouse qualified, marries someone below the qualifying age, will the eligible status be lost? Can the amount deferred to date continue to be deferred until the property finally changes hands?

- ♠ What happens if the homeowner moves out of the home but family continues to live there?

- ♠ What would happen if the proceeds of the eventual sale of the property were not enough to cover the entire debt? Would the homeowner or the estate be responsible for the outstanding balance?

- ♠ If an heir inherits the property on the death of the homeowner and wants to move in, what repayment arrangements, if any, could be made for settling the debt without selling the property?

Are there any questions I haven't asked that others usually do?
This question will often unearth tidbits of useful information.

SALE PLANS: SELLING AND STAYING

Sale plans have been used in Canada for a long time. However, as these are usually private transactions between two individuals, no statistics and few details are available. Two types of sale plans exist: **sale leaseback** plans, in which the seller becomes a tenant in the property; and **life estate** arrangements, in which the seller remains in an ownership position for life.

Sale plans are an extreme type of home equity conversion, because they convert all of the equity at once. The homeowner, here called the seller, sells the property to an investor, releasing all the equity. However, in true "have your home and money too" style, the sale has a twist: the seller then becomes a tenant. The property is rented back from the investor at an agreed-upon rent, subject to the tenancy and rental laws of that province. The rental period could run for a fixed term, or for the life of the seller or the surviving spouse.

Currently, the lender/investor for a sale plan is usually a private investor or a member of the seller's family. The arrangement is common in farming communities. Financial institutions may be involved in sale leaseback arrangements for their commercial and industrial clients but have not traditionally done so for residential customers.

The investor, as the owner, benefits from any appreciation in the value of the property. Therefore, the greater the potential for property values to increase, the more receptive the investor will be to entering into a sale plan. Some investors may be attracted by the prospect of having the property for their eventual retirement. Included in the investor's costs and responsibilities will be property maintenance, insurance, and taxes. The tenant (the seller) would probably pay utility and heating costs. Hiring a real estate lawyer with practical experience creating sale leaseback or life estate arrangements to help create a sale plan is wise.

On the other hand, the seller will receive cash for the sale of the property, either as a lump sum or coupled with regular instalment payments. The seller gets the benefit of selling, without having to pack one box or sort through one closet. Of course, the shift from owner to tenant may take some adjustment, especially if the seller has maintained the property meticulously. It is conceivable that the rent could be adjusted or offset by an arrangement by which the seller (the tenant) assumes some of the gardening and simple maintenance tasks. However, as one of the perceived advantages of sale leasebacks is having the pleasure of the home without the pain of maintenance, many sellers would probably be happy to relinquish as many maintenance responsibilities as possible.

The rent the tenant pays will probably be subject to increases. In drafting the sale plan agreement, the payment schedule for the investor who is purchasing the property should take this extra expense for the tenant into account. Otherwise, the rent could end up being greater than any payments the tenant receives from the investor. Another approach is to set the sale price of the property and/or the rent at less than market value. For instance, if the rent were reduced, the sale price of the property would reflect this reduction. (See Chapter 2, page 17, for an explanation of market value.).

Since a sale plan is an agreement between two individuals—the investor who becomes the landlord and the seller who becomes the tenant—the terms and conditions will be unique to each arrangement and to the circumstances of the participants. For instance, sale plans could also be set up for condominiums. Or the sale price of the home could be paid to the seller in a lump sum. Alternatively, the seller could receive regular instalment payments for a fixed term or for the life of the tenant (seller), or in a combination of these payment options. An annuity may also be involved: either one purchased for the seller by the investor personally, or one purchased by the seller. An annuity would give the seller a stream of income for a fixed period or payments would begin at a certain date and continue for life.

The selection of instalment payment schedules and rental plans should take into account tax considerations for both parties, as well as qualification for any social benefits programs applicable to the tenant. For instance, the investor will enjoy the tax advantages of owning a rental property. As well as, the costs of maintaining the property can be deducted from the rental income, and the seller will receive the tax-exempt proceeds of the sale of a principal residence.

As mentioned above, there are two types of sale plans. The difference between them lies in the seller's status and rights after the sale of the property. In sale leaseback arrangements, the seller becomes a tenant in the property, while in life estate, the seller remains in an ownership position for life.

Sale Leaseback Plans

In a sale leaseback plan, the property is sold to an investor, with the provision that it be immediately leased back to the homeowner or seller. The seller's tenure, or the period of holding and occupying the property, could be a fixed term of 10 or 20 years, or it might run for life. The

After selling the home, the seller becomes a tenant in the property for life or for a fixed term, paying the investor rent each month, while the investor is responsible for property maintenance and taxes.

rent, usually set at market value, would probably remain fixed for the term of the agreement. The tenant would be protected by the tenancy and rental laws for that province. The investor, as owner, is responsible for maintaining and insuring the property, as well as paying the property taxes.

A number of issues need to be addressed in creating a sale leaseback arrangement. For example, what are the consequences if the investor resells the property? If the investor has the right to resell, what provisions have been made in the arrangement to protect the tenant's income and rights? The death of the seller or investor, default of the investor, security of the seller's income, and length of the tenancy, as well as many concerns similar to those raised for reverse mortgages, must all be covered in the sale lease-back arrangement.

Sale leasebacks should be set up in a way that suits the investor and the seller. The potential for variation is enormous. At least two, and perhaps three, separate agreements are incorporated into the sale leaseback arrangement. An Agreement of Purchase and Sale, along with a Tenancy Agreement, form the basic arrangement. A traditional mortgage contract or an annuity may also be drawn up. Since each of these agreements contains a different set of terms and conditions, the permutations are almost endless. Usually an overall agreement outlining the sale plan must be agreed to before the details to be included in the different documents can be determined.

The complexity of a sale leaseback arrangement makes it vital for the seller to have independent legal, financial, and housing advice throughout the process. For example, the sale leaseback arrangement could pay the seller a lump sum that represents the full market value of the property. This money could be used by the investor or the seller to buy an annuity for the seller. The seller, as tenant, would pay fair market rent. Even in this simple variation, though, it becomes evident that the seller must have professional advice in determining the market value of the home and the rent. The seller will also benefit from professional support to verify that the annuity is competitive in its rates, terms, and income. (See Chapter 7, "Getting Good Advice," for ideas on how to make the most of the support available to you.)

In another case, the investor may not pay market value for the property, or the investor could give the seller a downpayment to be used by the investor or the seller to purchase a deferred annuity for the seller. The investor would also make regular payments towards the purchase of the property. In a few years, the final purchase payment would be made by the investor. At this point, the annuity income would begin, continuing for the rest of the tenant's life.

In another sale leaseback variation, the investor could give the seller a cash down payment of at least 10 percent of the agreed-to sale price. The remaining balance would be registered against the property as a traditional mortgage, held by the seller as mortgagee. The investor would then make regular payments to the seller until the mortgage was paid off, using one of a number of payment methods: payments of interest only; payments of interest with periodic lump sum instalments of principal, or payments of principal and interest. The mortgage would have a term equal to the term of the lease or to a fixed number of years, for example, 15 or 20 years. The investor, as owner, would be responsible for taxes, insurance, and maintenance of the property, and the tenant would pay a monthly rent that would be less than the income from the mortgage. The tenant would also insure the contents of the home, under a tenant's insurance package. If all parties found the terms agreeable, a $200,000 house could be sold with a 15 percent down payment of $30,000 to the seller. A traditional mortgage for $170,000—the balance of the sale price—

would generate an income for the seller that would depend on the interest rate and frequency of compounding. The length of time given to the investor to pay off the mortgage debt completely, referred to as the *amortization period*, would also affect the seller's income. The shorter the amortization period, the larger the individual payments.

Registering the balance of the proceeds of the sale as a traditional mortgage protects the seller (now the mortgagee) if the investor (the mortgagor) defaults. Before you panic at this though, remember—the same rules regarding mortgages that were discussed in Chapter 2 apply here. The seller, as mortgagee or lender, can take legal action against the investor, who is the mortgagor, if the payments are not made or if any covenants are broken. If, however, the debt has not been registered as a mortgage, the investor could default on the payments, declare bankruptcy, and leave the seller with nothing. If the house were seized in bankruptcy proceedings, the tenant would be left without shelter. The seller's mortgage also prevents the investor from mortgaging the property and putting the property at risk, should subsequent mortgages be in default. No one said these arrangements were simple—*that is why you need professional advice.*

Rents in sale leaseback arrangements are usually preset for the entire term or for life. A word of caution about sale leasebacks involving term lease arrangements in which the seller purchases a fixed-income annuity: if the investor increases the rent at the end of the term, the seller may be unable to afford to stay. Establishing a fixed rate of rent increase on renewal of a rental term in the arrangement would remove this problem. Rents are usually set according to market value. Keep in mind that concessions such as lower renewal rates or below-market-value rents would decrease the investor's returns, and may reduce the amount the investor is prepared to pay for the property initially.

Locating an investor may be the first challenge in arranging a sale leaseback. Your family and friends are probably the most likely candidates. Talk to your lawyer and/or accountant about the financial terms necessary to make the sale plan both feasible for you and attractive to an investor. If you have an unusual property or a waterfront location, try looking for an investor interested in using the property for retirement. With some ballpark figures on paper, you will be able to test the practicality of the idea with your potential investors. Your lawyer or accountant may also be able to contribute the name of a potential investor. Take your time in formulating the sale leaseback arrangement. Independent legal and financial advice will be vital to making an informed decision. (See Chapter 7, page 165, for a discussion about advisers.)

Life Estate Arrangements

After the property is sold, the seller remains owner of the property for life and lives in the home rent-free. In a life estate arrangement, the seller enjoys the benefits of home ownership, as well as the cash from the sale of the property. Once again, in this arrangement the property is sold to an investor, thereby converting all the equity at once. The difference, though, is that property ownership does not transfer to the investor on the date of the transaction, even though the investor must pay the seller for the property. The seller has security of tenure, that is, the right to possession for life. A life tenant is not a tenant in the usual sense of the law and cannot be evicted. On the seller's death or the death of the surviving spouse, ownership transfers directly to the investor. In technical terms, the investor purchases a **remainder interest** in the property. This gives the investor full ownership on the seller's death or on the death of the surviving spouse. Since the property has been sold, the seller cannot leave it as part of the estate.

In essence, a life estate is a prepaid lease arrangement. Since the seller lives in the property for life rent-free, the sale price is adjusted to reflect this benefit. In this type of plan, the seller usually sells the property for less than market value, but there is no rent to pay. For example, if the home were worth $115,000 and there were no mortgages against the property, the investor might agree to pay the seller $50,000 in cash. The remaining $65,000 would represent the cost of the life estate. The value of the life estate, or the value representing the seller's right to occupy the property for life, is based on life expectancies; therefore, the age, sex, and marital status of the seller are taken into account. Because any appreciation in property value belongs to the investor, properties that promise greater potential for appreciation or increased value in the future would be more attractive to investors.

Usually, the seller has full responsibility for the property during the seller's lifetime and must pay all costs for maintenance, insurance, and property taxes. Unlike sale leaseback arrangements, the seller here is in control of the property and its upkeep. The seller is entitled to make minor changes to the property without the investor's prior approval, although the investor would probably have to approve major renovations in advance. The seller would be expected to use the cash portion of the sale price to purchase a life annuity. The income from the annuity would more than cover property maintenance expenses. For instance, in the example above, the $50,000 received by the seller would be used to purchase an annuity that might generate a monthly income of $470. If monthly expenses were $270, the seller/tenant would have $200 left to spend.

Regardless of how reassuring and concerned an investor may appear, the potential for loss and abuse for the homeowner makes it imperative that the homeowner/seller have knowledgeable, and independent legal, financial, and housing advice throughout the entire negotiation process. For example, the sale price may be unfairly low or the lease may turn out not to be a lifetime arrangement. Professional support is essential in determining a fair and reasonable sale price and in setting forth the terms of the agreement. Verification that the annuity is competitive in its rates, terms, and income may also require professional expertise. Read Chapter 7, "Getting Good Advice," for tips on finding the right professional support.

TO GET YOU STARTED

As well as the points made above, the questions starting below highlight the key issues to address in designing your sale plan arrangement, whether you have chosen a sale leaseback or a life estate. You will also find many of the concerns raised regarding reverse mortgages in Chapters 5 and 6 apply to these plans as well. The following questions are also important for advisers to bear in mind while helping you negotiate the sale plan:

- ♠ Are the sale price of the property and the rent set at fair market value? If not, how were they established?

- ♠ Is the lease for life, that is, will it run longer than your statistical life expectancy? If not, do you have the right to renew the term indefinitely?

- ♠ Is the rent set for life? If not, what control exists to prevent the investor from raising the rent unreasonably [sale leaseback arrangements]?

- ♠ What would happen if you fell ill and had to move from the house, temporarily or permanently, before the end of the rental term?

- ♠ Does the tenancy agreement fall under provincial tenancy and rental laws, even if the rent is below market value?

- ♠ Can you sublet the home?

- ♠ If you were to die, what compensation would your estate receive, if a fixed-term or a life-term arrangement had been signed?

- ♠ Are the interest rates and terms for any mortgage or annuity involved competitive for the duration of the arrangement? If the mortgage interest rate varies over the length of the plan, what is the rate set against?

- ♠ Have responsibilities for both parties been carefully outlined?

- ♠ Who pays for maintenance, utilities, insurance, and property taxes?

- ♠ How are you protected against investor default, whether failure to make payments or to maintain the property [sale leaseback arrangements]?

- ♠ What tax considerations have been taken into account to maximize your income from the sale plan?

- ♠ Will the sale plan income affect eligibility for, or benefits derived from, any social benefits programs?

Joint Ownership

Sale leaseback and life estate plans are "selling *and* staying" approaches to accessing equity in the home. Once again, there are many variations on basic sale leaseback and life estate plans. Instead of purchasing the property outright, the investor could purchase an interest in the property so that the owner and investor would become joint owners of the property. In this way, only a portion of the equity is converted. For example, the investor could purchase a 50 percent interest in the property. The purchase price, based on market value, would be discounted or reduced by an amount that would represent the value of renting back this portion of the house for life. Eventually, when the home is sold or when the homeowner dies, the investor would be entitled to half the value of the home, including half of any increase in the value of the property from the original sale date.

Joint or concurrent ownership involves two or more unrelated people owning a property at the same time. In this case the homeowner and the investor, either an individual or a company, will be joint owners of the home. See Chapter 12, page 277, for an in-depth look at joint ownership.

The summary chart provided in Chapter 11, page 240, will put the various home equity conversion methods into perspective.

CHAPTER 9

Right from the Beginning

T he question, "Should home equity conversion be available?" is obsolete. Home equity conversion is a reality, and
reverse mortgages are gaining acceptance. The question to ask at
this stage is not, "How will the home equity conversion market
evolve?" but, "How can we—consumers and the government—get
this market *right*, right from the beginning?"

In Canada, the market for reverse mortgages and home equity conversion represents a clean slate—a start from scratch. Home
equity conversion and reverse mortgages involve an entirely new
concept and require a new way of thinking. We stand at the
threshold of this exciting new marketplace with the opportunity
to create a consumer-friendly marketplace—to get everything
right from the beginning.

Typically, industries come under government scrutiny and
regulation only after problems have arisen for consumers. Once a
number of consumers have suffered, governments may respond.
Since the family home is at the heart of home equity conversion,
consumers are putting their futures on the line while governments wait to see what might go wrong.

If problems with reverse mortgages and home equity conversion programs arise, consumers risk significant financial loss
and great personal stress. The largest group of consumers at risk

will be older homeowners, a group that has the least opportunity of recovering—financially or physically—if something goes wrong. People's lives and often their entire financial future, hang in the balance. Why should consumer "horror stories" continually supply the impetus for consumer protection measures, when so many of the problems can be anticipated and avoided? Isn't it time governments at all levels took responsibility for ensuring things are done right—from the beginning?

Chapters 5, 6, and 8 discussed the terms and conditions that should be included in home equity conversion contracts. Chapter 7 continues the theme of consumer protection. This chapter outlines the developments necessary to ensure the consumer-oriented environment that will permit the evolution of home equity conversion in Canada.

SIMPLICITY IS VITAL

Since reverse mortgages are legally and financially complex, the forms, contracts, and procedures should be designed for clarity, comparability of lenders and products, and full disclosure of risks and costs. Industry-wide standardization of all documents and procedures is the ideal solution. Standardization would allow consumers to compare apples with apples, instead of wondering whether they are dealing with oranges and apples, as is the case with registered retirement savings plans (RRSPs). **Ideally, this market should become "user-friendly." That is, consumers should be able to deal directly with lenders without having to hire someone to explain everything to them.** Particularly beneficial improvements would be:

- **Plain language**: Legalese, or formal legal wording, should be avoided as much as possible. Documents should be written in simple, but accurate, unpatronizing language that uses little or no jargon. In this form, contracts could be translated more easily.

- **Standardized calculations**: Lenders should be required to present, in a standard format, the costs of setting up and administering each of their programs. Using standard formulas and statements to describe reverse mortgages would enable even individuals who are not mathematically inclined to compare products fairly and intelligently.

- **Translations**: Ideally, documents should be available in languages that reflect the particular multicultural nature of the population in the area where a specific product is sold.

- **Legibility**: Large, legible type should be used whenever possible.

- **Audio alternatives**: If illiteracy and/or failing vision restrict a consumer's comprehension, the standard contract could be made available on audiocassettes. Having a simply worded contract read aloud on tape would ensure clarity and enhance opportunities for discussion. If the document is lengthy, the lender could group terms and conditions into subtopics and present them in manageable sections.

- **Disclosure**: Full details of all fees, commissions, and costs should be revealed to the consumer well before the final contract is signed. This information should include the total amount of interest that will have accumulated by the end of the term, or, in the case of a lifetime plan, projections of possible life expectancies and related interest amounts. An industry-wide standard format for disclosure would allow easy comparison by consumers.

- **Accessibility**: Documents should be made available to borrowers with time enough prior to their signing that they may be carefully examined by the borrower and the borrower's professional advisers.

The issues and details related to home equity conversion contracts were discussed in Chapters 5, 6, and 8. The following recommendations address the main concerns raised in that discussion:

- **Frequency of interest compounding**: A limit should be legally set on the frequency of interest compounding against a home equity conversion debt. For instance, reverse mortgage balances grow rapidly towards the total value of the property, because interest is compounded. The Federal Interest Act already restricts the frequency of interest compounding for most commercially offered traditional mortgages, to annual or semi-annual compounding. At least for reverse mortgages covered by the proposed lender insurance program, interest compounding could be limited to annual compounding.

♠ **Full disclosure:** The importance of disclosure cannot be overemphasized. The complexity of the financial and legal aspects of home equity conversion make detailed cost and benefit information crucial. Details about the covenants, interest calculations, prepayment penalties, default standards, and termination procedures should also be readily available to the consumer. This information should be presented in writing, and in plain language, well in advance of the consumer's signing any home equity conversion contract.

♠ **Regular reports:** A biannual or annual statement should automatically be sent to *each* homeowner named in a conversion program—rather than one copy per family. The report should include the current balance owing, a breakdown of costs with details related to interest charges, and the exact cost of terminating the program at that point. Receiving this information regularly would enable homeowners to monitor their financial situations and evaluate their options accurately.

♠ **Lender default:** Consumers should have recourse if their lender cannot make the required equity advances. This consumer protection may require starting an industry-wide contingency fund, extending the current reverse mortgage insurance coverage to include home equity conversion lender default; or setting up a separate home equity conversion insurance program for this purpose. Also, an industry-wide consumer protection plan should be initiated so that homeowners can be compensated for losses caused by misrepresentation or fraud. And, if the lender does default or go bankrupt, consumers should not be held responsible for any interest charged during the period of default.

♠ **Consumer default:** If a homeowner fails to keep the home equity conversion contract in good standing for health or financial reasons, the lender should be limited in taking legal action against the homeowner. For example, if the property falls into disrepair, taxes are not paid, or the insurance lapses, the lender should not be able to correct the disrepair or nonpayment and add these costs for correction to the mortgage balance, until a certain period of default has passed. This would give the borrower an opportunity to rectify the situation. In default situations the lender should not be entitled to force the sale of the property until a longer period elapses, perhaps six months or even longer, if a lifetime reverse mortgage is involved.

- ♠ **Cooling-off period**: Consumers should have a period of time to reconsider their decision and evaluate the complete costs, without excessive penalty for changing their minds. If they have not received full written disclosure of all financial and legal details relevant to an informed choice the time is particularly important. This period should be of a reasonable length relative to the term of the home equity conversion program— at least a few weeks. A cooling-off period would also serve as an incentive to lenders to put a high priority on informed consumer decisions and to assist consumers in educating themselves on the complexities of home equity conversion.

- ♠ **Renewal of fixed-term reverse mortgages**: Before they sign up, consumers should receive full written disclosure of the status of the reverse mortgage at the end of the term. In turn, they should be required to provide written acknowledgement of their receipt of this information. Independent financial and housing counselling should be available to help consumers make alternative living arrangements at the end of their reverse mortgage if the home must be sold to settle the debt.

- ♠ **Nonrecourse provision**: The lenders' right to repayment of the debt should be limited to the value of the property. Calculations and costs should be designed to control the growth of the debt so that it does not exceed the value of the home. Consumers should not be made to pay when they do not have a say in the method of calculation. Nonrecourse provisions should automatically be included in any government-backed home equity conversion programs.

- ♠ **Rights on termination**: Within a short time after the home equity conversion program ends, homeowners or their beneficiaries should have the right to give written notice to the lender that they wish to pay off the conversion program and keep the property. They would then be given a reasonable period of time to pay it off.

♠ **Prepayment privileges**: Government-backed programs should impose a ceiling on the size of the prepayment penalty a lender can charge for a lifetime program, especially if it has already run for a considerable period, for example, more than 5 years.

PUTTING THE CONSUMER FIRST
Consumer Protection Legislation

The "wait until it's broken" approach to government regulation should be replaced with a preventative, proactive method that anticipates consumer needs. After all, the "players" in the home equity conversion industry are well known to government regulators: insurance agents, mortgage brokers, real estate professionals, financial planners, and lawyers. Consumers' problems in dealing with each of these groups have been well documented. The solutions to these kinds of problems that have evolved into the consumer protection measures in effect in other markets should be extrapolated into the home equity conversion market so that it can benefit from them. For example, 1992 amendments to the Ontario Mortgage Brokers Act included the provision for pre-signing cooling-off periods for both borrower and investor. These requirements should be incorporated into reverse mortgage transactions.

Advertising, promotion, and marketing campaigns including printed material should be designed to prevent consumers from being misled or misinformed:

♠ **Program names**: Names that include "pension" or other misleading words should not be allowed. Perhaps a logo could be required so that home equity conversion programs can be easily identified by consumers.

♠ **Government approval**: Organizations selling home equity conversion products should not lead consumers to assume any connection with or approval from government, where none exists. Company and product names must be carefully selected to avoid any confusion in this area. For example, when the CMHC insurance program begins, lender participation in this program must be carefully and clearly explained, so that consumers are not led to believe that the approval is a guarantee or a signal that they can let down their guard. For instance, the proposed insurance program will be in place to protect lenders against borrower default. If lenders display "CMHC insurance approved" or a similar slogan, consumers may feel they are completely protected by a government insurance program, which may not be true.

- **Endorsements**: Seniors' organizations, other nonprofit groups, and groups with many older members that promote specific home equity conversion lenders and products to their members, must disclose, in detail, all financial connections, commissions, and other gains made by the organization, staff, or board members. Every advertisement, flyer, and seminar should prominently display this disclosure. Organizations allowing their names to be used by those selling home equity conversion programs should publicize and make available the research that led to the endorsement. Each organization should form a watchdog committee to monitor its relationship with the company that is selling products to its members. This committee would support and assist members, not the professionals, should any complaints or misunderstandings arise. Disclaimers should be used to explain that celebrities and public figures who appear in home equity conversion campaigns have been paid for their endorsements.

- **Sales seminars**: Seminar speakers and workshop leaders should state their relationship with the sponsoring company at the beginning of a sales presentation and disclose any agreements regarding compensation immediately. For example, if the speaker is to receive a percentage of the sales resulting from the presentation, the audience is entitled to be told of the speakers' vested interest. If only one reverse mortgage product is going to be presented, advertisements should notify consumers of this bias.

- **Sales literature**: Promotional material should be clearly marketed as sales literature, not disguised as unbiased informational pieces—pamphlets or booklets—when only one product is being discussed.

Heading off con artists and consumer scams is another important aspect of consumer education and protection programs. While fraudulent activities have not yet been reported, great potential for abuse exists. For example, the reverse mortgage contract obligates the homeowner to keep the property in good repair. An unscrupulous lender could sell the homeowner inflated or unnecessary maintenance services by fraudulently presenting them as requisite to the contract. Or consumers could sign up for a home improvement program that first requires a reverse mortgage be arranged. When the con artist takes the money from the mortgage and disappears, the homeowner is left with a reverse mortgage to pay off.

Existing consumer protection legislation may need to be amended to include reverse mortgage and other home equity conversion options. Or perhaps new laws must be passed. In either case, legislation should place an explicit obligation on those involved in selling reverse mortgages. Lenders should be required to anticipate the information a consumer would consider relevant to an informed decision, and to provide those details clearly and thoroughly. If a consumer is induced into a contract by false or misleading information or through unscrupulous actions, the consumer should have the right to rescind or cancel the contract without penalty. The right of *rescission* (cancellation) should be in effect for a reasonable amount of time after the signing, lasting perhaps even into the second year for lifetime programs. Yes, cancelling the reverse mortgage would be a tremendous, and possibly expensive, inconvenience to the lender. However, the consumer's right to rescind would be a powerful incentive to lenders and their sales staff to ensure that consumers are treated fairly from the beginning. This right to rescind would be quite distinct from a much shorter cooling-off period, which would not be linked to unfair practices, but which would give consumers recourse after they signed and received full disclosure of the details of the reverse mortgage. (See Chapter 6, page 122, for further details.)

The greatest security for homeowners lies with lifetime or tenure-plan programs, as with these programs they will not be forced to leave their homes at the end of a few years. For home equity conversion products, all financial institutions should be able ideally to create and sell lifetime products.

Currently, only insurance companies can offer products based on life expectancy.

Ideally, the reverse mortgage market and the home equity conversion industry should develop as a model marketplace within a model industry. A national home equity conversion standard and a stringent regulatory program could be established, instead of waiting for varying degrees of consumer protection to evolve in each province and territory. The home equity conversion market should be rigourously monitored to protect homeowners against exploitation and loss. CMHC's involvement may provide an important catalyst for the home equity conversion movement. Canada's home equity conversion industry could become a trendsetter, both for other countries and for other Canadian financial and housing industries.

Consumers who need information should not have to spend hours tracking down a lender. Nor should they be vulnerable to misdirection or

In 1989, retired homeowners Ron and Marina Ringler formed Consumers for Home Equity Conversion (CHEC) from their Mississauga, Ontario, home. Ron became interested in lobbying for home equity conversion when he found it difficult to access the equity in his mortgage-free home. Over the years, Ron and Marina have shared their personal knowledge of home equity conversion with hundreds of older homeowners, professionals, and politicians from across the country.

CHEC is an information resource, not an association or a charitable organization. It is funded by the Ringlers and by contributions from supporters. To receive an information package, the Ringlers request you send a donation (whatever you can afford) to CHEC, P.O. Box 623, Streetsville Post Office, Mississauga, Ontario L5M 2C1.

misinformation. A central lender registry and a product evaluation system are necessary now. A home equity conversion (HEC) centre, a one-stop, government regulated resource, would make programs more accessible to those who need them, provide a standard format to facilitate product comparison, and reinforce consumer protection laws. Using computers and a 1-800 number, the HEC Centre could eventually also match homeowners with private investors. This centre could be administered by CMHC or another government agency or department. It could even be a project for the Seniors' Advisory Committees set up by CMHC. Or the centre could be run through a consortium of national and provincial seniors' organizations, assisted by CMHC. Ideally, a HEC Centre should have the power to intervene on behalf of consumers should problems arise and to require unscrupulous lenders to repay money they received unfairly.

In the meantime, lenders who stand behind their products should be prepared to fully disclose all costs and risks, in writing, before contracts are signed.

Case Study: Cannibals in the British Home Equity Conversion Market

"We had cannibals selling dangerous schemes very aggressively," explains Cecil Hinton, British home equity conversion specialist and independent adviser. "If clients' needs had always been put first, the risky type of home income plans [home equity conversion] that caused untold misery would never have been sold."

The British home equity conversion market has been the victim of unscrupulous sales practices by a handful of "make-a-quick-buck" product providers and salespeople. Hinton calls them "cannibals" since they "feed on" the savings and lives of older homeowners.

British companies offering the popular and safe home equity conversion plans called home income plans have had an excruciating time for many years. They have had to cope with a bombardment of bad press over a scandal that "tarred the entire marketplace" although it affected only a small fraction of those who had bought conversion plans. After more than 20 years of hard work, Hinton has had to watch helplessly as disaster after disaster ripped the home income plan business to ribbons. One newspaper made a crusade of exposing unscrupulous salespeople who advised elderly people to take out inappropriate investment bond schemes. Negative press coverage has overshadowed the virtue of safe home equity conversion schemes that do provide homeowners with a good way of releasing equity from their homes and have an excellent track-record. One "rotten apple" (the investment bond income scheme) has certainly ruined Great Britain's "home equity conversion barrel."

Between 1988 and 1990, investment bond income schemes (IBIS), a variation of the home income plan, were aggressively marketed to older homeowners in Great Britain. When IBIS were introduced, real estate values were rising sharply and interest rates were low. Since 1989, this situation has been completely reversed.

Investment bond income schemes used the proceeds of a mortgage to purchase a bond that fluctuated in value much as stocks do. In traditional British home income plans, the home-owner makes regular payments of mortgage interest using the income from a lifetime annuity so that the debt against the home does not increase. The homeowner receives the balance of the annuity payment as income. At the end of the home income plan, the home is sold to pay back the mortgage. The homeowner receives the remaining home equity and the full annuity payment.

With IBIS, the bond was to increase in value each year and provide income to pay off the interest and provide a larger income than with the conservative home income plans. The homeowner's risk arose from the fact that the bonds could also fall in value, which they did with decreases in value of 15-20 percent per year. On the other hand, the home-owner's interest payments on the mortgage were increasing as British interest rates rose. Homeowners had substantial losses, up to 30 percent per year, because of the drop in bond value coupled with the increase in interest rates. A drastic drop in real estate values further compounded the problem for these homeowners.

Bond-based schemes were sold by independent financial advisers and life insurance agents who rarely, if ever, explained the risks inherent in IBIS. For example, less than half of the 500 homeowners who had purchased an IBIS from one company were aware of what they had bought and the risks involved. These schemes were marketed on their great potential to increase 20 percent each year and give older homeowners the income they so desperately needed. While home income plans are monitored and closely regulated by the financial institutions offering them, bond-based schemes were not. Some older homeowners are now in danger of losing their homes as the size of their outstanding loan exceeds the available equity (nonre-course limits were not set).

Although Hinton first alerted people to the dangers of investment bond plans in 1988 when they appeared, it was not until late 1990 when the first media stories began, that regulators finally decided to ban such schemes. In 1991, regulatory bodies for the insurance companies and the independent financial advisers banned IBIS. For cases in which homeowners were not made aware of the risks, the insurance regulatory body required its members to refund the funds invested in bonds and cover any costs involved in doing so. However, one large IBIS company dissolved without repaying any of the funds. IBIS plans have not been banned by the government or even all of the regulatory bodies involved, and can still be sold, probably without detection until problems arise again.

If it had not been for Hinton's Safe Home Income Plans campaign, the damage to the home equity conversion industry would have been worse. SHIP—Safe Home Income Plans—is a collective initiative launched in 1991 by the 4 largest home income plan providers in Great Britain. The major lenders of safe home income plans pledged to observe a SHIP Code of Practice which includes a guarantee that you cannot lose your home—whatever happens to the stock market or interest rates. Fair, simple sales presentations and full written disclosure of all risks, costs, and obligations are also guaranteed. Companies complying with this Code use a ship logo on their printed material. Hinton, the SHIP Secretary, was named Great Britain's Independent Financial Adviser of 1993.

Although it is true that home equity release schemes (home equity conversion programs) have been available in Britain for over 20 years, the development of the home equity conversion market has been stalled over the past few years by high interest rates and depressed real estate values. The IBIS scandal compounded this situation. However, Hinton strongly believes that home equity conversion will continue to steadily gain popularity as the population ages.

Note: In Canada, homeowners might be encouraged to arrange a reverse mortgage to invest this tax-free money in stocks or bonds. For the unsophisticated or naive investor, using home equity conversion to purchase stocks, bonds, or any type of investment, can be dangerous. If your home is your only or main asset, minimizing risks is important. Remember, the salespeople receive their commission whether you make money or not. Always consult independent financial and legal advice before signing a home equity conversion contract.

Regulating the Professionals

Lenders offering home equity conversion products do not carry a special licence to sell reverse mortgages. Those offering reverse mortgages—lenders selling directly or agents brokering another's products—encompass a tremendous range of backgrounds, including insurance brokers and chartered accountants. However, among them are also people possessing few formal financial credentials. Many selling have had few or no dealings with mortgages of any type. At the moment, anyone can be called a "reverse mortgage specialist." And yet consumers assume that they are speaking to reverse mortgage and financial experts when they are buying a home equity conversion product. Consumers tend also to believe the government will protect them at every step of the way—but this is far from true.

In setting standards for the home equity conversion industry, registration as a mortgage broker seems a good place to begin, since above all, reverse mortgages are mortgages and other conversion programs also involve registered legal claims against property. For instance, in British Columbia and Ontario, reverse mortgage lenders must register as mortgage brokers. However, these regulations only cover the originators of products not the army of agents selling lenders' reverse mortgage products. Regulations should also set standards for establishing the financial strength and stability of organizations offering home equity conversion.

What type of professional structure will the home equity conversion industry support eventually? Will there be a separate professional designation for home equity conversion, comparable to those of insurance brokers and chartered accountants today? Or will existing industries add a new dimension to their businesses by offering services and counselling in home equity conversion? Governments may increase the educational requirements for mortgage, insurance, and real estate brokers, as well as for legal and financial advisers, and then regulate their activities through their individual industries.

Most industries are monitored and kept in check by a combination of self-imposed rules and government regulations. In many industries, trade organizations or professional associations set professional standards and codes of business ethics. These professional guidelines establish the acceptable minimum levels of

disclosure, responsibility, and service for the industry's professionals. Membership and compliance with standards and ethical codes
may be entirely voluntary, or may be regulated by local branches,
depending on the industry. The government regulates professionals through legislation; for instance, each province has laws for real
estate brokers and mortgage brokers. These laws cover specific
procedures and criteria for qualification, registration, education,
advertising/marketing, and conducting business. Penalties for
breaking these laws may include fines and/or jail terms. The professional association may be involved in supporting government
regulatory activities, especially educational requirements.
However, the success of the system described here depends on
knowledgeable consumers who complain if their rights are violat-
ed, as well as on stringent enforcement by regulators.

The timing and extent of CMHC's involvement in the reverse
mortgage market may greatly influence the development of regulations for those selling reverse mortgages and home equity conversion plans. As mentioned in Chapter 1, CMHC is ideally
positioned to provide reverse mortgage lender insurance that
would reduce the risks for those offering reverse mortgages. CMHC
could set standards for those eligible to sell under their reverse
mortgage lender insurance program. Approval to use this insurance could be linked to provincial registration requirements, or a
separate reverse mortgage lender designation could be created.

Historically, regulatory measures have been difficult to introduce on an industry-wide basis once an industry is established.
However, these measures could be built in from the beginning
fairly easily. For instance, educational upgrading requirements are
often "grandfathered." That is, established professionals are ex-
empted from having to participate in new education and upgrading programs; only new registrants must comply. Ideally, from the
beginning, educational requirements should be designed to
ensure industry-wide compliance with increased standards and
upgrading requirements.

Professional standards of conduct and a clearly defined code
of ethics are important, but they are not enough. Governments
must regulate and monitor the professionals who make their living selling home equity conversion products. Consumers deserve
government support with "teeth."

Independent Counselling

As reverse mortgage products are relatively new and sparsely distributed, few legal, financial, and housing advisers have had extensive practical experience with reverse mortgages or home equity conversion. Many advisers are unfamiliar with the public benefits programs available to older homeowners. Consumers looking for unbiased, experienced input may be hard pressed to locate a suitable professional adviser at this stage.

As mentioned earlier in this book, there are two levels of decision making and, therefore, two kinds of independent counselling that consumers interested in home equity conversion will require:

1. Independent counselling is needed to analyze the "big picture" in order to see whether reverse mortgages are the best solution and to help locate the ideal supplier. This level of independent advice assists consumers in wading through the maze of marketing activities, promotional literature, and sales techniques. Professional support for these tasks would become less crucial if the home equity conversion marketplace became user-friendly in the ways discussed in this chapter (for instance, plain-language contracts and full disclosure of costs). (See Chapter 4 for details.)

2. Independent legal advice is needed in reading the contract to determine whether all the terms and conditions, as well as their implications, are clearly understood by the homeowner before signing. Lenders, who are interested in reducing their liability, often require the borrower to receive independent legal advice before the borrower can sign up with their firm. As reverse mortgages become more widely understood and as contracts produced in plain language become the norm, independent legal advice will become a less onerous obligation and more of an interactive verification of details. (Chapter 7, page 154, outlines the support that consumers may need and should expect from professional advisers.)

The concepts discussed in "Regulating the Professionals," on pages 215 to 216 of this chapter, are also important here. Consumers must be able to expect professional behaviour and expert information when receiving counselling and advice on home equity conversion. Tightening up professional standards and regulations will, in turn, improve the reliability and quality of the advice and services provided by professionals acting as independent advisers. Also, when CMHC enters the market with its insurance program, it may stipulate independent counselling requirements or procedures. For instance, if CMHC makes independent counselling a requirement for its program, it should be obligated to assume responsibility for developing educational programs and monitoring counsellors. This could be done either directly by CMHC or in conjunction with provincial groups, such as professional associations or nonprofit organizations.

However, mandatory counselling, beyond independent legal advice, could infringe on an individual's right to make decisions independently. Many older homeowners feel quite capable of making their own decisions and would resent mandatory assistance. Others may have very helpful and knowledgeable family and friends. However, a number of older homeowners, especially those without family nearby, would probably welcome an unbiased sounding-board. In some cases, family members may want to explore home equity conversion on behalf of ailing or frail family members who can no longer make decisions for themselves. However, everything comes back to choice. Governments should establish and regulate the standards of independent financial, housing, and legal advice across the country. In this way, should a consumer want counselling the quality and consistency of this service would be assured.

Once home equity conversion becomes a household word, independent counselling may be unnecessary for most consumers. Furthermore, if the home equity conversion industry evolves with an emphasis on consumer education and protection, instead of on marketing and sales, consumers may have less need for a watchdog. Until then, consumer accessibility to independent housing, financial, and legal counselling is vital to creating a safe consumer marketplace.

"Who pays?" is an important part of the counselling issue. In general, consumers have shown a reluctance to pay direct fees for counselling advice on financial and housing matters. Even if skilled independent home equity counsellors exist, they may not be able to generate the fees necessary to make their practice viable. Eventually consumers will realize the value of financial and housing advice that is not linked to commissions for the adviser. (See Chapter 4, page 83, and Chapter 7, page 166.)

Seniors' organizations may be able to provide the necessary independent resources, at no or low fees, until the government decides how it will proceed. Many older consumers have the experience, time, energy, and interest to see that appropriate counselling, support, and consumer protection programs are established. Counsellors in legal outreach clinics and programs (usually no or low fee) also have an important role to play, especially as many are also on the watch for elder abuse (which is not only physical abuse, but also includes intimidation or coercion by friends or family members).

Reverse Mortgage Insurance for Lenders

One impetus to increasing lender activity may be the introduction of reverse mortgage insurance to reduce lender risks. Canada Mortgage and Housing Corporation is the most likely candidate to become the primary reverse mortgage insurer. The security of a government-backed reverse mortgage insurance program would encourage lenders to enter the reverse mortgage market and to offer a greater variety of features and options. If lending risks were reduced, reverse mortgages would become a viable option in areas where real estate appreciation is slow or unpredictable. Government involvement might also facilitate the development of independent counselling programs and consumer protection legislation.

CMHC's current traditional mortgage lender insurance program, regulated under the National Housing Act, protects lenders from borrower default while ensuring that borrowers across the country have equal access to traditional mortgages. The fundamental characteristic of this insurance program, is that CMHC is mandated to guarantee that the program is financially self-sufficient. Although the insurance policies must compete with others commercially in the open marketplace, essentially there is no net cost to the federal government. Expanding the program to include reverse mortgage lenders would require that the reverse mortgage insurance program also be self-financing.

This "no cost" feature may hasten the implementation of the reverse mortgage lender insurance program; however, this characteristic may have a few negative effects on program design from the borrower's perspective. What would the borrower's premiums be? Would this insurance lead to restrictions on the types of housing that qualify and on possible uses for equity advances? Would qualification criteria for the borrower include an upper limit on the homeowner's income? Would the program also include consumer protection against defaulting lenders who fail to make the required equity advances? When CMCH reverse mortgage insurance is introduced, use the questions for reverse mortgages in Chapters 5 and 6 to evaluate its flexibility, security, and value from your perspective. Additional concerns about the insurance program are explored on page 63 in Chapter 3.

A Consumer-Driven Future

Lenders have made it clear that development of home equity conversion options, including reverse mortgages, will be consumer-driven. Once demand is measurable, lenders will act. In a market responsive to consumer demands, the consumer has ample opportunity to play a key developmental role.

In this consumer-driven market, consumers can influence the types and features of home equity conversion programs that appear. Direct requests for specific features have already led to the creation of an innovative reverse mortgage line of credit and to the ongoing modification of existing products to suit individual consumers. Eventually we may see an integration of home equity conversion into many consumer areas. For example, in real estate sales, having a property pre-approved for a reverse mortgage may become a common sales feature when listing retirement properties.

Insurance companies, trust companies, mortgage brokers, credit unions, and banks are closely monitoring the rising consumer awareness of home equity conversion and reverse mortgages. The pioneering reverse mortgage products that have emerged are firing consumer interest and, therefore, also getting the attention of financial institutions and entrepreneurs. There are a number of home equity conversion programs in development now. Already, finañcial institutions feel that they must offer some type of conversion program to "stay in the game" with older consumers.

Can all of this creative energy and expertise be channeled to create a consumer-friendly marketplace? As home equity conversion builds momentum, this marketplace will also attract negative elements. In the United States, a few home improvement con artists have already found a way to exploit the government-backed reverse mortgage program. Credit cards that allow consumers to draw directly on home equity, but charge more than twice the standard loan interest rates, are an example of how home equity conversion can take a dangerous twist. How would you like the Canadian home equity conversion market to develop? What are you going to do about it? Answering these two questions is the first step towards making your contribution to financial stability for yourself and for other homeowners. The squeaky-wheel approach is necessary to create a consumer-friendly home equity conversion marketplace. If you want choice you must speak up.

IMPACT ON THE COMMUNITY

Although governments are now promoting aging in place by funding social support programs to allow older individuals to remain in their homes as long as possible, a number of issues must be addressed as the home equity conversion industry develops: Should home equity be viewed as a resource to support over-extended government programs? When reverse mortgages become readily available, will eligibility for social support and health care programs be reduced or denied a homeowner unless home equity is converted first? Will income tax laws change to favour or penalize homeowners who convert home equity?

As home equity conversion can enable homeowners to live in their homes for many years longer than may be feasible now, it may also impact the community on another level. Homes could be tied up for longer periods, reducing the number and type of properties available for family housing and redevelopment in some neighbourhoods. The use of reverse mortgages and other conversion methods could result in a decreased demand for retirement housing, at least in some areas. Instead, homeowners

may choose to stay in their homes as long as they can live independently, moving into extended care facilities when they need
full medical support.

The resulting lower population density of age-in-place
households may not be favoured by some local housing and transportation policies. For instance, garbage collection or full bus service may not be cost-effective for some municipalities to provide
services for areas with high proportions of single owner households. In some areas, property values, and therefore property
taxes, could even be affected if older homeowners do not keep
pace with local modernizing trends.

Communities should generally benefit from the stability and
continuity that will result when homeowners remain in the neighbourhoods they have helped build. If aging in place becomes
common in a community, local home support, home maintenance, and renovation services will develop, providing additional
employment opportunities in the area.

At this stage, there is time to ensure that the negative aspects
are minimized or eliminated. One way or another, home equity
conversion and other housing innovations should have significant
impact on society as one quarter of the population will be over 65
years of age by the year 2031. We have to be sure the impact is a
positive one for all concerned.

There's More Than One Way

Home equity conversion is an innovative and powerful option for homeowners interested in improving their standard of living while retaining ownership and control of their home. But it is not the only alternative available to older homeowners, nor will it always be the best option. In fact, before using home equity conversion to resolve a problem, homeowners should thoroughly investigate and evaluate the alternatives presented in Part Four.

If, after reviewing your current options with a financial adviser you cannot find a way to resolve your financial or housing concerns, you can still consider other alternatives. Some ideas come quickly to mind. For instance, you might qualify for a traditional mortgage or a personal loan with a financial institution, or perhaps you could arrange a loan or mortgage privately through your family or with a friend. However, many other solutions are possible—solutions that may not occur to you immediately, or that you may not realize would apply to your situation.

In Chapter 10 the old saying, "It's not what you make, but what you keep that counts," is explored. Here the reader is reminded that reducing expenses and maximizing income tax savings, especially when coupled with another remedy, can be effective in lessening financial stress. Chapter 11, examines ways to put your home to work for you: buying down, that is, the sale of your current home and the purchase of a smaller and/or less expensive property; and starting a home-based business. As well, home equity conversion is briefly put in perspective. Life as a landlord and joint ownership, ways to generate income while gaining companionship, are the main topics in Chapter 12.

CHAPTER 10

It's What You Keep That Counts

I t's not what you make, but what you keep that counts. You have undoubtedly heard this saying before and would acknowledge the wisdom of the statement. What do you do to "keep" your money? Your income is constantly under attack: diminished by your spending habits, eroded by inflation, and devoured by taxes.

These strategies reinforce the "it's what you keep that counts" line of thinking:

♠ Spend wisely

"A loonie saved, is a loonie earned." Avoid impulse buying. Join a co-operative or a bulk-buying club, or form your own. Be a coupon hound. Save whenever you can, so that you can splurge on the things you love, even if you are on a tight budget. This incentive will help you stick to your regime the rest of the time.

♠ Get your due

- *Pension plan*: Long before you retire, learn what you can expect from your pension plan when you do retire. Spend time getting to know and understand the ins and outs of your pension plan. Ask your employer, pension adminstrator, human resources manager, and the pension specialists at Health and Welfare Canada. There are a number of questions to have answered in detail, including:

– How much will I receive?
– How much would payments differ if I were to retire early, for instance at 55, 60, or any age under 65?
– Is there a penalty or an incentive for early retirement?
– Is the pension plan indexed for inflation? If so, how will that affect the amount I actually receive?
– Will my spouse be entitled to receive benefits after my death? If so, how much and for how long?
– Are there any circumstances under which my spouse could lose pension benefits? For example, what would happen if my spouse remarried?
– Where do plan administrators invest the pension plan funds?
– What safeguards are in place to protect my pension?

• *Community support services:* Have you inquired at local municipal offices, community support agencies, and community centres to see what services and programs are available for older homeowners at no charge or for a small fee? For instance, many municipalities offer snow-removal services to those physically unable to do their own shovelling. Community and seniors' centres also sponsor services, support groups, and counselling programs. Public libraries frequently sponsor seminar programs and film nights. They are also usually very receptive to suggestions from the patrons. Seniors' groups often host information nights, social gatherings, and a number produce informative pamphlets and newsletters.

Also, investigate the services provided by students at local community colleges. Many schools offer free or discounted services and products in order to give the students an opportunity to put what they have learned into practice. For example, colleges with hospitality programs often have a student-run restaurant or bake shop that offers great food at great prices. Income tax preparation and home-based business consulting services may also be available.

- *Public benefits programs and other special plans*: Find out what grants, loans, property tax credits, home rehabilitation programs, supplementary benefits, and other government programs you qualify for? If your combined family income is relatively low, you may be eligible for the Guaranteed Income Supplement (GIS) or the Spouse's Allowance from the federal government. Contact your area Health and Welfare Canada office for details.

♠ Anticipate inflation

Although you cannot control inflation, which is the rate of increase in prices, you can plan for it. The impact of inflation on home equity conversion is discussed in Chapter 6, page 00. While inflation rates are low now, it is conceivable that they will rise over the next decade. Inflation has a similar effect on all income. For example, suppose you can live comfortably on a $20,000 annual income today. If inflation increased an average of 5 percent per year over the next ten years, the higher cost of living would mean that by then you would need an income of approximately $32,000 just to maintain your current standard of living. When you plan for inflation, look for strategies that protect your buying power, that is, investments that grow in value to compensate for the impact of inflation. If you put your money in long-term investments that generate interest income only, you will be financially vulnerable in periods of high inflation. Your income will stay constant, while the cost of living rises, lowering your standard of living in the process. The same investments would be less productive when interest rates are low.

Even though you are retired, there is still work to do to ensure your future security. Your savings must work for you. Do not just park your money, invest it—let it work for you. You will be rewarded for the time you invest in finding the most suitable products and the most qualified people. Keep in mind that there are no free lunches, and that "get rich quick" schemes don't work. Be an active element in your own future. Talk to your financial adviser about achieving a blend of growth and income investments that is right for your situation.

⌂ Use will power

Everyone should prepare for the unexpected. If you arrange your affairs now while you are able, others, including the government, will not make decisions for you in the future. A will is a must. If you die without a will or close relations your property may go to the government. What precautions have you taken for temporary or permanent incapacity? Not a pleasant though, I know. But would you rather recover from a lengthy illness to find your home has been sold out from under you by "helpful" people?

⌂ Bartering for services

You can improve your standard of living in two basic ways: by increasing your income or by decreasing your expenses. Bartering for services may be an ideal way to decrease your expenses. Bartering may also eliminate some of the maintenance jobs that are either too much for you or are simply no fun: eavestrough cleaning, lightbulb changing, and putting out the garbage. Bartering involves exchanging products and services for products and services, instead of money for products and services.

The barter movement is growing in popularity. To get things going in your area, set up your own service-exchange network among your neighbours and friends. While many neighbours are ready to help out without wanting anything in exchange, it is often easier to ask for help if you feel you can give something of value in return. Often the things we take for granted, amaze others. Those who can "bake up a storm" think nothing of it. Knitters are undaunted at the prospect of tackling a skiing sweater. Woodworking fans know exactly which tool will get the job done. Some people are wizards at reviving a dead toaster. On the other hand, everyone has certain jobs they hate to do. We can all name our "personal worst" job when it comes to home maintenance. Perhaps you can exchange skills, swap your personal worsts, or make payment in the form of fresh bread or changed light bulbs. As an added benefit, developing a neighbourhood barter network may also serve to strengthen community spirit and give everyone a stronger sense of belonging.

Your barter network may evolve gradually with a group of friends exchanging talents and tasks, or it may gather momentum and become a thriving neighbourhood exchange system. However bartering develops, keep a few basics in mind:

- **Remember, value is in the eye of each barterer.** One person's "trivial" is another person's "amazing."
- **Be sure you can keep your end of the bargain.** Taking on too much does everyone a disservice.
- **Avoid behind-the-back evaluations.** If you have a grievance, discuss it with the other barterer first to iron out what may have been a simple misunderstanding.
- **Keep an eye on your expenses.** Although fun and companionship have value as well, be sure you don't end up "paying" for a service you have provided or "overpaying" for one you have received.
- **Enjoy yourself**—otherwise, you might as well pay a stranger to help you with disagreeable chores.

Note: If you have a service or product to exchange you may want to look into joining a commerical barter network, which is a business established to manage the barter accounts of members. The members are usually businesspeople and companies interested in bartering business services. For example, printing companies often barter their services for home repair services with construction firms.

KEEPING THE TAX COLLECTOR FROM THE DOOR

"It's not what you make; it's what you keep" is an important distinction for those looking for ways to subsidize their retirement income. Before you tackle any of the ventures described in this book, contact your financial adviser and describe your idea to find tax snags or overlooked tax benefits. Remember, "If I'd only known" is an expensive approach. "Thank goodness I asked" is a much better strategy when it comes to the complexities of income tax.

With an income tax system that is a maze of often baffling rules that allow and disallow transactions, professional assistance and tax planning are important. Tax planning involves maximizing investments while minimizing taxes paid. Change is a constant with taxes. Each year new rules are introduced and old tax benefits, are discontinued. Tax strategies must be regularly updated to accommodate these changes.

A financial adviser with income tax experience that is relevant to your financial situation is an important asset. Be aware that the designation "accountant" can be used by anyone, whether they have financial qualifications or not. To protect yourself look for a chartered accountant (CA), a certified general accountant (CGA), or an equivalently accredited financial adviser. See Chapter 7, page 165, for suggestions on selecting a professional adviser. You will usually get the adviser's full attention if you get the information for filing your tax return well in advance of the crush of latecomers who do so in March and April.

Accurate, up-to-date information is important in exploring many of the ideas and concerns raised in this book, but none more so than taxation. The changeable nature of the Federal Income Tax Act makes it difficult to detail particular aspects of the Act in a book that may serve as a reference for years. Instead, for the latest on taxes, read newspapers, personal financial planning magazines and newsletters, or listen to tax planning discussions on television and radio. These are all good sources of information on the latest changes. However, if you really want to know how a new tax provision or the termination of an existing tax advantage affects you and your money, contact your financial adviser.

Home Equity Conversion

Being able to earn tax-free profit on one's home makes home ownership a very attractive investment strategy and allows for a tremendous advantage in retirement planning. Home equity conversion gives the homeowner access to this tax-free money without selling the property. Revenue Canada, the administrator of the Income Tax Act, has not made a general ruling on home equity conversion or even on reverse mortgages, and so the taxability of each conversion product must be considered separately.

However, some broad statements concerning home-equity conversion and liability for taxation can be made. The equity advances from simple reverse mortgages and lines of credit are not considered taxable income but are seen as equivalent to the loan advances from a traditional mortgage. The income from a reverse annuity mortgage is not taxable, if the taxable annuity income is cancelled by the tax-deductible mortgage costs, which are technically the cost of borrowing the money to invest in an annuity. These costs are the interest charged and the borrowing expenses, such as the appraisal fee. As long as the annuity income is less than or equal to the mortgage costs, the net result will be a "tax-neutral" situation with no taxes to be paid. If the taxable annuity income is greater than the mortgage costs, there may be a net taxable income. (See Chapter 6, page 149, for more information on reverse mortgages income tax implications.) The proceeds from a property sale in a sale leaseback or life estate arrangement are also tax-free.

Capital Gains

The Capital Gains section of the Federal Income Tax Act allows for the taxation of profit made on the sale of property. Here "property" refers to the legal term that was introduced in Chapter 8 in our discussion of real property taxes on page 179. Legally, property includes real property and personal property. *Real property* is immoveable property such as land, buildings, and the rights of ownership attached to a piece of land, whereas *personal property* is moveable (e.g., stocks, works of art, vintage cars or jewellery). The Income Tax Act dictates that when the sale of property of any type results in a profit, that profit may be liable for taxation. "May," not "is," since there are some exemptions under the Income Tax Act. Note that while personal property is not taxed as part of property tax, it may be taxable under this Act.

The distinction between the legal and everyday definitions of "property" should be understood. However, this discussion of capital gains will avoid the legal jargon. For simplicity, I will use the common substitute, "real estate," as equivalent to "real property," even though in legal language these terms are not interchangeable. If you are interested in the the legal terminology, see the definitions of these three words in the Glossary; however, these technical details are not relevant to the discussion here. Also note that I shall continue to use "property" to mean merely a house plus land, or a condominium, including the rights of ownership, and to consider "property" equivalent to "home."

Capital gains is the difference between the sale price, after deductions for the cost of selling and either the purchase price on the date of purchase or the property value on December 31, 1971, if the sale took place on or after that date. In other words, if you bought your cottage on March 12, 1960, any increase in value between that date and December 30, 1971, is tax-free profit. On the other hand, if your cottage was purchased in 1972 or anytime later, all the profit from the eventual sale of the cottage would be included in the capital gains calculation. However, a lifetime $100,000 capital gains exemption may reduce the profit figure— more will be said about that later on page 234. Any capital gain or profit that accumulates on one's home or *principal residence*, as it appreciates in value over time, is exempt from taxation under the Act.

Reverse mortgages generate tax-free income and preserve the principal residence exemption. Discuss the investment management and tax planning implications of reverse mortgages and the other income-generating alternatives with your financial or tax adviser.

Jeopardizing the Principal Residence Exemption

In Chapters 11 and 12, home-based businesses, rental of all or part of the home, and the sale of an interest in your home are discussed as income-generating methods of having your home and money too. Under certain circumstances these options may affect the principal residence status of your home and therefore, its eligibility for exemption under the capital gains provision of the Federal Income Tax Act.

Preserving the exemption is not difficult or even complicated. However, maintaining the principal residence status of your home does require forethought, tax planning, and probably some professional advice. For example, a business is entitled to a tax deduction for depreciation, the reduction in value of the business premises due to obsolescence of the building created, for example, by the aging of the heating system. A home-based business is permitted this same depreciation deduction, this time on the home. However, by taking advantage of this deduction, the home-owner is jeopardizing the prinicipal residence status of the house.

The homeowner must decide whether to use the deduction for depreciation as a business expense or to use the principal residence exemption from capital gains. Professional advice will be useful here. If your home is located in an area that historically shows low or no real estate appreciation, your financial adviser will be able to determine whether there would be any advantage to taking the depreciation now. Do some long-term thinking here, though. Play the "what if" game with your adviser. What would happen if real estate values did suddenly go up in your area? Most home-based business people do not take the depreciation deduction for the house in order to preserve the principal residence status of the home. See page 235 for a discussion of common home-based business deductions.

Renting out your principal residence may also jeopardize the capital gains exemption. Again, long-range thinking will start you out on the right foot and ensure the exemption remains intact or that you at least understand the impact of the reduced tax status.

First of all, renting out your home means you are running a home-based business—a property management business. As such, the caution about deducting depreciation would hold true for rental situations as well. However, there is another aspect to consider here. Depending on the circumstances and extent of the rental, the capital gains exemption may not be affected while the home is rented out. However, in a few cases the exemption may be jeopardized. In other words, the profit earned, should your home appreciate in value during this time, may be subject to capital gains and may have to be added to your taxable income for taxation at your personal rate. However, any profit earned on the home before the loss of principal residence status would remain exempt. The Income Tax Act, like all laws, is constantly being revised. Check with your financial adviser or Revenue Canada. (When dealing with Revenue Canada, verify all verbal responses by asking for the pamphlet or bulletin covering the topic you are investigating.) Even the temporary loss of this exemption would not necessarily be a sufficient reason to decide against the rental option if it suits your needs in all other respects.

You may miss out on a great solution for your financial or housing concerns if you let the fear of affecting your capital gains exemption colour your actions. Make your decisions regarding a home-based business or the renting out of all or a portion of your home only after you get the facts and discuss your intention with a professional adviser.

Real Estate as an Investment

Owning a cottage is an attractive way to have your holiday and money too. Real estate is considered one of the most attractive types of investment. It has proven to be a stable, familiar, and low-risk investment, and one that also carries some tax advantages. However, if you own real estate other than your principal residence, capital gains tax will affect your profits when you eventually sell.

The termination of the $100,000 lifetime capital gains exemption for real estate came into effect on March 1, 1992. (The $100,000 lifetime exemption for stocks and similar investments was not affected at that time.) Before that date, if you sold a piece of real estate, perhaps your cottage, and made a profit of up to $100,000 on the sale, there would be no capital gains tax to pay (if you had not used any of the exemption to date). If the recreational or investment real estate was purchased before March 1992, a portion of the capital gain may be eligible for the exemption. The government's formula prorates the capital gains by introducing a factor created by dividing the period of ownership before March 1992 by the total period of ownership. For example, if you bought a cottage on February 2, 1988, and sold it after March 1, 1992, you would have 48 months of ownership eligible for the captial gains exemption. If you owned the property for a total of 60 months, the factor would be $48/60$, so that $4/5$ of the capital gains on the sale of the property would have been eligible for exemption. If you sell on March 2, 1996, you would have owned the cottage for a total of 96 months and the factor would be $48/96$ or $1/2$. Other deductions, as well as future changes to the Act may come into play here, so check with your financial adviser or Revenue Canada to find out how the capital gains calculation would apply to your specific situation. If you contact Revenue Canada, ask for a pamphlet or printed material answering your question, as well as the verbal explanation.

Capital Gains and Your Estate

People who own cottages now have the worry of having to pay capital gains when their cottage changes hands. Capital gains could be deferred, however, until the surviving spouse's death by transferring the property to the spouse's name. Joint tenancy, a method of registering joint ownership that is discussed in Chapter 12 (page 277), can be used to defer capital gains. For example, the ownership of a cottage is automatically transferred to the surviving owner of the death of the other joint owner.

None of the tax-minimization approaches for reducing the capital gains liability for your estate is simple. Each has advantages and disadvantages that must be weighed against your circumstances, goals, and stress tolerance level. Investigate each option thoroughly with your legal, financial, and/or estate planning adviser(s). Find out what the strategy will cost you and weigh this cost against the gain. Sometimes the savings are greatly reduced or cancelled out by the adviser's fees. Your local Revenue Canada office may also be helpful. Some seniors' organizations and legal clinics provide literature on estate planning issues and strategies.

Operating a Home-Based Business

A home-based business can support you in the running of your home, as you will be able to deduct some home maintenance expenses. You can also reduce the taxable income from your business by receiving credit for the costs of running your business and your home. Reasonable expenses incurred in giving service or producing products—in other words, anything that you must buy or pay to earn money—would probably be eligible, including salaries for your spouse or children.

Check with your financial adviser or Revenue Canada to be sure. For example, if you were running a guest house or taking in boarders, you would be entitled to deduct anything from a tablecloth to tulips if these purchases were legitimately made to provide service or comfort to your paying visitor or boarder. As well, for this business or any other, the homeowner would be able to deduct the expense of advertising, extra furniture, smoke detectors, fire extinguishers, painting, wallpapering, cleaning, accounting expenses, bank account charges, stationery, legal fees for incorporating (if necessary), and so on. In addition, a portion of the expenses of maintaining the home are eligible for tax deduction. For instance, if your business occupies 35 percent of your home, you may be able to deduct 35 percent of the following expenses against the business income: traditional or reverse mortgage interest, property taxes, property insurance, utilities and heating or cooling costs, home maintenance, gardening service, and home repairs. Take the time to find out the full range of deductions available to your home-based business; this research really pays. See Chapter 12 for more on home-based businesses.

CHAPTER 11

Putting Your Home to Work

Home has an active role to play in a homeowner's sense of satisfaction and in future plans. Many homeowners are attracted to the idea that their home can make a financial contribution to their retirement rather than merely consuming time, energy, and resources. Today, people are not content to accept the narrow set of housing options that was open to their parents. They are searching for creative alternatives that will keep them independent and allow them to live in the community of their choice.

Exploring every option open to you means looking for ways to use ideas instead of reasons not to. Innovation begins with your imagination. Build on the ideas of both other homeowners and professionals to realize your housing dreams. Innovation is not restricted to new concepts but can include novel uses for existing options and approaches.

The alternatives discussed in this chapter, all follow the formula:

$$100 \text{ percent ownership} + \text{privacy} + \text{income}$$

In other words, all of the options discussed allow you to maintain full ownership, as well as the privacy and independence associated with being a homeowner. At the same time, these alternatives can generate the cash flow that may enable you to remain in your home. These income-generating options can be adapted by an individual to earn a few extra dollars, to make a major financial contribution to an increased standard of living, or even to launch an entrepreneurial venture. This chapter offers practical suggestions for how best to start out in order to achieve the desired results.

As with all of the alternatives presented in this book, the homeowner must feel comfortable living with an option, that is, accept and take to its advantages along with its disadvantages. Avoid selecting an alternative and starting a project for the money alone. Take on an option because you enjoy the process, the relationships and the lifestyle—and, finally, the money.

TAKING TO HOME EQUITY CONVERSION

If you should decide that home equity conversion does not suit you now, do not rule out the possibility that it could be an ideal solution at some time in the future. For example, although a reverse mortgage may not appeal to you at the moment, suppose you eventually want to move into a smaller, less expensive house or condominium that is well suited to aging in place. Arranging a reverse mortgage on this home may enable you to stay there in comfort for many years, or for the rest of your life. Or, you may again decide to wait for a few years before getting a reverse mortgage for the new property. In fact, one of your buying criteria should be the property's eligibility for the greatest number of home equity conversion options. In the future, checking out a property with local reverse mortgage lenders or seeing a "pre-approved reverse mortgage" sticker on the "For Sale" sign may become a prerequisite for buyers.

Acquaint yourself with the full potential of reverse mortgages, property tax deferral, sale leasebacks, and other methods of home equity conversion. Follow Louis Pasteur's maxim: "Chance favours the prepared mind." The more you understand about home equity conversion, the more you will be able to use innovation and inspiration to put the concepts to work for you when an opportunity arises. You will also be better able to create your own opportunities.

If you investigate the reverse mortgage products available to you now and find all of them unsuitable, remember that the industry is in its infancy. You are only saying "no" to the products available today, not necessarily to the basic principles of home equity conversion. Once the market develops, product variety and flexibility should increase. Keep an eye on the growth of home equity conversion, so that if circumstances in your life suddenly shift, you will be prepared to make an informed decision.

Locating commercial home equity conversion products can be a frustrating task, since national lenders may not be listed in your telephone book and many of the home equity conversion advertisers are actually agents for reverse mortgage lenders. Until a central registry, such as the one mentioned in Chapter 9, page 211, exists, the consumer is faced with a challenge. The resource groups listed in the Appendix, page 287, may provide names and addresses for new lenders. Current lenders are listed on page 289 of the Appendix. The consumer is still responsible, however, for evaluating the existing home equity conversion products.

Commercial home equity conversion options are not readily available to all Canadian homeowners as yet. The greatest opportunity for many owners will lie with individual investors and family members who have funds to invest in long-term ventures such as home equity conversion. Local lawyers, mortgage brokers, financial consultants, and retirement planners are likely sources of private investors. You must have your facts and figures together though, so that you can create a win–win situation, that is, one which has clear benefits to the investor as well as for you. Independent lenders and small financial firms like credit unions may also prove useful. Although this will not necessarily be an easy or a quick search, if you believe it is your best option, you will do well to keep asking. The worst you will get is a "no"—unless you sound too desperate. If people feel you are vulnerable or frantic, you may not be able to get the best financial return. Or worse, they may try to take advantage of you. Once again, the best time to pursue private home equity conversion arrangements—in fact, any and all of the options presented in this book—is before you *must* arrange something quickly.

Homeowners who see home equity conversion as a money management tool, might also consider reverse mortgages as an

HOME EQUITY CONVERSION AT A GLANCE			
Concerns Once HEC* Program in Place	**Reverse Mortgages**	**Property Tax Deferral Plans**	**Sale Plans**
Property owner	Homeowner	Homeowner	• **Sale Leaseback:** sold to investor; home-owner becomes tenant • **Life Estate:** Homeowner owns for life; on death ownership transfers to investor
Who is respon-sible for mainten-ance, insurance, and taxes?	Homeowner	Homeowner	• **Sale Leaseback:** investor • **Life Estate:** homeowner
Equity liberated as...	Cash	Credit for payment	**Both:** cash and option to rent for life
Amount of equity released	Usually less than 60% of value of property	Could be all or maximum of 75% of value of the property	**Both:** all equity liberated as property is sold, but may not be sold for market value
Residual equity	Possibility of none remaining in tenure plan unless equity preservation guaranteed	Possibility of none remaining, or 25% left if plan limit set	**Both:** property was sold at start of program
Property appreciation belongs to...	Homeowner, un-less shared appre-ciation provision for lender	Homeowner	**Both:** investor
Status of debt	Rising debt against the property	Rising debt against the property	**Both:** sold so no debt for homeowner
Availability of products	Commercially in some areas (see Chapter 3, page 55).	government programs: B.C., P.E.I., plus some municipal plans (see Chapter 8, page 183).	**Both:** private arrangements only (see Chapter 8, page 193).

* Home equity conversion

investment. Check with your financial adviser to see whether they would be a suitable investment for you. But before doing that, real the discussion on lenders' risks in Chapter 3, page 63, to see whether you would be comfortable with the realities of this investment. Then read the rest of the book to see how best to present your investment opportunity to a potential borrower.

TAKING A STEP DOWN: SELLING AND MOVING

Selling your home is the most direct and most common way to use your home to subsidize your retirement. Liquidating this asset will liberate your home equity and give you cash to reinvest, use, and enjoy. However, you will still need a place to live. Unless you have other financial resources, part of the proceeds from the sale of your home will go towards putting a new roof over your head.

Chapter 11 explores the process of selling your home and buying another one. The following suggestions should help you make astute decisions, so that you get the greatest possible benefit from both the sale and the purchase. See Chapter 4, "Decisions, Decisions, Decisions," on page 79, for suggestions on making the decision to move.

Throughout this book, "home" has meant property that you own and reside in: a detached house, townhouse, semi-detached house; condominium-townhouse, or apartment condominium. "Home" may also refer to property you hold under a life tenancy arrangement, or a leased land agreement. As housing innovations emerge, the concept of home ownership will undergo further modifications. (See the discussion of "property" in Chapter 1 or look it up in the Glossary.)

Obviously, if home ownership is no longer one of your priorities, you will probably rent a house or apartment, or move in with family after you sell your home. This way you will liberate all of the home equity and remove the responsibility of maintaining a house or a condominium. Once again, good advice is vital, both in selling your home and in managing the proceeds of the sale.

The following ideas are slanted towards traditional types of home ownership. For more innovative home ownership, the contractual arrangement will spell out exact procedures and requirements of the sale. It is beyond the scope of this book to explore all these variations in detail. However, this chapter will explain the seller's rights and how the sale price may be enhanced.

Step One: Developing a Selling Attitude

Getting the most out of the sale of your home is important, especially when the property is your major asset. There is a lot more to selling your home successfully than simply putting a "For Sale" sign on the front lawn. Selling your home does not mean sitting down to *wait* for buyers to appear. To sell successfully, you should do all that you can to *attract* buyers.

For years, real estate professionals have said that three things determine the value of a property: location, location, location. External factors also affect the real estate market in your area; for example, the state of the economy, buyer demand, interest rates, unemployment, and number of competing sales, to name just a few. There are, however, many things you can do to maximize your gain when selling.

Tips for Selling Successfuly

♠ **The buyer is interested in a "house," not in "your home."**

The pride of ownership can be an expensive burden if you do not get it under control. Make an effort to distance yourself from your emotional attachment to the house. You must be able to look at it with the critical eye of a stranger. When prospective buyers look at your house, they will compare it to their idea of the "perfect" house. They will also compare your property to the other houses on the market that they could select instead. Don't take this comparison personally. To keep things in perspective, stop referring to "my home" and start calling the property "the house" or "the condominium."

♠ **It's the little things that count.**

No one really likes anything second-hand. Make your house look as "new" and fresh as possible. If you remove all the bumps, scrapes, and sticky fingerprints of your life, a prospective buyer can pretend that the house is "new." Fresh, neutral-coloured paint and a good cleaning—windows included—go a long way. Fix all those things that you meant to, but got used to instead: cracked light switch plates, damaged moulding, broken tiles, poorly hung doors, discoloured toilet seats, squeaky stairs, loose handrails, and anything else that needs attention. Details add up to an overall impression. Make the first impression a good one.

♠ Space, glorious space.

One of the most common buying incentives is to get more living space. If your house seems cluttered, buyers may not realize how large the rooms are and how spacious the closets are. Get rid of as much stuff as possible. Organize a garage sale before the house goes on the market; you may be able to pay for paint and wallpaper from the proceeds. Put extra furniture and boxes of books in storage.

♠ People buy with their noses.

Smells mean dirt and neglect. To a buyer, they also mean time must be spent cleaning and repairing. Give everything a good scrub. Don't cook fish and aromatic foods the night someone is coming to see the house or condominium. Invest in air fresheners and a vent in the kitchen. Or simply bake bread.

♠ Look before you leap.

Stop and think before you get talked into re-siding the house, overhauling the kitchen, or making a major structural renovation to the house. Exactly how much value can you reasonably expect this change to add to your property? Remember, cost does not automatically equal value. Spending several thousands of dollars does not guarantee a higher selling price. A real estate professional can give you an informed opinion as to what could add significant value to your home.

Usually, home improvements that add space and function give the greatest return for your money. Extra storage cupboards, a walk-in closet, an additional shower, or an extra bedroom or bathroom usually add value. However, spending more will not necessarily net you more. A bathroom renovation that costs $5,000 and one that costs $2,000 could add the same amount of value. Get expert advice before you start spending.

If your kitchen is outdated, spending thousands to renovate it may be a risky investment. Try a face-lift, instead. Fresh paint, new hardware (door knobs and hinges), or new flooring or cupboard doors can transform a kitchen at a fraction of the cost of a total overhaul. Use white and neutral shades to give the room a fresh new look. Plants and collectables can create a charming, "We can live with this for now" look. Done properly, these touch-ups will convince the buyer that the advantage in buying your house is that they will be able to do exactly what they want and in the way they want.

Whatever you decide to do, find out exactly what the total cost will be before going ahead. Get estimates from at least two contractors. Make sure you use the same job description for each construction quote, so that you are comparing apples and apples.

♠ Get out on the street.

Check out the "curb appeal" of your home. This is the first view that prospective buyers have of the house, and it is also the view that is photographed if you decide to use the Multiple Listing Service. Cast a critical eye. What needs painting? cleaning? pruning? digging up? Would a plant or two brighten up the doorway, fill in a gap, or camouflage the gas meter? "Inviting," "well cared for," and "welcoming" are words a prospective buyer should use to describe your home when you have finished your improvements. Your dreams may die at the curb if you neglect this selling perspective.

♠ Anticipate objections.

If there is something wrong or something that appears to be wrong with your house, fix it before putting the house on the market. For instance, if your house is located in a known termite area, have the house professionally certified as termite-free before you put it up for sale. Research any known problems to see if there are new products available to solve them. If the defect is too expensive to repair yourself, get at least three estimates from well-known contractors to show to prospective buyers. Face the possibility that if something is wrong with the house its value may be diminished. However, concentrate on accentuating the positive aspects of the property.

⌂ **Timing is everything.**

Time plays an important role in three ways:
- In most areas, the best times to sell are the spring and the fall;
- The greatest opportunity to sell is in the first few weeks the house is on the market. At this stage, a well-presented property can generate considerable interest from buyers. "Well-presented" means priced right for the market, given the condition and limitations of the property;
- The more flexible your closing date—the day the property changes hands—the greater strength you will have in negotiating the price you want. If you can adjust to the buyer's ideal moving date, the buyer may be willing to give you a better price. However, if *you* are bound to a fixed moving date, you will be asking for a time concession from the buyer. This may be represented as dollars in the sale price. For instance, if you have already bought your next house and have a closing date set for 90 days from today, you will need the buyer's cooperation in honouring that contract. Otherwise, you may be faced with additional costs for extending or defaulting on that agreement.

⌂ **Remember your house is worth exactly what someone will pay for it.**

This is the golden rule of real estate. What you spent for the house and on the house are less important than what buyers are currently paying for comparable houses. You may have paid $310,000 for your four-bedroom house and spent $25,000 renovating the kitchen and landscaping the lot. But if buyers today can purchase a similar four-bedroom house in your area for $290,000, why would they spend more for your house?

What is "Market Value"?

Market value is the worth of a property, or the amount of rent that can be collected, relative to a specific time or real estate market. Market value is the largest amount of money a knowledgeable, rational, unpressured buyer or tenant would pay for a particular property in an open, competitive market. In other words, a property is worth what someone is prepared to pay either to buy or rent it. The market value focuses on the buyer's or tenant's actions not on the owner's costs, needs, or dreams.

The same property in a fast-paced sellers' market will carry a higher market value than it would during a buyer's market. The difference? Demand. In a sellers' market, there are more buyers than there are properties. The demand drives up the sale price or the rent. In other words, the market value will be higher than it would in a buyer's market, in which purchasers have lots of choice and can negotiate a good price for themselves. Low demand brings the price or the rent down.

To estimate market value, similar properties currently on the market are surveyed. Research into the actual sale price or rent paid in recent transactions for similar properties provides information essential to establishing a buying pattern. These two sets of data are compared to properties that did not sell or rent, to give a complete perspective on what buyers or tenants seem ready to spend for that type of property and its location, at that specific time. Appraisers and real estate professionals normally provide estimates of market value. Lending value, used by mortgage lenders to establish the amount of money a consumer may borrow, is a very conservative estimate of value and often considerably lower than market value.)

Hiring a Real Estate Professional

Once you have decided to sell your home, you are faced with the challenging task of getting the best possible price in the shortest time, with a minimum of hassle. Where do you start? *Acquaint yourself both with the real estate market and with your consumer rights.*

You may decide to follow up on a couple of the "free, no obligation" market evaluation flyers that are left in your mailbox. Steel yourself in case you meet with heavy salesmanship, and remember the "no obligation" promise. By seeing the real estate people in action during the evaluation, you will get a feel for what is involved in selecting and working with a real estate professional. Remember, until you sign an agreement, you do not owe anyone anything.

Research the buyer perspective on your neighbourhood. Read local real estate publications; visit open houses. Knowing what choice a buyer has in your price range may help with your

WHAT ABOUT FSBO (PRONOUNCED "FIZ-BOW")?

In a flat real estate, or buyer's market, or when you are under pressure to sell quickly, professional real estate help will usually expedite the sale. A real estate professional should be able to negotiate a better deal for you. FSBO or "For Sale By Owner," could be your approach when the market is fairly hot—that is, in a seller's market.

If you decide to sell your own house, be committed to doing a professional job. "Be prepared" is an excellent motto. Research marketing approaches, the ideal list price, competing properties, negotiating strategies, and contract preparation. This work will pay off in the long run. An information sheet that lists the physical details and features of the property will save you from having to answer many of the same questions. If you include a picture of the house, as well as the benefits of living in the house and the neighbourhood, you will have an excellent marketing tool. Independent legal advice from a real estate lawyer will save you headaches later. Be ready to work "hard and smart" for your money. To sell your home on your own, you must develop a "selling" attitude.

If a family member or a friend is interested in buying your house, have a lawyer and, ideally, an appraiser assist you in getting the best price while pre-serving the relationship. Don't let anyone "guilt" you into acting against your best judgement.

decision making. In doing so, you will also have more opportunity to see real estate professionals in action.

If you decide to hire a real estate company to help you sell your house, keep following in mind:

 Exercise consumer caution.

In spite of the fact that consumer laws offer you some protec-tion, "Buyer Beware" is the best attitude to adopt when hiring a real estate service.

 You're the boss.

When you sign the listing, you have not transferred ownership of your property to the real estate company. The listing—Multiple Listing Service or exclusive—merely gives the real estate broker (that is, the real estate company) the authority to act as your agent or representative. The salesperson with whom you deal is an employee of the broker, not an agent. Real estate professionals must, according to agency law, tell you—the one who pays them and therefore, the client—everything they learn, from any source, that concerns you or your property. This includes information from other salespeople about buyers who are thinking of "testing the waters" with an offer. Further, whenever there is a decision for you to make, they must explain your options and the implications of your choice so that you can make an informed decision. Whether lowering the list price or signing back an offer, the decision is yours. Obviously, you should have confidence in your real estate representative's abilities, negotiation skills, ethics, and thoroughness.

♠ Beware of the highest bidder.

Avoid selecting your sales representative on promises to get you more than a realistic value for your house. Look for real estate professionals who provide you with information on recent sales, unsold listings, and the current competition so that you can, with their guidance, arrive at a realistic list price.

♠ Arm yourself with knowledge.

A mixture of federal laws, provincial statutes, business standards, real estate board bylaws, and traditions guide real estate practioners through the hundreds of real estate transactions that take place across the country each week. The more you understand about the real estate industry, the better equipped you will be to protect yourself. Consumer protection is the main focus of the laws associated with real estate but this security is only possible if the consumer takes some of the responsibility. Consumers must know how things are supposed to work and what to do when things go wrong.

Do these suggestions sound like too much bother or effort? The alternative is putting your faith and your future blindly in a stranger's hands. The sale of their home is one of the largest financial transactions in most people's lives. In fact, for many older property owners their home represents 60 percent or more of their financial worth. A smart real estate move may set an individual up for life; poor judgement or poor advice can result in a financial nightmare.

The real estate industry's current movement towards written disclosure will reinforce consumer protection laws and strengthen the consumer's position. Disclosure refers to the responsibility of real estate professionals to tell sellers and purchasers exactly who they are working for and what each person can and should expect from the real estate broker and salespeople. For instance, when sellers hire a real estate broker to sell their home, they are entitled to any and all information that may or may not be significant in the seller's decisions.

See Chapter 7, page 165, for more information on selecting professional support and Chapter 4, page 79, on decision making.

Step Two: Buying Smart

Selling and buying expose you to two opportunities to come out ahead financially. When the shoe is on the other foot and you become a buyer, remember the smart seller's list in step one. You will be paying for these ideas when you buy your new home.

Keep the "buyer beware" perspective in mind. In your dealings with real estate practitioners do not assume they are working for you, even if they let you call them "my agent." Legally the brokerage or real estate company is the agent or broker; buyers and sellers usually deal with the broker's employees—real estate salespeople. The salespeople are not agents, merely employees of the agent, but the word "agent" is often used to describe anyone in real estate. As a buyer, ask a direct question, "Are you working for me as my legal agent?" If the person responds, "Yes, I'm your agent" or "Yes, I'm your salesperson," and adds, "I'm working for your best interests," get that statement in writing. If the real estate professional is not working for you, the individual's being paid to be the seller's agent. The professional could also be a salesperson of the agent. If that is the case, everything you say will be relayed to the seller. For instance, if you discuss your upper spending limit with a real estate professional who is working for the seller, then this information must be relayed to the seller.

The trend towards real estate professionals acting as buyers' agents and working for the purchasers' interests has prompted the move to formal written disclosure, to consumers, of the working relationship between the real estate professional and the seller, as well as between the professional and the buyer. According to the Canadian Real Estate Association's 1993 amendment to the Real Estate Standards of Business Practice, written disclosure, by professionals who belong to a real estate board, of exactly whose interests the brokers and the salespeople are representing, will be required, beginning in January 1995. From then on, written disclosure of a real estate professional's relationship with and responsibilities to each party in a transaction—the buyer and the seller—will be clarified at the outset of their work together. Some brokers may begin disclosure procedures before the deadline; others will not. Assumptions can be dangerous. Your best protection is to ask exactly what you can expect from each real estate professional regarding loyalty, fairness, and disclosure of information.

Many homebuilders' associations, real estate boards, government consumer departments, and libraries offer free seminars and literature on home buying. There are also many books available on the subject. If you have been out of the home-buying market for a while, you may benefit from seminars and literature aimed at the first-time home buyer.

Financial counselling can help you determine exactly how much you can afford to spend on your next home. After you have bought down to a smaller home, ownership responsibilities remain, but on a more manageable scale. Buying down may also mean buying a home that is similar in size to your present one, but in a less expensive area. However, you now have the added concerns of money management as you put the remaining liberated cash to both short- and long-term use. (These considerations also exist for those who sell, then rent.) See Chapter 7, "Getting Good Advice". "Taking to Home Equity Conversion" on page 238 explores the advantages of buying down and shows that using foresight in buying a home that would qualify for a reverse mortgage gives you options for the future.

You may wish to reread the discussion of housing options in Chapter 4, "Status Quo or Pack and Go?"

Putting the Sale on Paper

Agreement of Purchase and Sale

The most common type of real estate sale contract is the Agreement of Purchase and Sale. However, there is no standard format or universal set of terms and conditions for this agreement. Each is as unique as the people and the property involved. The agreement describes in detail what the buyer offers the seller, and what the buyer will do once the contract is signed. The responsibilities and rights of the seller are also set out in detail. (The real estate professional representing the seller, as well as the seller's lawyer if necessary, can explain the background and the significance of each clause and condition in the offer to the seller.) All conditions of the transaction must be contained within the agreement, rather than in side agreements. In Canada, according to federal law, contracts for the sale of land must be in writing to be legally binding. If an agreement is "legally binding," each party will have the right to seek legal recourse if the other party does not live up to the obligations agreed to in the contract. Verbal agreements for the sale of land may be legal, but they are not legally binding, that is, legally enforceable.

The sale price is an important element in the contract, but not necessarily *the* most important. The amount of money the seller *nets* is more significant. The real estate professional working for the seller will present the calculations dictated by the conditions of sale to determine the amount of money the seller will net, or receive, after deductions, such as the real estate commission. The terms of the contract also influence the seller's net return. For instance, if the buyer asks for a completion date that is 30 days in the future, everything would be fine as long as the seller had accommodation lined up. However, if the seller did not have another place to move into, possible storage and interim housing costs should be calculated before the seller accepts the buyer's offer. If the buyer is prepared to assume the seller's mortgage, the seller may save thousands of dollars in penalty payments to the mortgagee. Whereas if no buyer is willing to take on the mortgage, the seller would have to discharge the mortgage ahead of schedule and pay the penalties for prepayment.

The decision to accept or reject the buyer's offer rests with the seller. If the buyer makes an offer that meets, or exceeds, the requirements of the seller, the seller is still not under an obligation to sell, even if the seller has signed a listing agreement with a real estate company. While the real estate professional can interpret the implications of accepting or turning down the offer, the decision to accept or reject any offer rests with the seller. However, the owner cannot legally discriminate against a buyer, that is, turn down an offer only for racial or religious reasons.

The seller's third alternative is to sign back the buyer's offer, which means to change the buyer's offer. Once the buyer's offer is altered in anyway, it becomes null and void. Then, the seller signs what is now an offer from the seller, or an offer to sell the property under certain terms and conditions. If the buyer accepts the offer to sell, the contract is finalized and the property is sold. However, the buyer may choose to decline the offer outright. Now, there is a third alternative for the buyer. The buyer can sign back the seller's offer, and so the circle is complete. Eventually, either the parties will agree to agree and the property will be sold, or they will agree to disagree and everything will go back to square one.

Vendor Take-Back Mortgage

When the buyer does not have enough cash to buy a home outright, but is a good credit risk, a vendor take-back or VTB mortgage may solve the problem. The seller, also known as the vendor, gives the buyer credit in the form of a mortgage for the balance owing. Ownership is transferred to the buyer, with some cash changing hands. The seller holds a mortgage for the balance. The term, *vendor take-back mortgage*, originated with the seller's selling the property to the buyer, then taking back an interest in the property as security for the mortgage debt, which represents the balance of the sale price.

Now, whether there is an actual transfer of interest back to the seller or not, the seller has a registered claim against the property as security for the debt, that is, mortgage. For example, if a property sold for $150,000, the buyer might give the seller $70,000 cash at the time ownership is transferred to the buyer. The balance of the sale price, $80,000, would be registered against the property as a traditional mortgage. The seller would become the mortgagee, with all the accompanying mortgage rights and legal powers. The buyer would become the mortgagor, with all the responsibilities of repayment.

The sale price, contract conditions, interest rate, and repayment terms should all reflect the degree of risk for the seller and the gains made by the buyer. The risks to the seller must not be taken lightly. The early 1990s showed us that there's no such thing as a sure thing. Even when the buyer seems to present a rock-solid, low-risk profile as a mortgagor, the possibility of buyer default on the VTB mortgage still exists. The seller should understand the financial and legal implications of default, before agreeing to a vendor take-back mortgage.

Once again, many questions have to be answered, including:

- Why did the buyer simply not arrange the mortgage through a financial institution?

- Will a credit check and perhaps a personal consumer report be arranged to determine the buyer's credit history and financial stability, before the seller commits to the mortgage?

- How competitive are the interest rates and the mortgage terms in the mortgage contract being proposed, relative to the current mortgage market?

- In calculating the return on the VTB mortgage for the seller, has the interest earned on the mortgage balance been compared with the return this amount of money would earn in another form of investment?

- To what extent would provincial mortgage laws enable the seller to prevent the mortgage from being assumed by or transferred to a new mortgagor who had not been checked out and approved by the seller (if the property is resold before the mortgage is paid off)?

- How will the buyer pay off the mortgage when the mortgage is due at the end of the 1- to 5-year term? (Sellers are usually not advised to make the mortgage automatically renewable to the buyer.)

A variation on VTB mortgages is to have the VTB mortgage purchased by an investor, probably through a mortgage broker.

When the buyer and seller negotiate the Agreement of Purchase and Sale, this option should be kept in mind when they first put the house on the market, sellers may wish talk to a mortgage broker to determine what interest rate, term, and other conditions are necessary to make the VTB mortgage saleable with the minimum discount. The mortgage is discounted when it is sold, that is, the seller receives a reduced amount, not the face value. For example, a $60,000 VTB mortgage would not yield the seller $60,000 cash if it were sold to an investor. The mortgage broker handling the sale of the mortgage would calculate a discount using factors such as interest rate, term, balance, and percentage of the equity to be mortgaged. If the home is being sold through a real estate company, the real estate professional involved can explain discounting in detail to the seller and ensure that the seller does not lose anything by offering a VTB mortgage to a buyer. Independent advice may be sought as well.

VTB mortgages can help achieve the price and terms necessary to buyers and sellers in a difficult real estate market, or with a hard-to-sell property. However, unless the seller sees the mortgage as an excellent investment after speaking to a financial adviser, or unless it is truly in the seller's best interests, not the buyer's, a VTB mortgage should not be the first option explored in negotiating the contract. Investment in a mortgage carries risk, which may not be attractive to all sellers. Independent legal and financial advice can help the seller determine whether the benefits outweigh the risks. (See Chapter 2, page 14, for background on mortgages.)

Agreement for Sale

An Agreement for Sale puts the risk inherent in the purchase and sale arrangement on the buyer. It is a contract in which a seller agrees to transfer ownership of the property at a later date, by which time certain terms and conditions of the agreement will have been met by the buyer. In the interim, the seller gradually receives the money from the sale of the property. The buyer has the pleasure of living in the property while paying for it. Both the buyer and the seller know exactly how much money is involved, the size and frequency of payments, and when the final payment is due. The agreement is registered on title, so that the rights of both the buyer and the seller are protected. Once the selling price has been paid in full, the seller transfers ownership to the buyer.

An Agreement for Sale might be useful when a homeowner wants to move immediately, but the house is located in an area where properties sell slowly. Or, if a buyer is willing, but lacks the cash to purchase the home outright, an Agreement for Sale may be the answer. This agreement also suits situations in which the buyer has a good income and is perhaps expecting money later, for example, an accident settlement or an inheritance, but does not have enough cash at the moment. An Agreement of Sale may also be appropriate when a large traditional mortgage exists against the property. If the mortgage contract does not allow the debt to be paid off during the current term, or if the penalties for paying it off early are prohibitive, the homeowner could choose to sell the house under an Agreement for Sale. Payments from the buyer would cover property taxes, house insurance, mortgage payments, and payment of the balance when the mortgage comes due. This type of agreement works only for sellers who do not need the full amount of equity immediately, but can manage comfortably while receiving the money over time, for instance 10 years or so.

If the buyer misses a payment, the seller may have the right to terminate the agreement and evict the buyer, depending on the terms of the agreement. The seller may also have the right to keep the money received to date. For these reasons, the VTB mortgage alternative is usually favoured over this arrangement by the buyer. With a traditional mortgage, even if a number of payments have been missed, the buyer (mortgagor) would have the right either to bring the mortgage back into good standing by making the missed payments and paying the lender's costs. Or a mortgagor could redeem the property by repaying the mortgage debt in full and paying the mortgagee's costs. **An Agreement of Sale, on the other hand, clearly favours the seller in its remedies for buyer default.**

The terms and conditions of the Agreement for Sale can take any form mutually agreed to by the seller and the buyer. As with all contracts, the details of an Agreement for Sale define the rights and responsibilities of both the buyer and the seller. As this is not a common arrangement and because each agreement is different, understanding the contract is vital.

There are a number of variations of this basic concept. For example, the buyer may purchase an option to buy the house at a later date, but at a sale price set today. Or, the value of the option may be included in the purchase price of the house. An Agreement for Sale alternatively may require the buyer to pay the seller a down payment, or lump sum of cash at the time of signing the agreement, and pay interest on the balance.

The buyer takes possession of the property, while the seller remains the property owner. The buyer lives in the house and, if it is a farm, works the land, gradually paying off the balance of the previously agreed-upon purchase price. The buyer, although assuming the role of tenant, is not a tenant and therefore is not protected by provincial tenancy laws. The regular payments made by the buyer are not rent, but contributions to the purchase price.

The advantage of this sale agreement, for the buyer and seller alike, is that the buyer will regard the property with the eye of ownership. The buyer often improves the property, in accordance with any limitations or restrictions set forth in the agreement. (However, the owner may not allow major structural changes until the property is completely or substantially paid for.)

Experienced independent legal advice is essential to ensure that all the "what ifs" are covered in the Agreement for Sale, and to make sure that the seller is completely protected, however things turn out for the buyer.

TAKING TO BUSINESS

If the current trend continues, self-employment will become common after retirement—an integral part of the Third Age mentioned in Chapter 1. Early retirement is becoming very common; many people are retiring while still at their peak. The average retirement age has dropped to 62 in Canada, while many people are retiring in their 50s as corporations downsize or leave the country. The retirement income from 25 or 30 years of work may not be enough to cover the 30, 40, or even 50 years ahead. Self-employment has become a financial necessity for some retirees, and a mental necessity for others.

One of the most interesting aspects of the self-employment wave of the 90s is the heightened credibility of home-based businesses. Creating a home-based business (HBB) can be an exhilarating and rewarding investment at any stage of life. Investing in self-employment—in your abilities and your future— can take many forms: learning a new skill such as word processing or public speaking; broadening horizons through travel with a trip to a conference in San Francisco or a visit to the National Archives; or applying your talents to an industry you know well by working under contract to your former employer or for a company that was previously a client. Financial gain, independence, and personal satisfaction are the most obvious rewards. New friends, new skills, and new adventures may also result from operating a home-based business.

Coming Out of the Basement

Home-based businesses and cottage industries have existed for a long time, however, never before have they commanded such widespread acceptance and as much attention from the media as they do now. The wave of interest in HBBs has increased their credibility and brought many HBBs out into the open.

The HBB wave has also been fueled by manufacturers, retailers, and service suppliers keen to develop new markets for their products and services. In an economy that has drastically reduced the steady markets of the 1980s, businesses are targeting these entrepreneurs as consumers of everything from photocopiers, fax machines, and computers, to office supplies, furniture, and business services. This business motivation and the drive of unemployed or early-retirement individuals rebounding from the recession, who are its market, have combined to form a new market. A growing number of magazines, books, seminars, and conferences cater to HBBs, and further validate this expanding business segment.

Keep in mind, though, that the HBB movement focuses on one common element—location. That is, the business has its headquarters in someone's basement, dining room, spare bedroom, or garage, instead of in an office tower, a factory, or an industrial park. However, the similarity among HBBs ends with the common location and the special requirements of self-discipline and time management it involves. The range of businesspeople who use "home" as the headquarters for their business is amazing: word processing and marketing specialists; home renovation and repair contractors; management and human resource consultants; real estate and insurance brokers; childcare and homecare providers; importers and exporters; video producers and film directors; financial planners and accountants; computer programmers and software designers; interior designers and architects; portrait painters and craftspeople; embroiderers and seamstresses; fashion consultants and hairstylists; bed and breakfast operators and property managers; manufacturers' sales representatives and inventors; and on and on. The rental option discussed in Chapter 12 would also be managed as a home-based business (see page 268). Also, many employers are turning to freelancers who work from home to save on the expenses of salaries and benefits that must be paid to full-time employees.

The HBB movement will give you a business community, a skill reservoir, and perhaps a social outlet, but your focus must always be the customer. When you are designing and developing your business, a customer orientation is vital. The focus of a business must be its customers, not its location. Location is strategic only if it contributes to customer service and the quality of your work. Home may be an ideal location if it enables you to serve your customers more effectively. For example, a home office may permit you to keep prices down because your overhead costs are low, to offer unusual service hours, or to maximize accessibility by serving those living in the immediate area.

Having a home-based business does not necessarily mean customers come to your home. Some of the business people listed above may do much of their work on the client's premises (for example, home contractors and management consultants). One retired administrative assistant who offers stenographic services for board meetings, has never had a client visit her home office—a spare room in her home. She enjoys getting out and going to clients' boardrooms as much as she enjoys being able to prepare the minutes from a meeting in the comfort of her own home, on her own schedule. In contrast, one weaver runs a combined studio and showroom from her ground-floor family room and welcomes visitors.

The following discussion explores the issues and concerns behind deciding to start an HBB and then designing the business itself. *This is not a guide to starting a business*: rather than examining the "how to" of home-based businesses, the section below looks at the more preliminary, "Why not?" aspects of whether to start a home-based business. If you are interested in finding out how to create your own HBB after reading this section, visit your public library, take a course at your local college or night school, and talk to as many people who are doing what you want to do as you can.

Is a Home-Based Business Right for Me?

When considering a business enterprise for your retirement years, examine the patterns of your life and design a business that enhances your lifestyle. Incubating your business idea by giving it hobby status first, or by building on a lifelong interest can be a productive, low-stress approach to designing your business. Or you may want to keep up the momentum of your pre-retirement business career and build a business that you can sell after a few years. The same options open to any budding home-based business person are open to you when you retire, or even before you retire. You could buy a business, operate a franchise, or telecommute for your former employer using your computer and a telephone connection to your old office. Before you decide which business road to take, or whether to take one at all, it may be wise to give yourself at least a few months, if not a year or so, of pure retirement. If starting a business has a "gotta keep busy" motivation, give retirement a chance first. Many people find their lives fuller and richer than expected after retirement.

If you loved your previous work, there are probably many ideas you could pursue. A note of caution, though: spend some time analyzing what you really enjoyed about the work. Was it the hands-on work itself, or managing a department? The adjustment from executive to home-based entrepreneur can be difficult for some people. Consulting may appear to be a viable alternative, but this still involves a big adjustment to being "on the outside."

Your personal values and goals must be the foundation of your business design, to ensure that you enjoy personal satisfaction as well as monetary gain. How you thought of success before retirement may no longer apply. Some will expect the HBB to generate a certain income, but not at the expense of golf games or summers at the lake. Some entrepreneurs want a continuation of prestige and recognition. Others would like to earn the same amount each year, but with less and less time required to bring in the dollars. Still others wish to see the community benefit from their efforts, while they supplement their income at the same time. How will *you* define success for your retirement venture?

If you decide a home-based business is right for you, make sure it centres on something you can do even on days you do not feel like working. Connecting your personal interests to income-generating activities ensures your enthusiasm will be reinforced, even on the bad days. For example, if you value your winter trip south or your summers at the cottage, you might select a "portable" business that you run from anywhere, based on such activities as photography, knitting, painting, inventing, jingle writing, or jewellery design. Of course, with a lap-top computer and a modem, your office is open whenever you are near a telephone. Marketing campaigns, strategic plans, course proposals, or financial plans can be produced from any location. If you prefer a more low-key business venture and are off to Florida in the winter, perhaps you can collect shells to use in the crafts you create to sell during your summers at the cottage. Or, if you summer at the cottage, you might do carpentry work or repairs for neighbours, or offer property management services to absentee cottagers.

The cooperation and support of your family are essential to the success of an HBB. "Family" may consist of your spouse, your children, and/or your close friends. Resist the urge to commandeer a room for your office. Let family members have a say in how the business is to operate in their home. Keep them up to date on your progress and involve them whenever possible. The business will inevitably become a nuisance at some point. It may prevent you or the family from doing something. Or it may require everyone to pitch in and help you finish a project on time. Build goodwill until that day by keeping the business from cluttering up the house and by letting everyone know they are an important part of your success. Say "thank you" and treat the family to an outing "on the business" once in a while.

If you live alone, your greatest challenge may be to find a way to stop the business from taking over your home and your life.

For example, a fashion designer, who worked long hours, used a spare room as a workroom. However, she found the room drab and felt cooped up in it. She also liked to have the television on for company while she worked in the evening. But it was in the living room, so enjoying it meant relocating. Before she knew it, her business had spread all over her living room. Eventually she got tired of putting things away every night. She began to feel overwhelmed by the business. The solution proved to be very simple: painting the workroom, adding better lighting, and buying a small television put the business back where it belonged. The moral? Make your work area a pleasant place to spend your time during your business hours.

Effective time management is vital to your mental and physical health. When you design a business to retire into, the scarce resource is *time*. What hours would you like to work? Will your business be full-time or part-time? Will it operate all year round, seasonally, or target a particular time of year, like tax time or Christmas? Consider this carefully. Once you get your business rolling, it could "take over" your retirement. At an earlier stage of life, rapid business growth is wonderful. In retirement, this is not necessarily the case.

Also, consider these factors when designing a home-based business:

- **Type**: The types of businesses to choose from are endless— some of the best businesses for next year don't even exist yet! As new technologies are developed, new business opportunities will appear, while others disappear. You can do anything from freelance writing and newsletter production, to interior design, home crafts, market research, or importing. Take your time and find the right niche for you, so that you can avoid getting stuck in a rut.

- **Style**: Your home-based business should have your personal stamp on it. How will you express your individual style?

- **Communication**: Even if you have the best products or services, your business will not succeed if no one knows that you exist or how to find you. How are you going to communicate with your customers? What will be your marketing strategy?

- ⌂ **Customers**: Who are your potential customer or clients? Do they know you already? Do you plan to deal with one, a few, or many clients? Will your client base be a large one with little repeat business but a lot of referrals? Your marketing and advertising will hinge on how you design your customer base. One HBB focuses on grandparents with grandchildren under the age of two, while another services customers who are avid golfers. They use very different approaches to reach their clients, that is, two very different marketing plans. The first entrepreneur reaches clients by attending craft shows frequented by older consumers, while the other HBB is a financial planning company operated by an avid golfer who does his best marketing on the golf course.

- ⌂ **Support**: Will you wear all the "hats" in your business: office manager, accountant, salesperson, receptionist, word processor, mail clerk, and so on? How will you handle the jobs you do not like doing? For example, every business needs at least one salesperson to sell products or services. You can either do the sales yourself, hire a salesperson, or contract out your sales requirements. A lack of sales experience does not mean you cannot or will not enjoy selling. However, if you decide that sales is not for you, research alternatives very carefully.

- ⌂ **Inspiration**: Working alone can be difficult, especially if you are used to a noisy, interactive workplace. Treat yourself to "outings" for social and mental stimulation. Join an HBB association. If you work with your hands, you can organize an idea-exchange network, or arrange group buying trips for supplies. Use your ingenuity to find ways to satisfy your need for contact, sounding boards, or distraction.

Launching a home-based business does not necessarily require huge cash outlays or drastic renovations. But when you start out, try to keep your costs down. Getting carried away has crippled more than a few HBB with unwieldy debt. Remember, your goal is to keep more than you spend. If you have unlimited funds for electronic gizmos, that's great. However, most home-based businesses are on a tight budget. For example, do you really *need* a fax machine? If most of your client contact is by fax, or if you work after normal business hours, having your own machine is probably essential. Otherwise, use the fax machine at a nearby copy shop or corner store. Keep track of what you spend on faxes so you will know if buying your own fax machine would be more cost-effective. However, consider whether owning a fax machine would make operating your business easier, as it would save you from having to go out for faxes. Convenience has value too.

To reap the benefits and not the whirlwind of self-employment, consider the following guidelines when designing your business venture:

- **Thriving Not Surviving**. Planning and research should keep you from getting in over your head. Maintaining a balance between your work and your life is essential. Books, seminars, video tapes, and courses on self-employment and HBB abound. Take advantage of free government literature and the resources in your public library.

- **Setting It Right With the Government**. Find out exactly what registration and licences are required for your type of business. Your provincial government's business registration office can give you the information you need. Most of the businesses mentioned in this article would probably not require a special licence.

- **Design Taxes In**. Talk to an accountant *before* you get your business rolling. Unless you have an accounting background, balancing the business income and expenses against your current tax situation requires professional skills. Decisions regarding incorporation or other methods of protecting your family's assets, including the home, from loss or law suit should be made with professional input. Be careful not to unknowingly jeopardize your eligibility for public support and tax benefit programs. Setting limits on your business income could generate a net benefit to you. Also make sure your insurance policy covers the business.

- **Experience Speaks**. Talking to people who are doing what you would like to do can often give you valuable insight. Ask them what they might do differently, given the benefit of hindsight. What pitfalls should you avoid? How might running a home-based business affect your life? One person who had the lifelong dream of owning a retail store, but no practical experience, got a job as a sales clerk during the Christmas rush to "try it out." Sitting in the store, surrounded by inventory proved too much for her: all she could think of was the debt the inventory represented, and this was too stressful. She abandoned that idea and happily went on to develop another business project.

⌂ **Be a Good Neighbour**. Keep in mind that many municipal zoning bylaws do not allow businesses in most residential areas. However, many municipalities cast a blind eye on HBBs in their area, provided there are no complaints from neighbours.

Apply the KISS principle, Keep It Simple, Sweetheart, to most aspects of your business. Picture yourself using a certain procedure when you are in a hurry, not when you have all the time in the world. Anticipation is the best form of troubleshooting. For example, how are you going to ensure that your customers pay you on time? Collecting bad accounts is time-consuming and can be frustrating. One entrepreneur relies on a prepayment scheme for his photograph-enlarging business; another uses a COD approach to keep things simple in his printing business, and a third has clients pay in instalments, so that when the project is finished the account is paid in full. Make it advantageous for the customer to pay in advance or upon delivery. Perhaps you could offer extremely fast delivery, a discount, or extra service for prepaid accounts. If you need help designing your services or products, ask your customers and potential customers to tell you what they want.

The unique challenge in designing a retirement business lies in incorporating the possibility (not the inevitability) of physical limitations. Many retirees remain active well into their 80s and 90s, even when some physical disabilities develop. Their stories have become too numerous to be "extraordinary." Check your local newspaper or a national television program for examples.

Yet, you must consider the possibility of physical limitations, because the business represents income that you may now depend on. How will your business continue, should your mobility, or any other aspect of your life, gradually or suddenly be affected? The same considerations discussed in Chapter 4's "Decisions, Decisions, Decisions," on page 79, apply here as well.

One thing is true for many people as they age: they find so many other interests in life that, ideally, they would like to spend less time generating income. In terms of a business design, this implies a business that requires decreasing amounts of your time "down the road." For some older homeowners, this could also become a physical necessity. If you picture yourself thinking along these lines in a few years, do some long-range planning now. The business design should incorporate your intentions from the beginning. For example, will you build a business for your grand-children to take over, so they can put themselves through school? Will you create a business to franchise or to sell? Will you take in partners, perhaps even family, to carry the bulk of the load one day? Will you work hard to develop your reputation as an expert, a specialist, or an artisan so that you can charge "big bucks" for your time, eventually? Will you create a business that gives you the money you need now, but that can also gradually be transformed into a community service organization or an institute of learning? Use your imagination to flesh out these ideas and, perhaps in doing so, find your own niche.

Spotlight on the Mature Market

One final idea: home-based businesses with their natural community connections may have particular success in offering services that support and enrich the lives of older residents. The age in place movement has already given rise to new financial options, such as reverse mortgages, as well as new safety products, for example, personal alarms. The demand for products and services that promote and preserve personal independence will grow as the population ages. One of the basic tenets of business is "Know your market." If your target is the very market that you belong to, you may have some distinct advantages.

CHAPTER 12

More Than Money

A re you often overwhelmed by the physical responsibility of maintaining your home? Is the beauty of the change of seasons overshadowed by the worry of getting the extra gardening and maintenance work done? Are you fighting a feeling of uselessness? Do you lack something on which to focus your energy? Do you feel trapped in your home, isolated from the world, especially in the winter months? Would a few extra dollars each month make a difference?

The options presented in this chapter provide suggestions for answering these questions. The ideas explored in the first section of this chapter, "Life as a Landlord," fit the following formula:

100 percent ownership + income + companionship

They may also be viable alternatives to hiring home maintenance and gardening services, housekeeping assistance, or even personal care providers. As explained in "Joint Ownership," on page 277, the formula would be altered slightly for this alternative, as a portion of the ownership is cashed in for a lump sum for regular payments through a traditional mortgage.

MONEY is not the only retirement benefit to be derived from your home. Companionship and a sense of purpose may hold an equal or greater value for many older homeowners.

In Chapter 8, page 200, joint ownership with a nonresident co-owner was examined as a method of maintaining the homeowner's privacy and full control of the home, while liberating a portion of the equity. The joint ownership arrangements discussed in this chapter focus on live-in co-owners, a relationship that also reduces isolation and one's share of home maintenance responsibilities. *For background on decision making see Chapter 4; Chapter 7 will be helpful in selecting advisers.*

LIFE AS A LANDLORD

Regardless of your reasons for considering the landlord option, the rental variations possible for your property are limited by a number of factors: local zoning bylaws that regulate property use, the number of renters available, the rents you can charge, the physical layout of your home, and the degree to which renovations are necessary. One of the most significant factors in assessing the feasibility of becoming a landlord is the cost effectiveness of renting. In other words, after subtracting the costs of renting from the rental income, will you make any money? Be conservative with your estimates. For instance, base your income projections on 10 or 11 months of rent instead of 12. Having the unit unrented for a month or even two, or being unable to collect a month's rent should not be enough to financially collapse your project.

In evaluating whether to become a landlord, give credit to any other worthwhile benefits provided by tenants or boarders at no charge, that could improve the quality of your life, remove an expense, enhance your independence, or provide you with a sense of purpose. For example, the tenant or boarder may provide gardening or home maintenance services or help with the shopping at no charge. Also, having someone in the house with you may give you a greater sense of security and reduce feelings of isolation. Some howeowners may consider a break-even financial situation acceptable as they place the greatest value on nonmonetary benefits. Others may feel that the companionship and services they receive from a tenant or boarder far outweigh financial considerations. (In fact this approach may be more economical than hiring service providers.) The ideas presented in the section in Chapter 11 called "Is a Home-Based Business Right for Me?" page 259), also apply here, as renting out your home is a type of home-based business.

You may not be able to generate rents large enough to cover your costs or create the amount of profit you feel would make your venture worthwhile for any of the following reasons: rents are regulated by law in your province or the rental market for your type of rental unit is saturated; opportunities are limited by the small number of potential tenants, or demand is low for rentals of that type.

Accessory Apartments

An accessory apartment is a private, self-contained residential unit, built within an existing house. The apartment contains a bathroom, kitchen facilities, living/dining area, and sleeping quarters. Usually a one-room or a one-bedroom apartment, the unit has a private entrance which is either inside the house or leads directly to the outside. Basements, attics, and one or two floors of a house are all common sites for accessory apartments. Unless an apartment is being built for a family member, so that cost effectiveness is not an issue, building an addition to a house is usually not financially feasible. Another exception could the creation of an accessory apartment, perhaps a wheel-chair-accessible unit, *for* the homeowner and the renting out of the rest of the house.

A homeowner can decide to take on long-term or short-term tenants. There are advantages and disadvantages with each decision. For instance, short-term rentals can carry greater maintenance costs, because repainting and cleaning must be done more frequently. However, short-term rental rates are often higher. Long-term rentals can be advantageous if you are away from the house for the summer, but can be a liability for the same reason, depending on your relationship with the tenant.

Accessory apartments allow older homeowners to remain independent while eliminating the stresses of isolation. With a tenant close by, the homeowner can enjoy greater safety and security, while preserving privacy. An accessory apartment also enables an older homeowner to stay in a well-loved house, that has become too costly or carries too much responsibility for one person. The rental benefits may include additional income, decreased costs, emergency support, and perhaps maintenance or personal services received in lieu of rent, as well as the personal satisfaction of running a business venture.

Boarders

Building an accessory apartment is not always practical or desirable. In some cases, the rental income may be needed for only a short period of time, for instance, to pay off a new furnace. Furthermore, companionship may be as important, or even more important, than the rental income. If it is, you may want to consider boarders.

A boarder may have a separate bedroom and no eat-in privileges in the home; a separate bedroom plus meals; a bedroom and bathroom with limited private kitchen facilities; bedsitting-room and a microwave oven; or a two-room suite with its own kitchen; or any arrangement that suits you and the layout of your home. Unlike arrangements with tenants, a boarder shares either the kitchen and/or a bathroom with the homeowner and/or perhaps another boarder. The boarder may also have general or limited access to other areas of the house, for example, the laundry room, family room, workshop, or garden. Obviously, if you decide to take in a boarder or boarders, you must decide beforehand what degree and extent of access they will enjoy.

Language schools that offer live-in immersion opportunities for students interested in learning English or French may be a good source of short-term boarders. These students often want to participate in the everyday activities of a Canadian home and so can offer the older homeowner companionship. These schools may be able to provide you with student boarders for a few months to supplement your income or to pay for your annual holiday. Teaching hospitals, colleges, and universities may also be a good source of boarders. If the boarder proves to be incompatible, the institution may be able to help you resolve the problems or find a replacement.

References are important in any rental situation, but especially so when the renter will have access to your private living quarters. Protect yourself against theft by being sensible with your valuables. The local police department can give you a few safety hints. However, if you are nervous at the idea of having strangers in your home, perhaps you should forget this idea.

Homesharing

Homesharing is based on the concept that the owner and the housemate are not merely sharing a house but a home. This arrangement goes beyond just taking in a boarder. Counsellors who work for the nonprofit organizations that run this type of program match up those who have space with those who are looking for housing. Individuals are matched on the basis of compatible lifestyles, preferences, needs, likes, dislikes, and hobbies. Each person has a private room, however, they share the rest of the home, including the kitchen, bathroom, and garden. This arrangement is also available to apartment dwellers who find the benefits of homesharing appealing. Contact the local community information centre, seniors' information service, or provincial housing department to find out if a program is operating in your area.

After a match has been made, the homeshare counsellors follow up, offer advice, and mediate any disagreements until both parties have settled into the relationship. Homesharing is more than a landlord-boarder relationship. Companionship, security, and the pleasure of sharing your days are the real bonuses of this arrangment. In exchange for having someone to share day-to-day acitivities, the homeowner charges a reasonable rent. If the housemate takes on cooking, shopping, cleaning, and/or gardening, the rent is probably reduced. The arrangement may even involve bartering for personal care services, with minimal or no rent changing hands. As with all rental arrangements, clear communication, both verbal and written, is important. A commitment from both parties to work out any misunderstandings is essential.

A counsellor can help you determine whether homesharing might suit you. If the idea of sharing space with strangers is unappealing to you, perhaps sharing with a family member or a friend would be preferrable. For instance, a grandchild looking for reasonable accommodation while starting out in life may be interested in a homesharing arrangement that suits both of you.

Rental Variations

Once more, put your imagination to work. Do you have space you are not using or that has become a liability? For example, your liability—the garden—may be an asset to someone else. Why couldn't a house-bound homeowner, perhaps, rent out the garden to a neighbour in a near-by highrise building? The homeowner would find the view from the window a wonderful tonic; the neighbour would have an audience for the garden's glory. In the winter, they could gain a great deal of pleasure pouring over seed catalogues and redesigning the flower beds. The rent could be paid in fresh vegetables and cut flowers. In fact, a small business could evolve from this relationship. They may be able to make a few dollars, at least to cover the cost of gardening supplies, by selling some of the produce, plants, or flowers. Or, they could run a plant clinic in the neighbourhood, passing on their gardening expertise to the less well informed. The homeowner could handle the research, administration, and promotion; and the neighbour would carry out the hands-on aspects of the business. This could happen, not in every home or neighbourhood, but for someone. **All it takes is imagination. Remember, the impossible merely takes a little longer, that's all.**

Here are a few more rental ideas:

- ♠ Rent out a room or two for a few months to save some money for a great trip or a new roof.

- ♠ House swapping for a few weeks or months can give you an inexpensive holiday in another province or country.

- ♠ Short-term rental of your furnished home may be an alternative while you are at the cottage or away during the winter.

- ♠ Don't restrict your rental plans to your peer group; inter-generational relationships can work really well, too. Explore the potential for a rental relationship with someone who is your junior. Intra-family arrangements might be feasible, particularly if money is not the main focus. However, discuss how you can avoid conflicts and what you might do to resolve differences of opinion should they arise, in order to protect the relationship.

The Garage

Renting out your garage may not make you rich, but it will bring in a few extra dollars. If you garage is old, the rental proceeds may help pay for repairs. Since garages usually add to property value, these repairs could make an important contribution when it's time to sell the property. If your home is in a highrise condominium, you may be able to rent out your underground parking space. Check your bylaws to be sure.

Obviously, demand will have a major impact on the rent you can get. Check local newspapers and bulletin boards for an overview of the going rents. The larger and dryer the garage, the more rent you may be able to charge. Power and water outlets in the garage may add to the rental, since the garage may be rented by someone who wants to use it as a workshop.

Payment in advance may be a good idea, at least first and last month's rent if not the full winter rental. Also, for insurance reasons, find out exactly how the tenant intends to use the space and what will be stored in the garage. Your insurance agent can give you a few ideas on potential insurance premium increases, so you can build this charge into the rent beforehand.

Is Life as a Landlord Right for Me?

The role of landlord does not suit everyone. Having a tenant living in your home can be the most difficult type of landlord arrangement because there is no escape if problems arise. However, renting or sharing your home can also be a pleasant and rewarding experience if you are well prepared and make everything clear to the tenant/boarder from the beginning.

Other issues need to be resolved in making the decision to become a landlord, including:

- ♠ **Control**: As the homeowner, you have made the decisions concerning your property. Nothing can be changed or added without your permission. No one may enter the property without an invitation from you. Should you decide to share your home with a tenant, boarder, or housemate, your control of the property will be modified somewhat, depending on the terms of your arrangement. You will have to relinquish some control over at least a section of the property to the person with whom you are sharing your home. Before arranging to rent or share your home, carefully review the dos and don'ts you would like the other person to respect. Are you being reasonable? fair? realistic? or too permissive?

♠ **Tolerance**: A very important influence on your decision to become a landlord is your level of tolerance. Sharing your house with a tenant who lives in a self-contained apartment is not as great a personal adjustment as sharing your home with a housemate who has the run of the property. However, in both cases, your patience will be tested. Flexibility, a sense of humour, and resilience are essential characteristics for anyone tackling a rental project.

♠ **Possession**: Since you own your home, you hold the right of possession, that is, the right to occupy and use the premises. When you decide to share your home with a tenant, boarder, or housemate, you will relinquish your exclusive right of possession to certain sections of the house and grounds, or to the entire property, depending on the specifics of your written agreement. Talk to a lawyer, accountant, or property manager with rental experience before you enter into a sharing arrangement. You may need help developing the written tenancy agreement or lease. Be absolutely sure you understand your rights and responsibilities under the agreement and provincial laws. Do you know exactly what your rights are should you wish to cancel the arrangement? You may have to take legal action to regain possession, should you wish to terminate the arrangement.

♠ **Privacy**: For many people, privacy is a valued benefit of home ownership. Privacy means different things to different people. To some, it guarantees a degree of seclusion. To others, it means being able to close a door whenever you wish. To yet others, privacy means not having to talk to anyone until after the first morning coffee, or the freedom to walk around without your teeth in. When you are deciding whether to share your home with a tenant, boarder, or housemate, ask yourself precisely what degree of privacy is essential to you, and whether this degree can be preserved within the new living arrangement.

♠ **Stress**: Changes in living arrangements are bound to cause stress, but, not all stress is bad. The rental income and the companionship that result from sharing your home may balance or outweigh any emotional, mental, or physical strain you experience in adjusting to the change. If you accept the fact that there will be some stress, the issue then becomes how to cope with it. If the tenant/boarder repeatedly leaves a bike or car in what you consider the wrong place, how will you react? If you hear hammering from the apartment, what will you do? If you notice that the boarder forgets to turn down the heat when going out, how will you handle it?

You *know* how things are to be done, since this is your house and it has been for many years. However, your way is not the only way. Are you ready to give the tenant/boarder time to get used to your methods? Can you accept the fact that you may have to compromise, and perhaps occasionally, change your habits? Renting or sharing your home is definitely a "live and learn" experience. Are you ready for it?

♠ **Running a business: However you decide to earn rental income from your home, treat the exercise like a business.** Keep all receipts and records during the set-up process, because these expenses are tax deductible. Do your homework. Talk to landlords, lawyers, and tenants, and contact the provincial ministry of housing. Review your financial situation with your accountant, who will also help you set up your rental business. Local community information and legal programs such as Dial-a-Law may also be helpful. Once again, the public library and local seniors' groups are good sources of information. Chapter 11, page 259, provides more background on home-based businesses.

♠ **Zoning bylaws**: Government and community support is growing for programs that allow seniors to remain independent in their homes and communities, rather than entering institutions. However, zoning bylaws are still a major barrier. Homeowners interested in building accessory apartments may find their plans altered, delayed, or aborted by municipal zoning bylaws. Even those who wish to take in boarders may have to change their plans if zoning bylaws limit the number of unrelated people who can live in one dwelling.

Zoning bylaws vary from street to street, and even from house to house, so check carefully to see whether you will be allowed to carry out your rental plans. Zoning bylaws are municipal codes that define uses of land in intricate detail. They set minimum frontages for residences and parking requirements. Many municipalities cast a blind eye to apartments that violate zoning bylaws, provided neighbours do not complain. Check with your local elected representative to gauge the rental "climate" in your area.

If you decide to build an accessory apartment, the municipal building department will help you understand the significance of local zoning bylaws, building code requirements, health and fire regulations, and building permit procedures. The building department can explain the steps involved in creating your accessory apartment and help you get information on your legal rights and responsibilities under provincial laws. They can also link you with any provincial or federal programs designed to assist you with renovations.

♠ **Support network**: Instead of the older homeowner taking on all the responsibilities of a landlord, a family member or friend could share the workload or function as a property manager. This would free the homeowner from some of the stressful aspects of the tenant/landlord relationship. The homeowner's legal or financial adviser, or a professional property manager may also be available to back up the homeowner or handle rent collection and disputes.

Provincial laws regulate rental and tenancy agreements; thus, procedures and legalities vary from province to province. In general, you will need information or people to help you do the following:

♠ locate government programs to assist you with renovations.

♠ draw up your written tenancy agreement;

♠ find a suitable tenant, boarder, or housemate;

♠ locate troubleshooting support should problems arise with the property or the tenant/boarder;

- ♠ learn how to collect the rent and deal with nonpayment;

- ♠ understand the legal grounds for eviction;

- ♠ explain your rights if the tenant is noisy or destructive; and

- ♠ evaluate the tax implications of the rental income (see Chapter 10, page 232.

Two Notes of Caution

If you live in a condominium, check the bylaws first, to see whether rental of your unit or parking space is permitted. Also, if you have a reverse mortgage, reread the terms of your contract to see whether you are allowed to rent out all or part of your home without violating the reverse mortgage contract.

JOINT OWNERSHIP

Joint or concurrent ownership is ownership in which two or more unrelated people own a property at the same time. Joint ownership can be achieved in two ways: an owner could sell an interest in the property to another person or persons; or, two or more individuals could buy a property together and take ownership at the same time. In this way, joint ownership may be a "Selling and staying" option or a "Selling and moving" option, respectively. In Chapter 8, page 200, joint ownership with a nonresident co-owner, the investor, was examined. Here, joint ownership with a live-in co-owner will be explored. To avoid repetition, the bulk of the discussion on joint ownership is contained on the following pages. However, the points made here are also relevant to joint ownership with a nonresident co-owner.

Selling an interest in your home to someone other than a family member, or buying a house with unrelated people, can be a housing alternative that offers a very supportive atmosphere. This ownership option is ideal for individuals who have the resources to live comfortably alone but prefer to share their lives, or for those who must pool their finances to acquire or maintain their preferred type of accommodation. Any of the benefits of sharing—reduced maintenance responsibilities, security, increased standard of living, preservation of independence, and enjoyable companionship—can be the driving force behind creation of this relationship.

Joint ownership could involve any number of co-owners. In selecting a co-owner you think might be compatible, a few questions should be answered: What are the long- and short-term goals and objectives of each co-owner and their combined objectives? Are the individual and combined objectives and goals compatible? Is joint ownership the best way to achieve the objectives and goals for both or all parties? Will one type of joint ownership be more suitable than the other, if there is a choice?

Once again, variations on the basic concept of joint ownership are almost endless since the property, owners, uses, and relationships differ in each case. There are, however, two legal types of joint ownership: tenancy in common and joint tenancy.

The chart on page 279, " Joint Ownership at a Glance," summarizes the differences between the two types of joint ownership. However, examining the differences requires an understanding of the similarities. Both types of joint ownership have the following important concepts in common:

♠ *Undivided interest:* **Everyone owns everything**, that is, no one owner can point to a corner of the garden or a room in the house and say, "That is mine, not yours." Even if a clear division such as a fence exists between farm fields, or if the house is divided into separate apartments, everyone still owns everything. The only way to create a concept of "my half" and "your half" is to have a users' agreement drawn up and signed.

♠ *Limitation of relationship:* When individuals are joint owners of a property, their personal estates do not merge. They only hold one asset—the property—together. They are considered separate people in other respects unless they are married or living common-law. Being tenants in common does not mean you are living common-law. The legal concepts are completely different. (Married and common-law couples may have ownership rights and options under provincial family laws.)

♠ *Choice:* When you are buying a new property with another person, you will be able to choose between the two types of joint ownership. However, joint tenancy requires that all owners take ownership at the same time from the same person in the same document. Therefore, if you were selling an interest in your current home, ownership would have to be taken as tenants in common.

Each type of joint ownership has different characteristics. The chart below summarizes these differences. The following discussion highlights the key difference between the two types of joint ownership—the right of survivorship.

JOINT OWNERSHIP AT A GLANCE		
	Tenancy in Common	**Joint Tenancy**
When must owners take ownership?	• may buy at different times or at the same time	• *must* buy at the same time
Who must each owner take ownership from?	• different sellers or the same seller	• same seller only
What is the size of share held by each owner?	• may or may not be equal shares	• *must* be equal shares
What happens to the property on the death(s) of each owner?	• each owner can name own heir(s); • owner's share of the property always becomes part of the deceased's estate	• cannot name heir(s)—even if heir named in will, not binding; • share of ownership is automatically transferred to the surviving owner(s) on the death of one owner (this is called *right of survivorship*).

Joint Tenancy and the Right of Survivorship

The rights of home ownership can include the right to leave your property as part of your estate, that is, to bequeath your home in your will to whomever you wish. Tenancy in common provides this right of ownership for each co-owner. Further, each owner will probably leave their interest in the property to a different person.

Under joint tenancy, co-owners have given up the right of ownership discussed above—the right to leave the property as part of the estate. On the death of one of the owners, that interest in the property automatically passes to the surviving owner or is divided equally among the surviving co-owners. This right of the surviving co-owners is referred to as the "right of survivorship." A will bequeathing the interest to someone other than one of the joint tenancy owners would have no meaning, as the property did not become part of the deceased co-owner's estate. Technically, at the moment of death, ownership passes to the other joint tenancy owner(s). Each owner's interest automatically goes to the surviving co-owners. The last surviving owner, who will be sole owner of the property, will be able to leave the property in an estate and specify an heir or heirs. Should the relationship between the joint tenants change, ownership could be changed to tenancy in common— a change that would end the right of survivorship.

Joint tenants give up an important ownership right. To prevent an unsophisticated homeowner from being taken advantage of, joint tenancy can only be created under very specific circumstances; the following four *unities* or conditions must exist simultaneously:

1. all the owners have equal interest;

2. all gain simultaneous possession;

3. all take ownership from the same person in the same document; and

4. all take title at the same time.

Choosing Joint Tenancy

Even if you have family living, you may feel closer to nonrelations who have become your "family." In fact, extended family is becoming an appealing alternative to the traditional family: living à la *Golden Girls* can be wonderful. If you are drawn to this kind of arrangement, buying the property with joint tenancy in mind will seem quite natural. Couples also often use this method, as the transfer of ownership is automatic and there are no taxes to pay. There is also no delay caused by having to wait for probate should the survivor wish to sell the property. However, if you invest with individuals who are not related to you, you would probably prefer to leave your interest in your estate, unless your investment contribution was meant to include agreement to joint tenancy.

The following variations illustrate what will happen with the sale of one co-owner's share. (Note that usually, but not always, the other owner(s) have the first option to buy the co-owner's share.) If an owner, Bill, sold his share in a property, that interest must be held in tenancy in common by the new owner, Susan. If originally there were two joint tenants, Bill and Lee, then joint tenancy would be ended, and Lee and Susan would be tenants in common. However, if there were four joint tenants originally, the new owner, Susan, would hold ownership as a tenant in common for one-quarter of the property. The remaining three owners would still hold three-quarters of the property in a joint tenancy relationship between themselves. If one of the joint tenants died, the remaining two would then divide the deceased owner's share equally between the two of them; Susan would not receive anything. If Susan died, her share would be part of her estate.

Defining the Joint Ownership Arrangement

Joint ownership, whether tenancy in common or joint tenancy, combines the complexities of law and of relationships, so care must be taken to avoid further complications that might result from confusion. Compatibility is vital. You may even decided to experiment by first renting or taking a long holiday together.

If you sell an interest in your property to someone, you will become tenants in common with the new owner(s). Each owner will have the right to do what they wish with their interest—sell it, mortgage it, or give it away. One owner cannot speak for the other owners without their consent. The same would also be true if you bough a property together, regardless of the type of ownership involved.

With each owner acting independently, chaos may result. Therefore, defining the joint ownership relationship is essential. To preserve the relationship and your sanity, create a detailed joint ownership agreement that will legally define your relationship now and in the future. The details of the agreement should be worked out before the Agreement of Purchase and Sale is signed. To protect individual interests, each owner should have a legal adviser, a lawyer who has recent practical experience with residential joint ownership arrangements.

Everything from death to disputes should be covered in the joint ownership agreement. Daily, seasonal, and annual responsibilities must be described in detail as well. The following topics should be dealt with in the agreement, whether you sell a share in your home or buy a new one with at least one other person:

- ♠ a clear description of the required contribution, financial and otherwise, of each party to the agreement (the homeowner may sell any percentage of the property, such as 30 percent or 60 percent; buying together, the owners may have equal shares or any split they agree on, depending on the contribution each makes to the purchase and maintenance of the property);

- ♠ a system for the daily and annual management and main-tenance of the property (which should include a description of the method for each co-owner to pay their share, for example, in proportion to their degree of ownership, that is, with a 30 percent share an owner would pay 30 percent of the expenses, or each owner would make lump sum payments, splitting each bill or contributing time or expertise);

- ♠ detailed descriptions of each owner's responsibilities;

- ♠ a system of decision making and dispute resolution that would dictate how everything from disagreements over which lawn care service to use to arguments that require mediation such as those concerning the arrangement itself are to be handled;

- ♠ an accounting system that outlines who keeps the books for the property, who signs the cheques, how large purchases are to be made, and whether an emergency fund is to be developed;

- ♠ a detailed explanation, with plans and/or diagrams if neces-sary, describing the areas of exclusive and shared use for each owner;

- ♠ policies on rentals, visitors, redecorating, landscaping, park-ing, marriage of owners, and absences from the property;

- ♠ arrangements for termination of the arrangement under a variety of situations, including provisions for handling profits or losses, and prolonged illnesses or incapacity of one owner (answers to such questions as, for example, will there be a penalty for leaving within a certain period of time? How would the arrangement be dissolved if if terminated?).

Buying Together

If you and your partners buy a property together with the intention of becoming joint tenants, making sure your commitments and expectations are clear and in tune before the property is purchased is vital. Check with an experienced real estate lawyer first to find out the ins and outs of joint tenancy in your province. You should also draw up a rough legal agreement, like the one outlined on page 282, that will also give each owner clear rights to a specific portion of the property, for example, one apartment or a floor of the house.

Once you are committed to each other and to the project, begin the search for the perfect property. Do all the deciding and planning before you start looking at properties or you may get swept away in a buying frenzy and regret it later. You might consider finding a real estate professional who is a buyer's agent (see Chapter 11, page 249). You may not have to pay a fee for this assistance if the buyer's agent is paid by the seller through the Multiple Listing Service. Remember to ask for written confirmation of the real estate professional's responsibilities to you and of any fees involved. Asking for references is a very good practice.

Allow time for the search for an ideal property. Give the real estate person a written outline of what you want so you will only see properties that suit your plans. Be prepared, however, for the possibility that, if your real estate representative is effective and luck is with you, the first property you see may be the right one.

Zoning Bylaws

The zoning of the property is an important consideration as municipalities have occupancy codes that may limit the number of unrelated indivduals who can live together. Get the answer from city hall so you know where to look or how feasible a zoning bylaw change would be. If you are buying a new property, your real estate representative will be able to clarify zoning concerns for you.

A Final Word

From one squeaky wheel to another: If we want choice and change in any aspect of our lives, we must speak up and speak out—be a squeaky wheel. If we want choice and change in housing, we must speak up and speak out about home equity conversion and other innovations, as loudly and a often as possible— alone and in groups. "If it is to be, it's up to me" should be the squeaky-wheel slogan for change.

To be successful in this campaign, we must overcome ageism and make people understand that age is not a disease. I sadly acknowlege the tendency of individuals and society to lump everyone over fifty into one homogenized group. Do they believe that people, on their 50th birthday, are suddenly transformed through an "Invasion of the Body Snatchers"-like plot into a homogeneous, monolithic group—seniors? In fact, this group is many groups—a mosaic of differences. No two 55-year olds or 85-year olds are any more alike than any two 25-year olds. For this reason, a one-size-fits-all approach to housing or life will not work.

Technology is allowing society to shift from a mass mentality— mass production, mass marketing—to a customized approach— targeted production to service specific small groups. This evolv- ing environment is ideal for the customized-financing approach of home equity conversion. The evolution of new housing products and services should be a collaborative process with consumers having direct influence on design and delivery. Society must begin producing products, services, and programs that suit the individual, instead of forcing individuals to adapt to what is presented.

Have Your Home and Money Too was written to remain relevant and useful as new products appear and the government "gets into the act" since I believe that we are moving towards a strong national home equity conversion market. As The Catalyst, I will continue to advocate the development of a consumer-friendly marketplace. This will not be my final word. I will be gathering ideas as well as chronicling your experiences in order to provide you with a closer look at the next stage of this Canadian housing revolution—whatever and whenever that is.

In conducting countless seminars and workshops on home equity conversion, innovative housing options, and change itself, I have gathered many questions about these topics. I have also received hundreds of telephone calls and have had an even greater number of conversations with older homeowners, their friends, family members, professional advisers, and members of nonprofit groups. What these conversations have reinforced for me is the realization that there will always be new developments, new ideas, and new perspectives on home equity conversion, housing, and living with change. If, after reading this book, you have an unanswered question or a suggestion, please drop me a line. I want to hear from you: P.J. Wade, The Catalyst, P.O. Box 77, Toronto Dominion Centre, Toronto, Ontario M5K 1E7.

Appendix

RESOURCES:

Canada Mortgage and Housing Corporation (CMHC) Regional Offices:

Atlantic Regional Office
(civic and mailing address)
P.O. Box 7320
1 Brunswick Square
Suite 1410
Saint John, New Brunswick
E2L 4S7
Phone: (506) 636-4460
Fax: (506) 636-4607

Quebec Regional Office
(mailing address)
1010 de La Gauchetiere Street
West
Montreal, Quebec H3B 2N2

(civic address)
11th Floor
Place du Canada
Montreal, Quebec H3B 2N2
Phone: (514) 283-4464
Fax: (514) 283-7595

Ontario Regional Office
(civic and mailing address)
Atria North, Suite E222
2255 Sheppard Avenue East
Willowdale, Ontario M2J 4Y1
Phone: (416) 495-2000
Fax: (416) 495-2004

Prairie and Northwest Territories Regional Office
(civic and mailing address)
Suite 300
410–22nd Street East
Saskatoon, Saskatchewan
S7K 5T6
Phone: (306) 975-4900
Fax: (306) 975-5134

British Columbia and Yukon Regional Office
(civic and mailing address)
World Trade Centre
Suite 450
999 Canada Place
Vancouver, British Columbia
V6C 3E1
Phone: (604) 666-2516
Fax: (604) 666-3020

Provincial Credit Union Centrals

B.C. Central Credit Union:
604-734-2511
Credit Union Central of Alberta:
403-258-5900
Credit Union Central of
Saskatchewan: 306-566-1200
Credit Union Central of Manitoba:
204-942-6331
Credit Union Central of Ontario:
905-238-9400
Credit Union Central of New
Brunswick: 506-857-8184
Credit Union Central of Prince
Edward Island: 902-566-3350
Credit Union Central of Nova
Scotia: 902-453-0680
Credit Union Council of
Newfoundland (Non-Central):
709-753-2701

Provincial Property Tax Deferral Program

The Land Tax Deferment Program

Surveyor of Taxes
Ministry of Finance and Corporate
Relations
Box 2900
Victoria, British Columbia
V8W 3G4
(604) 387-0599

Tax Deferral Program for Senior Citizens

Department of Finance
Revenue Division
P.O. Box 880
Charlottetown, P.E.I.
C1A 7M2
(902) 368-4070

ADDITIONAL RESOURCES:

Consumers for Home Equity Conversion (CHEC)
P.O. Box 623,
Streetsville Post Office
Mississauga, Ontario L5M 2C1
*Ron and Marina Ringler,
Co-ordinators*

Public Interest Advocacy Centre
Suite 1204
1 Rue Nicholas
Ottawa, Ontario K1N 7B7
Phone: (613) 562-4002
Fax: (613) 562-0007

P.J. Wade
The Catalyst
P.O. Box 77
Toronto Dominion Centre
Toronto, Ontario M5K 1E7

Home Equity Information Centre
American Association of Retired
Persons
601 East Street NW
Washington, DC 20049

Reverse Mortgage Lenders

This information is provided with the understanding that it does not promote or endorse any of the products, individuals, companies, or organizations mentioned. Readers considering a reverse mortgage are urged to consult professional independent advisers. Contact the head office listed below for the office or agent nearest you. You may wish to ask for two or three referrals in order to locate the managers and sales staff you feel most comfortable working with.

Canadian Home Income Plan (CHIP) Corporation
Suite 2520
1660 West Hastings Street
Vancouver, British Columbia
V6E 3X1
Phone: (604) 737-2447;
Toll free 1-800-661-1190
Fax: (604) 685-2427
President: William Turner

Home Earnings Reverse Mortgage Corporation of Canada
(previously **Security Life Insurance Company Limited**)
Suite 401
216 Chrislea Road
Woodbridge, Ontario L4L 8S5
Phone: (905) 850-8717
Fax: (905) 850-8723
President: Bruce Hammond

Royal Trust offers a term reverse annuity mortgage product. Reaching the correct individual for information may prove to be a challenge. To locate the account manager or area lending manager who can arrange reverse mortgages in your area, contact the manager at your local branch.

Retirement Counsel of Canada
(private company)
Second Floor
19 Four Season's Place
Etobicoke, Ontario M9B 6E8
Phone: (416) 622-7262
Fax: (416) 662-2299.
President: Paul Tyers

Credit Unions

Credit Union Central of Ontario
2810 Matheson Blvd. East
Mississauga, Ontario L4W 4X7
Phone: (905) 238-9400
Fax: (905) 238-5008
Contact: Bob Bernstein,
Product Development Co-ordinator
Contact: Jonathan Barnes at Cataract Savings & Credit Union Limited in Niagara Falls, Ontario pioneered the program.
(905) 356-4467

Caisse populaire St.-René Goupil,
(514) 321-2610

Reverse mortgages can be arranged within the family or with a private investor. Lawyers, mortgage brokers or financial advisers may be of help in locating an investor. In all cases, seek informed independent legal, financial, and housing advice before you sign.

Glossary of Housing Terms

Also consult the Quick Question Index for Reverse Mortgages on pages 297–301.

ACCESSORY APARTMENT — a private self-contained residential unit built within an existing house (pages 269–70).

AGING IN PLACE — means staying in your home as you age rather than moving into an institution. Also called staying put. Could age in place as the owner of a home or a tenant in an apartment.

AGREEMENT FOR SALE — a contract between a seller who agrees to transfer ownership of the property at a later date, once certain terms and conditions of the agreement have been met by the buyer. The seller gradually receives money from the sale while the buyer lives in the property while paying for it (pages 254–56).

AGREEMENT OF PURCHASE AND SALE — a contract between a seller who agrees to transfer ownership of the property at a later date, and a buyer who in exchange agrees to provide payment in full on the same date (pages 251–52).

ANNUITY — a contract in which a purchaser gives an insurance company a lump sum of money in return for receiving regular payments for an agreed period of time extending into the future. These income-generating investment products, that often involve tax benefits, provide a guaranteed stream of income in monthly, quarterly, or annual payments; an income generating investment (page 45). Also see DEFERRED ANNUITY.

APPRAISAL — an unbiased professional estimate of a particular type of value, for example lending value or market value, for a specific property, that is based on analysis and interpretation by a professional appraiser.

APPRECIATION — increased value of a property.

BALANCE — the amount of principal in a mortgage still outstanding for repayment by a borrower.

BARTER — a commercial trade exchange that involves the exchange of products and services for products and services instead of cash (pages 228–29).

BROKER — see AGENT

BUYING DOWN — refers to the sale of a current property and the purchase of a smaller and/or less expensive property that may result in surplus cash from the proceeds of the sale (pages 249–50).

CAPITAL GAINS — a section of the Federal Income Tax Act that places a liability for taxation on the seller of property when a profit has been made, with some exemptions including the principal residence (page 231–35).

CLOSING DATE — the date agreed to in an agreement of purchase and sale or similar document on which the seller agrees to allow ownership to be transferred to the buyer and the buyer agrees to make full payment as described in the contract. Also called the completion date (page 245).

COMPOUND INTEREST — interest charged on interest (page 22).

CONDOMINIUM — a form of property ownership in which each owner owns a unit and a proportional share of the common elements or remaining property; also one unit in a condominium complex, which can take any form from a detached home or townhouse to a high-rise apartment or an industrial warehouse.

CONTRACT — a legally binding agreement (in real estate, written) between two or more parties, to do something or deliver something on mutually agreed terms and conditions.

CONVENTIONAL MORTGAGE — a traditional mortgage for less than 75 percent of the appraised value of a property.

COOLING-OFF PERIOD — a provision in a contract that, if the terms of the clause are met, allows the buyer to rescind or cancel the contract, usually after signing, without any penalties (page 81).

CO-OPERATIVE (CO-OP) — a variation on property ownership that involves the purchase of a share in a corporation that owns the apartment building or townhouse complex. The buyer is entitled to the right to occupy, but not own, one unit.

COVENANTS — legally binding promises or obligations written into agreements like mortgages which bind one party to a responsibility or action (page 17).

DEFAULT — breach of or failure to meet obligations in a mortgage contract, usually by failure to make repayment as agreed in the contract (page 22).

DEFERRED ANNUITY — an annuity in which the premium is paid in a lump sum, however, the income payments are delayed until a pre-arranged time in the future, for example at the end of the monthly payments from an investor in a sale leaseback agreement. If the beneficiary does not live until this date, the annuity is ended.

DISCHARGE OF A MORTGAGE — a release from the lender for the borrower on full repayment of the mortgage debt.

DUPLEX — a property legally zoned as a two-family dwelling.

EQUITY — is the homeowner's share of the accumulated value in the home; the monetary value of the home that belongs to the homeowner after mortgages and creditors' claims are deducted (pages 12–14).

EQUITY ADVANCE — the money released by a reverse mortgage as payments or a lump sum, that is not usually taxable income (page 36). (I coined the term *equity advance* to avoid confusing the money liberated by a reverse mortgage with taxable income — an important distinction as the home equity conversion market evolves.)

FAIR MARKET VALUE — see MARKET VALUE

FEE SIMPLE ESTATE — complete or absolute ownership of a property.

FIXED-TERM REVERSE MORTGAGE — a reverse mortgage that must be completely repaid if it can not be renewed at the end of the term, a period that is usually 5 or more years long.

FORECLOSURE — legal action taken by a mortgage lender as a remedy to default that involves an attempt by the lender to gain ownership of the property through the courts.

FORWARD MORTGAGES — see TRADITIONAL MORTGAGES

GROSS INCOME — personal income before income tax is deducted.

HIGH RATIO MORTGAGE — a mortgage for more than 75 percent of the appraised value of a property that requires mortgage insurance to cover the lender against borrower default (page 22–23).

HOME EQUITY CONVERSION — refers to methods a homeowner may use to release or to utilize the equity or accumulated value in the home while retaining ownership and possession. For example, reverse mortgages convert equity into cash, and property tax deferral plans use the equity as security in a pay-later approach (pages 7–9).

INTEREST — a charge paid to a lender by the borrower for the use of the money loaned to the borrower.

INTEREST DIFFERENTIAL — amount of interest equivalent to the mortgage lender's loss if the funds have to be re-invested and the current interest rate is lower than the current rate of the mortgage; also known as INTEREST RATE DIFFERENTIAL (page 140).

JOINT OWNERSHIP — two or more people, including a couple, owning a property together.

JOINT TENANCY — joint ownership with the RIGHT OF SURVIVORSHIP so that ownership is transferred automatically from owner to owner on the death of one owner.

LENDING VALUE — value estimated by an appraiser that represents the maximum amount of money that a lender would advance against a particular property (page 16–17).

LIFE ESTATE — a home equity conversion approach in which the seller remains owner of the property after it has been sold to an investor. The seller also has the legal right to reside in the property for life (pages 198–201).

LIFETIME REVERSE MORTGAGE — see TENURE-PLAN REVERSE MORTGAGE.

LINE OF CREDIT — also a type of reverse mortgage in which the homeowner has a credit account and can withdraw funds as required (pages 49–51).

MARKET VALUE — the worth of a property, or the amount of rent that can be collected, relative to a specific time or real estate market (page 17).

MORTGAGE — a contract between a lender or mortgagee and a borrower or mortgagor that represents the security given to the lender by the borrower in return for a loan. The definition varies slightly from province to province (page 15).

PREPAYMENT PRIVILEGES — an option in a mortgage contract that allows the borrower to repay a portion of the mortgage debt ahead of schedule according to the terms of the mortgage contract.

PRINCIPAL — amount of money advanced to the borrower (mortgagor) by the lender (mortgagee).

PROPERTY — personal property and real property (legal); in this book, equivalent to "home" and refers to the land and the house plus any other buildings or landscaping (page 231).

PROPERTY TAXES — real property taxes levied by municipalities.

PROPERTY TAX DEFERRAL PLAN — a home equity conversion method that involves postponing the payment of property taxes until the property is sold at some time in the future (pages 178–187).

REAL ESTATE — used here as equivalent to real property but legally refers to land, buildings, ownership rights plus businesses and leasehold (legal definitions may vary from province to province) (page 231).

REAL PROPERTY — land, buildings, and the rights of ownership (immovable property).

REGISTERED — legal documents are filed against the property ownership in the appropriate provincial land ownership registration office, to establish priority of legal claim and protect the creditor's rights.

RESIDUAL EQUITY — equity left for the homeowner or the estate at the end of a reverse mortgage.

REVERSE ANNUITY MORTGAGE (RAM) — a reverse mortgage coupled with an income generating annuity (pages 45–49).

REVERSE MORTGAGE — a home equity conversion approach in which a mortgage is registered against a property to release equity for the homeowner's use or to purchase an annuity of the homeowner (page 13).

RIGHT OF SURVIVORSHIP — see JOINT TENANCY.

SALE LEASEBACK — a home equity conversion approach in which a homeowner sells the home to an investor with the condition that the seller will rent it back on a fixed or life term lease without actually having to move out (pages 195–98).

SHARED APPRECIATION — a variation on the reverse mortgage in which the lender is given a share in the increased value of the property in return for a lower interest rate or larger payments for the borrower (page 51).

SIMPLE REVERSE MORTGAGE — a reverse mortgage in which the borrower receives a lump sum payment, regular payments, or a combination from the lender (page 44).

TERM — period of time for which the mortgage money is loaned to the borrower. At the end of the term, the mortgage must be repaid in full, renewed, or refinanced (page 15).

TENANCY IN COMMON — joint ownership without the right of survivorship in which each owner has the right to bequeath the property to whom they wish (pages 278–81).

TENURE-PLAN REVERSE MORTGAGE — a reverse mortgage that usually runs until the homeowner sells, moves permanently, or dies (page 42).

TITLE — property ownership registration.

TRADITIONAL MORTGAGE — also called a forward or straight mortgage; a mortgage with a decreasing balance that requires regular repayment by the borrower.

VENDOR — the seller or owner of the property.

VENDOR TAKE-BACK MORTGAGE — a traditional mortgage in which the seller or vendor becomes the mortgagee on the property just sold to the buyer or mortgagor (pages 252–54).

ZONING BY-LAWS — municipal codes that define the uses of property in detail (pages 275–76).

Quick Question Index for Reverse Mortgages

People often ask me, **"May I ask you one quick question?"** Listed in the **Quick Question Index** are the reverse mortgage questions I am asked most frequently. In Chapters 2 through 7, the issues and concepts at the heart of these questions are explained and QQI questions are answered. These questions are also "translated" into questions that the consumers can in turn ask lenders, salespeople, and independent advisers.

HOW TO USE THE QUICK QUESTION INDEX (QQI):

Before using the Quick Question Index, check in the Table of Contents, page v, the Glossary, page 291, and the Index, page 303, to see whether your question can be easily coupled with an entry or entries in these listings.

- If not, locate the (QQI) category that best fits your question. Then select the question in that category that best matches yours. The chapter and page reference for each question takes you to a key discussion point for the answer to your question.

- If you need more information after reading the section you are directed to by the QQI, then follow any chapter cross references provided in that section or use the Index.

- *What is ...?* questions can be answered by using the Glossary, page 291, it contains chapter cross-references for the key terms. Or check in the Index, page 303, or the Table of Contents, page v.

Although a question about reverse mortgages can be *asked* quickly, the question may not be able to be answered quickly nor can the answer necessarily be absorbed quickly. This index is included only to give you easy access to answers that you need right now, not to encourage getting superficial answers to your questions. The reader is urged to read all of the material in this book before making a decision concerning reverse mortgages, home equity conversion, and any of the other options discussed. Basing a yes or no decision on the answer to one or two questions, short-changes you in ways you will only fully appreciate once you have read the entire book.

QUICK QUESTIONS:

What is a reverse mortgage?

Is a reverse mortgage a good idea?

How do I select the right reverse mortgage for my needs?

What about the lender?

What are my rights?

Will my other income be affected?

Where can I get a reverse mortgage?

Index

Words in bold are also in the GLOSSARY on page 291.
Reference numbers in bold represent pages containing a complete definition of the term or words.